GOOD AS GONE

ANNA POTTIER

GOOD AS GONE

MY LIFE WITH

Irving Layton

DUNDURN
TORONTO

Editor: Michael Melgaard
Design: Laura Boyle
Printer: Webcom
Cover Design: Laura Boyle
Cover Image: Arnaud Maggs, courtesy of the Arnaud Maggs estate

Library and Archives Canada Cataloguing in Publication

Pottier, Anna, author
     Good as gone : my life with Irving Layton / Anna Pottier.
Includes index.
Issued in print and electronic formats.

ISBN 978-1-4597-2856-1 (pbk.).--ISBN 978-1-4597-2855-4 (pdf).-- ISBN 978-1-4597-2854-7 (epub)

1. Layton, Irving, 1912-2006. 2. Pottier, Anna. 3. Layton, Irving, 1912-2006--Marriage. 4. Layton, Irving, 1912-2006-- Health. 5. Poets, Canadian (English)--20th century--Biography. 6. Authors' spouses--Canada--Biography. I. Title.

PS8523.A95Z73 2015   C811'.54   C2014-907671-1
                                                      C2014-907672-X

1   2   3   4   5   19   18   17   16   15

  Canada

We acknowledge the support of the **Canada Council for the Arts** and the **Ontario Arts Council** for our publishing program. We also acknowledge the financial support of the **Government of Canada** through the **Canada Book Fund** and **Livres Canada Books**, and the **Government of Ontario** through the **Ontario Book Publishing Tax Credit** and the **Ontario Media Development Corporation**.

Care has been taken to trace the ownership of copyright material used in this book. The author and the publisher welcome any information enabling them to rectify any references or credits in subsequent editions.

J. Kirk Howard, President

Printed and bound in Canada.

Visit us at
Dundurn.com | @dundurnpress | Facebook.com/dundurnpress | Pinterest.com/dundurnpress

Dundurn
3 Church Street, Suite 500
Toronto, Ontario, Canada
M5E 1M2

To Grant Hickman
"... 'til the rivers all run dry ..."

Contents

Preface

WHENEVER I SEE an old photo of Irving, say from the 1960s, it is like glimpsing an icon in its natural setting, removed from ordinary life. If shown with a former mate, his children, or bygone friends, a feeling of subdued respect takes hold. Many came before me; each had their Layton moments — good and bad — all of which will forever be beyond my ken.

Taken to its extreme conclusion, that sense of awed respect could preclude any attempt to write about Irving. That, however, would be grossly unfair to him, to me, and to who we were as a couple. After nearly fourteen years at his side and twenty years of silence, I must share something of my story. To paraphrase Irving: "until I, fabulist, have spoken ..."[1] none of what transpired happened. Sophists might argue that even if all I saw, heard, and did with Irving took place, so what? Why should it matter that I know who he was at his most vulnerable, and during moments of hard-won triumphs? Does it ultimately matter that I can describe the afternoon he wrote the last complete poem of his career, or that I witnessed the effects of old age cutting relentlessly into his body and mind? He will always have his loyal detractors, just as he will continue to gather new readers. The best among the latter, like me, are never quite the same for having truly tasted his worth.

This book is my homage to and thanks for all that he lavished on me: his absolute trust, an Ivy League education taught at the table, during long walks, and in the pre-dawn light as he challenged me like the extraordinary teacher he was, all imbued with unconditional love.

Writing *Good as Gone* took close to a decade, partly due to the wrenching blows each memory of him loosed on me, like stinging jabs to the face and gut. Guilt and sorrow left me nearly mute for those first years after leaving him. I missed him. I miss him still, and wish I could have stayed on. That, however, would have meant my creative and emotional, if not physical, death. Because he loved me, he helped me to leave before the age difference transformed me into a hollowed-out, broken shell.

What I hope to convey in these pages is something of the sheer exuberance that marked our days and nights. He made pronouncements, some of them incendiary, but always, *always*, with compassion at the heart and root of the matter. Having practically no one to share my story with while living it, nor afterwards, I want now to take you by the hand and sit you down beside us, there to laugh, be surprised, and perhaps even be shocked at how very possible it is for love to conquer all. We had *it*, that secret ingredient that permitted us to overlook the obvious challenges and to nurture one another, cherishing the good that flourished between us. If I have done my best, the reader will come away feeling as if they, too, enjoyed a few moments in his company.

I regret nothing, but am pained to say whether I would do it all again. Very likely, yes. Yes, I would take the same risks, jump off the same cliff. It was worth it, though I could not survive another such aftermath.

Writing this book has been tantamount to building a long tunnel, fitted with a leather-bound, brass-studded door at the far end. *Good as Gone*, now done, enables me to open that door, step through, and close it ever so gently behind me with strength enough left only to whisper: *Thank you my wild, peculiar boy, thank you and adieu.*

A Note on the Quoted Material

THE DESIRE TO STAVE OFF oblivion by writing things down began when I was at least nine years old. Taking note of Irving's words thus came naturally. Whether prompted by him to record a poem's meaning or my own impulse to capture his thoughts, I scrambled for pen and paper, capturing his words verbatim. Underscores and bold lettering helped preserve his emphasis and rhythms of speech. Such jottings were "caught scraps," written on whatever lay at hand, and were meant to be transcribed into journals such as "The Blue Book" or "The Ledger." Most helpful, a near photographic memory enabled me to transpose entire conversations late at night directly into journal pages. Irving spoke with such forceful, well-crafted language that even casual remarks rang with memorable phrases. "Transient Notes" are snippets set down when I was away from the house and without my journal at hand. Some quotes are from "The Changing Book," a journal begun in November 1981 while travelling in France. Its purpose was to record events that, well, left me irrevocably changed. The slim hardcover book, filled to its inside back cover, spans nineteen years. Much of the dialogue attributed to Irving throughout this work is from these sources. They have been edited for grammar, the underscores replaced with italics, but not for content. The words quoted are all Irving's.

Leave-Taking

IRVING DIED ON January 4, 2006. It had been eleven years since I left him. There would be no more bedazzlements, no more schmoozing, laughter, or his annoyingly funny rendition of the 1928 hit song "Ramonaaa." No more of that brilliance coiled in his every gesture ready to blaze, startle, and delight. He was dead. Like Shakespeare, he would not trouble us with any new masterpieces, ever. He is dead. Shall I write it five hundred times? Will that show me the shape of his absence?

Days slip by me. Is this the feeling he had — "quietly circling his grief"[1]— when he stared at a page for weeks and weeks after his mother passed away? Any poem of his, any mention of him, brings him back. I hear the timbre of his voice; I see the forearms packed with muscle as if put there by decades of stonecutting. Reading a line of his work brings back his warmth, the smell of his sweet breath —

The coffin, so plain and simple, was brand new. Its freshly sawn pine gave off an unexpected tang, ricocheting me back to childhood days in the Nova Scotia woods, or playing in the sawmill my father had built. The scent linked my past with the unavoidable present. A fine layer of sawdust lay on the coffin's closed lid. I swept it gently away, one last bit of housecleaning. I stood by the coffin, needing these last moments to make up for the years without him.

The entourage — lifelong friends of Irving's, Leon Schwartz, his wife Musia, and Sandra Goodwin, widow of Irving's nephew Bill — soon arrived. Leon and Bill had been given power of attorney over Irving's affairs. Musia had helped hire and fire staff, even raised funds for his up-keep toward the end. I overheard Musia remark, "I always said, when he closed his eyes, I would be done." She was choosing not to take sides in the anticipated fallout. The entourage stayed grouped by the entrance. Their job was over and it looked like they were in a furniture showroom for all the bonhomie. Not one of them approached me.

Irving's fourth wife, Harriet, and their daughter Samantha arrived. They promptly went out for a smoke before joining the entourage, where they formed a tight group, their backs studiously turned to me in a wall of exclusion. It was so obvious and so hurtful that even the *shomesh* (funeral home attendant) was appalled. He rose from his chair and, shaking his head, said, "J'ai tout vu, j'ai tout compris. Ces gens-là ne sont pas intelligents. Quel théâtre! Pas d'intelligence du tout!" (I've seen it all now, and I understand. Those people are not very bright. What theatre! No brains whatsoever!) His words eased some of the sting at being unjustly ostracized.

Most of them had been guests in my home, and I in theirs. Every High Holiday, year after year, saw Irving and me in our finest duds, flying along The Boulevard in a taxi to the Schwartzes' splendid home for Rosh Hashanah and Passover. I learned to sing "Dayenu" in their dining room, Seder after Seder, beaming at their approval. Marrying Irving had meant, in many ways, losing my family; but, as I told myself, I gained a people. The entourage, however, began turning its back to me as soon I left Irving in 1995 — this despite Irving's profound under-standing and support of my leave-taking.

By the time of his funeral, the shunning was absolute. One of them, Sandra, became increasingly agitated, and started calling out that she had to sketch Irving like she had sketched her dead mother. She pulled a large drawing pad from her purse while pacing to and fro before the coffin. At least she said hello to me. And wasn't I almost as ridiculous, with nail scissors and an envelope in my purse, just in case I'd be per-mitted to cut a lock of his hair? Or the digital camera, in case I'd be allowed one photo, just for me?

Contrary to tradition, it was agreed they would open the coffin. When they did, Irving's name flew from my mouth. I was almost felled seeing him, his square hands discreetly folded underneath a white cloth, beyond my or anyone's gaze. I was grateful for the neat, simple covering. It would have been hard to see those hands, so familiar, now dead. To my immense relief, he had put on his round mischief-maker face, his best boy *punim*.

Photos from his last years had shown him ravaged, haggard, covered in age spots, and hauntingly distant. Now, in his coffin, he was full-faced — pale as death but without disfiguring furrows or blotches. His hair. So clean and white and beautifully combed. A white yarmulke sat lightly on the famous mane.

I knew the colour of his eyes beneath the closed lids to be blue — blue as the edge of the sky on a late summer day. Those eyes are what had first caught and held me.

Through the noise roaring in my head, I suddenly made out the word "cremation." This was more than a breach with tradition — it was an abomination. All I could imagine were his blue eyes melting, perhaps bursting in the heat. The trademark hair would go in less than a second. Two thousand degrees Fahrenheit, for two to three hours "… now black, now ash…."[2]

Irving never wanted to be burned.

I was gutted, broken. He was not supposed to die. To whom had I given the very best of myself? Now they were going to burn him. He was the only one who ever tried to bandage my hurts and cherished me so. There would be no more encouragement, no more heart's delight or that seamless complicity of ours. Nothing.

My only consolation, standing there by his coffin, was that I had kept the promise I made to myself after my leave-taking. Leaving Irving had, in a way, made him become old almost overnight; as long as we were a couple, he remained a force to be reckoned with, like a super-charged dynamo. He had laughed when I dubbed him my wild, peculiar boy. I could not imagine seeing him in an institution being spoon-fed, diapered, or whatever else befalls those rendered helpless by "the inescapable lousiness of growing old."[3] No, I would not see him on some geriatric ward. I vowed never to set foot inside Maimonides, the care facility in Côte-Saint-Luc where he spent his final years.

I did see him from time to time, however. The last encounter had been five years earlier. Concordia University had invited me to a reception marking the acquisition of the last batch of Layton material for their archive. By then, Irving was in Maimonides. He arrived at the Loyola Campus Faculty Club in a limo. I was not prepared for the sight of him in a wheelchair. Photos of that day show a vivid connection that still held us, one in the other's eyes, in the other's soul.

He asked the same questions several times over and I answered them brightly as if hearing them for the first time. My patience was still intact, my love was unchanged, but I was in pieces. I put my hand on his forearm, surprised at its burly strength. His eyes danced blue and then blank, disappearing a bit behind the cloud, then back again. "You look like one of the Pottiers from Nova Scotia!" Irving said, pleased to no end that he had made the connection. He was partly right. I was indeed one the Pottiers from Nova Scotia — *the* Pottier who had been his wife for nearly fourteen years.

I drew up a chair next to him. Pictures were snapped discreetly. Everyone left us alone in front of the tall window, the sun pouring in onto our laps. Perhaps they sensed, the way animals sense earthquakes, that we two would never see each other again. The reception over, I contained my sobs and kissed him goodbye as he was bundled into the limo. I knew I would not see him again until he was "in his box." That was the phrase. My mountain was turning into grains of sand, and I could not support the weight of such desolation.

At the funeral home, my hand instinctively reached for his face. It was astonishingly cold, much colder than ice. As tradition dictates, no embalming had been done, no artificial attempt at prolonging a likeness when the soul is already gone. His mouth was still full-lipped. I put my hand flat over his heart, half-expecting to feel the familiar thud. He was always proud of astounding doctors with that heart of his, beating with such a force and rhythm that it was almost an aberration. Now, as I moved my hand gently back and forth over his chest, there was a hard stillness, the ribs still strong and prominent, but they were just skeleton now.

There were only minutes left in which to confront an entire lifetime, to say hello and farewell all at once — not only to Irving, but to all that our life together had been. Where had it gone?

No one could know the awfulness of those last moments, or how utterly ruined my life seemed. The heat from my hand and the warmth of the room had begun to disturb his face. His lower lip fell away, almost imperceptibly, leaving a thin black line. It was so black a void, blacker than midnight, blacker and vaster than infinity. My love for him, beyond reason or measure, appeared in that blackness like tiny stars a million miles away in what had been our very own firmament.

Seeing the coffin wheeled into the chapel was surreal. Had Irving ever approached a podium in front of a packed house and not performed? The most impassioned eulogy came from Irwin Cotler, a former student and one of Irving's favourite spiritual sons. Cotler, now a renowned human rights lawyer and federal cabinet minister, had interrupted his election campaign to eulogize his teacher. He was visibly upset, unabashedly grateful for all that Irving had taught and shown, not only to him, but also to the world. Leonard Cohen sounded another note, alluding to their friendship as a private thing, and then read Irving's poem "The Graveyard."

I forget now who read the famous lines:

> ... They dance best who dance with desire,
> Who lifting feet of fire from fire
> Weave before they lie down
> A red carpet for the sun.... [4]

There was no rabbi — not that Irving had ever been a traditional Jew — because no rabbi would agree to preside over the funeral service of a Jew who was going to be burned. I was told afterwards we were lucky to be allowed to sing "Kaddish," the prayer for the dead. Service over, the coffin was wheeled slowly out. Beethoven's Ninth played, but I did not hear it. I folded in with the family and friends, but could not help walking faster until I was almost close enough to touch the coffin. Harriet shot me a look, seemingly annoyed by my visible and audible grief.

There was the hearse, waiting. People crowded past on either side. I saw the news cameras; saw the coffin lifted in. My hand clamped over my mouth as the finality began to hit home. Irving's teasing voice in my ear sounded out: "I take my Anna everywhere ..." [5]

Not this time. Not ever again.

Irwin Cotler embraced me, as did Moses Znaimer, another spiritual son, this one having gone on to practically invent MuchMusic and found a media empire. Then, Leonard Cohen came up and hugged me close. Taking my hand tightly, he thanked me for all that I had done for Irving, saying he knew how happy I had made his irreplaceable friend. "I'm a witness!" he said, smiling softly, "I am a witness."

I was terrified to both see and perhaps to miss seeing the hearse drive away. News teams, finished with Leonard, Moses, and Cotler, now gathered around me. It was strange, me answering questions after having removed myself from the scene all these years. I would have to sound good, deliver with punch and a flourish, the way Irving always had.

He once remarked that a man's funeral is the wife's report card. We laughed at that, and even pictured his funeral and send-off. We imagined the event taking place on a warm sunny day, joked about how traffic would be disrupted, how the crowds would no doubt spill down the steps and onto the street. It was not arrogance; it was whistling a duet in the dark.

Now, on this bleak January morning on Jean Talon the sun had not shown. A cutting wind pushed the damp winter air right through my body as I stood before the funeral home's open maw. Sickly yellow-grey clouds hung over the concrete departure zone. The news teams were already gone; and the crowd, homage duly paid, had thinned to nothing. I looked up and the hearse was gone.

PART ONE:

CHANCE AND APPETITE

1: The Bull Calf: Controversial Poet

SPRING, 1977. We were agitated and giddy with the end of high school in sight. I was, as usual, half-drunk on the salt-air breezes tendrilled with the damp earth smells that oozed in from the woods and fields that surrounded my village of Belleville, Nova Scotia. Three kilometres away, Ste-Anne-du-Ruisseau High School sat in the L-corner between two grassy expanses. One, more meadow than playing field, sloped down to a saltwater marsh sluiced by the Atlantic Ocean some twenty kilometres from Yarmouth, Nova Scotia.

My classmates were children of Acadian fishermen, carpenters, and other tradespeople. We spoke multi-accented versions of seventeenth-century French cut with English. We were all Catholic, shaped more by family ways and tradition than by dogma. Country music played on the town's one radio station, though I had a small radio by my bed that could catch Boston at night. Some locals considered my family fortunate, but to Yarmouth's townies, we were just Frenchie hicks. Ours was the only house without a phone, as my mother detested the "party lines" that were shared between several houses, and insisted on waiting until private lines became available. In our big sea-green kitchen we had a black and white wood-burning stove. There was one road, no store, and two lakes: one fresh, one salt, and no other girls my age for nearly four kilometres.

The Class of 1977 was divided into three groups of twenty. Mr. Meuse, our English teacher, played Leonard Cohen's "So Long, Marianne" over and over on the battered record player in his classroom.

It was, to put it mildly, unlike anything we'd heard before. The mournful voice and strange music spawned irreverent asides. More peculiar, however, was how the song mesmerized Mr. Meuse. He stared at the dusty turntable, oblivious to our nervous discomfort.

He also had us read a poem called "The Bull Calf" by the "controversial" Irving Layton, though the controversy went unexplained. Mr. Meuse, no more than I, could not know that I was destined to leave my Acadian village of some 150 people and become Layton's fifth, and final, wife. Equally unimaginable, that I would one day greet Leonard Cohen at my door, that he'd hand me a bouquet of flowers, smile, and say "Hi, Darlin'!"

As I had done the previous summer when school ended, after graduation I left for Cohasset, Massachusetts, an affluent suburb south of Boston, to serve as au pair for the Babin family. The duties were light, their two young girls a snap to watch over.

Charles and Anna called me "Honey" and said "Thank you" for anything I did, a novelty I responded to like a lost dog to a loving hand. My Acadianisms and wit developed apace with their appreciation.

The Babins introduced me to a world of sophisticated urbanites, in-ground pools, and my first sip of Tanqueray gin. People in Cohasset owned grand pianos, wore cologne other than Aqua Velva, and took ailing pets to the vet instead of into the woods to be shot. One day each week, Charles ferried me to Boston where I wandered the streets and museums, too young to exploit it fully. On the crowded Cohasset beach I stood out as the only chubby teenager, fully dressed both in and out of the water. With one eye on my charges, the other on the lifeguards, I wished for invisibility while observing beach life. Uncouth and awkward as I was, the Babins fostered a sense of personhood that had been sorely lacking and for which I remain profoundly thankful

The Babins were very different from my family. My father, best described as a self-taught engineer, was the man in the white hard hat supervising commercial construction jobs for Kenny Construction and, later, Boyd & Garland. He was held in high regard by architects as well as the crews under his careful eye. My mother worked at Dominion Textiles, the big cotton mill in Yarmouth. She manned her looms ten hours a day, six days a week, for ten years, and continued working after marriage, though with better hours. She was good at what she did, her canvas chosen for the sails on the HMS *Bounty*. In 1964 a car accident prevented her from ever working again. My brother, four years older than me, said the accident changed her personality, though I was too young to make such a distinction.

Shortly after my seventeenth birthday in August 1977, the Babins brought me back to Belleville. Once home, I packed a blue steamer trunk for the start of my four years at Halifax's Dalhousie University to study medicine. No one doubted my desire to attend Dal. It was as close to the Ivy League as I could get, and so natural a next step that I did not bother applying to any other school. I was meant to do well at Dalhousie, like my father's uncle, the Honourable Justice Vincent Pottier, who had been sent to Boston at age eleven to learn English. He graduated from Dalhousie Law School in 1920, became a distinguished lawyer and professor, and founded Halifax's Legal Aid service. He was also the first Acadian from Nova Scotia elected to the House of Commons, and the first Acadian Justice of the Supreme Court of Nova Scotia. Our family was humbly proud of these achievements.

My parents drove me the 290 kilometres to Shirreff Hall, Dalhousie's stately women's residence, and left quickly, without ceremony, no doubt intimidated by the doctors and lawyers fussing over their well-groomed offspring. Framed by Shirreff Hall's massive doorway and the spray of fall-yellow leaves, I watched, heart crushed by pity and fear, as my parents' truck eased out from the Cadillacs and Buicks.

Did I want to be a doctor? Not really. I had initially planned on going into nursing, but at the last minute, to please my parents, changed programs. My desire to get into medicine grew, in part, from admiring my Aunt Bernadette, herself a nurse, whose bearing and knowledge epitomized what it meant to be a professional caregiver. If I could be half as adept, I would be able to write my ticket, travel the world, able to rent that all-important room of one's own.

Another early influence on my career path was the nurse who tended me after my first near-death experience, a car accident when I was five. A drunk driver had smashed into us head-on at ninety miles an hour. I was unhurt except for a friction-burned left cheek. I recall shards of glass coming silently toward my face in slow motion, pretty and shiny. Apparently, the drunk driver's flesh remained intact, with every bone in his body broken. At the hospital, a doctor and some interns materialized and, stupidly, lifted and shook each of my limbs in turn, as if unaware I might have something squashed inside me. In comparison, I thought my nurse to be far more capable. I studied her through half-closed eyes, deeming her ability to draw a smile from my swollen face commend-able. She acknowledged the doll Uncle Hubert and Tante Marguerite re-trieved from the wreckage, asking me its name. I never named my dolls, inventing "Nancy" on the spot in order to seem normal. Then, she helped me stand up on the bed so I could look into the mirror. Instead of making a big deal of my big cheek, she laughed, setting me to laughing too, earn-ing a gold star in my mind. Nursing thus became a possible future career.

Years later, however, my true desires were writing and travelling. But no one in my milieu encouraged such folly. For my parents, art was neither real nor valid, and I had not yet found the courage to oppose them. Not surprisingly, I went from being the high school valedictor-ian in June, to failure in December of my first year at Dalhousie. In retrospect, I should have majored in English, or enrolled at the Nova Scotia College of Art and Design, but that would have been like an-nouncing I wanted to be a weatherman on Mars. Much of my parents' life savings went toward my tuition. Personal choice was not an option. I still break into a cold sweat remembering my first chemistry exam, staring at the page for forty-five minutes, not daring ask permission to go to the washroom. Professor Terzis, an angry, pencil-thin Greek who made leftist speeches against the Junta all term, took pity. I left the exam room, returning to scrawl rambling equations for twenty points.

The Killam Library with its five floors of books attracted me like a cave of tantalizing delights. I ventured to it early that September. It should have been my second home, but its reading room, clotted with the cream of Eastern Canadian youth, who — to my mind — all knew each other and spoke unaccented English, so intimidated me that I did not set foot in the Killam again that year. Uncle Vincent had an office at the Law School but, paralyzed with fear, I could not approach him or an advisor to confess my terrors.

Overweight, with no definable style, I wore thick glasses that were ever on the brink of steaming up or sliding down a perpetually shiny nose. The only high point of my freshman year might have been pivotal if not for a Thomas Hardy–esque moment. My favourite class was English. Professor Michael Klug sounded like Faulkner, looked like Hemingway, and filled his pipe with movements so delicate they might have belonged to Emily Dickinson. I sat up front, eager but mute, crippled by a reluctance to reveal my Acadian accent.

Midway through the first term, we had run aground on "Dover Beach." "What did this poem mean?" Professor Klug asked. I sat there, lumpish, heavy, but with my spirits lightening. Epiphanies began to form. I pursed my lips, glanced up, and looked at the page, sucking air, not daring to speak. Klug boomed, "I'll give fifty cents to anyone who can tell me what this poem means." Up shot my hand as I blurted out something about Nature looking beautiful, but Man losing faith in God. "Miss Pottier," Klug intoned in his Missouri-like drawl, "you've earned about seventeen cents. Can you take it a bit further?" Another inspired burst about the Sea of Faith receding like the tide and Nature alone not being enough; Klug drove his huge fist into his pocket and plunked a mass of coins down onto my notebook with a gratifying bang. After class, with Klug's change burning a hole in my pocket, I contemplated buying him a coffee. The moment took on what I would later recognize as Prufrockian intensity. What I really wanted was to ask about the English program and becoming a writer. One word from Klug and I would have enough ammunition to confront my parents. I stood outside the classroom in King's College, gathering courage, imbibing the chalky, dust-flecked air. Just as I was about to take those nine or ten steps across the marble foyer, Klug's change barely contained in my sweaty hand, a teacher's assistant ran up to him, arms laden with exam papers. The moment passed. I never again found the courage to approach Professor Klug. Had I done so, who knows? Instead, I stayed in the science program for two more tortured years.

Buoyed perhaps by Klug's recognition and appreciation, I ditched my thick glasses for contact lenses after that first year at Dal. By summer's end, I was down thirty-eight pounds thanks to Weight Watchers, swimming, and biking six miles a day to a job as lab technician. My social life began to improve, but not by much. By my third year, unable to stomach more science prerequisites, I enrolled in Dal's four-year Nursing program and moved into Fenwick Towers in Halifax's south end. Filled with Dalhousie students, its windows clad in various Rebel and British flags, my mother pronounced this thirty-two-storey highrise "no better than a whorehouse."

Helen MacLeod, my roommate who came from Cape Breton with a Fender guitar and an acerbic take on life, introduced me to her music-making friends. She had a ringside seat for the fierce abandon with which I blew off my schoolwork in order to correspond with Vincent, a French artist I spent one memorable evening with the previous semester. It had been my first encounter with a Frenchman, and my second intimate encounter with a man. He had left Paris and zigzagged from Alaska to Halifax. His massive blue pack, road-hardened thighs, and hiking boots called to me as the Sirens to Ulysses. When he left, I watched from my fifteenth-floor balcony, barefoot on the frozen concrete in my red satin robe, until the blue speck of him disappeared in the distance. I was stuck; he was free. "Annette, anyone can be a nurse, but very few can be an artist like you," he said, kissing me goodbye. It was as if Hemingway's Paris had caressed my cheek.

Vincent set my imagination on fire with the desire be a female Hemingway. Concentrating on how to give injections or take blood pressure became nearly impossible. Helen exhorted me to do what made me happiest. So after two dismal years of pre-med courses, and that one horrible year of nursing (including a six-week practical in a full cap-to-shoes white uniform) handing in late but imaginatively written care-plans, I packed in Helping Professions and switched to English Literature. My parents were fountains of negativity and doubt-inducing scorn. A change in faculty meant, if nothing else, a change of scene. Enter Joyce Rankin, kindred spirit.

Oh, those nights dredging Barrington, Water, Argyle, Grafton ... Halifax's fog-bound, shadow-black streets, with our feverishly excitable voices muffled by wet leaves, mist, and the pungent salt and creosote-stained breezes. We were nascent writers. It was London. It was Paris. It was anywhere but the here and now of classes, parents, poverty ingrown and painful as a nail, and the ignorance we wore like Purple Hearts on our out-thrust chests. We skipped class for no better reason than the advent of a sunny day, wanting to taste the city's early morning routine as shouldered by delivery boys, lunch-counter waitresses, and other grown-ups. We trawled for anything that looked like adventure: walking through iffy alleys, peering into houses at night, scripting the lives we glimpsed, then sliding into greasy booths of greasy spoons to eavesdrop on the despair and hard lives all around.

Joyce was from Judique, Cape Breton, a Highland Scots girl with a mass of nut-brown hair decked out with a big fake magnolia. I, with my men's work pants and clothes so nondescript as to be distinct, made us a perfect pair of misfits. Luck threw us together in Comparative Canadian and American Literature taught by Professors Bevan Monks and Michael Klug, who, to my astonishment, remembered me from that freshman class three years earlier. "James-Joyce" and I arrived late for class, sat, left, and malingered together. A favourite trick: bothering waiters in good restaurants. The better the restaurant, the more polite they were forced to be when we, more locust than ladylike, devoured the bread and butter, asking for more as we pretended to scan the menu. We had hardly six dollars between us, but with great aplomb, and after much deliberation, we ordered coffee and one dessert.

Best seafood chowder in Halifax? I led her to the longshoremen's canteen on the docks, which I frequented when roaming the piers, sitting on capstans, with my journal as shield and foil. I ached to sail away on freighters whose vibrating hulls I would touch as one would touch the flank of a great horse. I had the harbour master's phone number by heart, and was keenly aware of all the ships at anchor. A British couple stumbled upon me once, gazing up at the Polish freighter they were on, and invited me aboard for lunch. One morning I watched a giant slip its moorings as I sat on a capstan on the corner of Pier 22. The ship was from Haifa and so close that I could hear the crew speaking what I thought was Arabic. Perhaps it was. I had not been exposed to geopolitics or world religions, and lacked the tools with which to distinguish Hebrew from Arabic, Jew from Muslim. My ignorance, velvety smooth and as yet unperturbed, kept me from knowing that Haifa was in Israel, not in Egypt.

Joyce and I often ended our rambles with the two of us safe in her little cave of an apartment on Church Street. We'd dream and make more plans in her boudoir suffused with orange light, eating homemade scones and drinking tea, spinning stories on the Ferris wheels of our imagination.

One day in February 1981, Joyce, breathless and clutching *For My Brother Jesus* amongst other books by Irving Layton, accosted me in front of the Library. *He* was giving a reading the next night, and we should go. I instantly recalled the controversial poet's "The Bull Calf," and needed no further persuasion.

2: Meeting

JOYCE CONTINUED on her way; I ducked into the Killam, no longer intimidating to me since I now worked fifteen hours a week in the bindery, typing labels and affixing them to new books. Driven by compunction as urgent as it was mysterious, I wanted to prepare myself for his reading, to acquaint myself with whatever the controversy had been. I had an essay exam the next day on short stories that I had yet to read. Mere detail. With a flair that has since become a signature trait, reality was put on Ignore as I headed to Special Collections.

To my bewilderment, there seemed to be twelve feet of Layton books on the shelves. Where to begin? Just above my head, a slim volume in white and blue shone from amongst the darker spines. I took it down and cracked it open.

"Peacemonger." The poem drew me in with its clever-but-simple title. There was nothing protracted or difficult about the poetry: simple words, simple sentences. Yet, he was famous enough to be invited all the way to Halifax. What was this fame made of? As I stood there reading the poem, images flew off the page with such clarity that it felt as if I was recalling a scene I'd once taken in with my own eyes: a Greek beach, a girl bringing chilled wine and cucumbers. I wanted — no, I was gripped by an overwhelming desire — to be like that girl. No, wait. Not like her: *better* than her. I would not serve. I would be shoulder to shoulder with the genius whose words held such indescribable force. This changing of simple language into astonishingly vivid, idea-filled lines was an alchemy against which I had no defence, no antidote. Nor did I want any. "Peacemonger" tumbled down on me like the proverbial ton of bricks.

I knew then — and to the marrow of my bones — that I was in the presence of one of The Greats. I was twenty-one years old, comically devoid of the knowledge upon which to base this opinion, but it was to me a hard, inalterable fact. Inspiration struck. Holding the book open at "Peacemonger," I floated to the nearest table, there to write my first poem.

The title makes me wince with embarrassment now: "I'm Coming to Layton Tonight." On some level it seems I was aware of his reputation as a sensualist. Years later this poem, still among his papers, became part of Concordia's Layton Collection. In February 1981, however, I still had no concept of what he looked like, and only the sketchiest notion of his life and career. Nevertheless, with each glance at "Peacemonger," a crazy notion took hold. I wanted to be with him — not as fluff — but centrally important to his life. Indeed, I imagined myself goddess equal to his god, alone with him on that beach, and, with my last breathless stanza, willed his audience to "turn into sea, the stage into sand / leaving only me and the poet-man." I hurried to Joyce's place, showing her my poem with the greatest of expectations. Madly, excitedly, she pronounced my oeuvre "perfect," insisting I give it to Layton, which of course propelled me to even giddier heights. The unimaginable became possible, within reach.

February 16, 1981. The date never passes without my recalling that night. We spruced ourselves up — Joyce with her magnolia and something sparkly — and arrived at the Rebecca Cohn Auditorium early enough to bag two front-row seats, me clutching my freshly typed poem.

The auditorium dwarfed us with its wash of purple seats and soaring wood-panelled walls. My father had been superintendent on the job to update the Cohn. He'd told me about how the panels were movable so as to tune the room. This and other mundane thoughts wildebeested across my mind. The initial bravura, however, was hissing out of me like steam from a vent. "Go up and put it on the podium," Joyce insisted. Was she insane? People began trickling in. Going up on stage, especially one prepared for Irving Layton, was out of the question. My poem was going limp in my hands.

At last, the dread gave way. With a very deep breath, eyes closed, I went up and placed it on the podium, returning to my seat like a soldier from a night raid. No sooner was I seated than an usher strode on-stage, grabbed the poem off the podium, came over, and crouched behind us. "What's *this*?" he bristled.

"Uhhh ... just a welcoming poem for Mr. Layton," I answered weakly. He fumed, glared, and stomped off backstage. Perhaps he thought it was something risqué or anti-Semitic. Either way, he was ticked, and I was mortified.

At last the emcee, Professor Andy Wainwright, materialized, relishing the moment. Through his introduction I learned that Layton had just been nominated for the Nobel Prize, had published some forty-five volumes of poetry, was translated into twenty-three languages, that he was a month shy of his sixty-ninth birthday, married to a woman in her mid-thirties, and the proud father of a month-old baby girl.

Wainwright ceded the spotlight. From stage right, out walked a short, stocky man in a velveteen suit the colour of mocha nougatine, his thick silver hair catching the light. He had a short, choppy stride and seemed to be crackling with energy. He set his books down, donned his glasses, and pulled a piece of paper from inside his jacket. His large handsome head turned slowly as he scanned the audience. His voice filled the Cohn. Its register was unlike any I'd heard before. Joyce and I were now on a rolling boil of giddy excitement. He said hello and thanked his hosts. But then, Layton paused and said, "Only two or three times in my entire career has someone so graciously written me a poem, and I would like to read it to all the gods and goddesses here tonight."

He held my poem in his burly hand and began to read it in his expert voice. It took a few seconds for the miracle to register, and when it did, I imploded, went boneless, clueless, heart pounding out of my chest. The only thing linking me to reality was the rather inelegant mantra of "Oh fuck. Oh fuck. *Joyce*! Oh fuck! *He's reading my poem!*" By the time he read the last line, I had recovered enough to hear his audience burst into applause. I was, save for the poem, completely unknown to him, still perfectly anonymous.

It took at least fifteen minutes for the blood to stop throbbing in my ears. He read "Shakespeare" and other poems that I would later come to know by heart. By the end of the reading, I was absolutely convinced that he was indeed the genius I had encountered earlier in Special Collections. Even more pronounced was the feeling that I, a mere student, had nothing remotely worthwhile to say to him.

After the reading, Joyce and I milled about, plotting how she would get his autograph. There was a reception, an usher said, but it was "strictly invitation only." My nerve dwindled. "That's it," I told Joyce. I had nothing valid to say to this genius. Besides, there was that exam to cram for. I turned and started for home.

Just as I began to walk away, the stage door opened and there he was. Joyce, now more eager than ever to get an autograph, lunged for my arm and yanked me in front of him. "Mr. Layton. I'd like you to meet Annette."

"Hello," he said politely, shaking my hand. Not quite the response Joyce hoped for.

"Um, the Annette who wrote the poem."

"Ohhhhhh ... " his blue eyes sparkled. "*That* deserves a better hand-shake!" He thrust his briefcase and raincoat at Professor Wainwright — who winced at being made valet — and squeezed my hand hard, confirming what destiny had already set in motion.

Whether real or imagined, it felt as if a surge of electricity coursed from his body into mine. Michelangelo's Sistine Chapel image of God sparking Adam to life flashed in my mind. Collecting his briefcase and coat, he thanked me very warmly for the poem, and asked what we were doing. I told him I was leaving to study for an exam. "Why don't you come up to my reception?" Wainwright flinched again — student riffraff were crashing his departmental party, and there was little he could do about it. We moved toward the exit, Layton now handing me his coat and briefcase to better negotiate the stairs. It would be the first of many such scenarios, me helping with his things, him the guest of honour.

There was a long white table with plastic stemware filled with Andrés Baby Duck wine in the brightly lit room. Within seconds, Layton was surrounded by Dalhousie English profs and a clutch of

Halifax's most stalwart literary matrons. Joyce, her magnolia, and I stood by the wine table taking it all in. I sipped two glasses of that enamel-stripper, rooted on the spot until the reception wound down. Layton and the pod of people around him began centipeding toward the coat racks. Uh oh ... the evening was coming to a close. If I did not grab this opportunity to say something, *anything*, to him, I would never again in my whole life have such a chance. With newfound audacity, I fixed him from across the room. Our eyes locked.

In a biblical moment worthy of a Cecil B. DeMille film, Layton held my gaze and emerged from the surrounding mob. It parted before him like a sea as he smiled devilishly at me and came over. His hands were very warm and vital as he took mine. He asked my name again and a few standard questions about our studies. I told him I'd just begun a B.A. in English, but what I really wanted to do was to go to Europe and write. "Finish your degree first so that you'll have something to fall back on," he advised gravely, his blue eyes dancing. We chatted for a total of about five minutes, no more. Joyce got his autograph, and asked if we wrote to him, would he answer? "Of course! 'Irving Layton, Niagara-on-the-Lake, Ontario, Canada.'" *That* was impressive. The man needed no box number or postal code!

Joyce and I made our way out, me feeling twelve feet tall. Without doubt, something bizarre and mysterious had just taken place: I had met my first husband. In letters to friends around that time, I wrote that one day I would "touch face" with him, my euphemism for all things conjugal. He had "the answers" to life's big questions. My next step was to go about finding the questions.

Joyce and I left the Cohn and tried to pull our "fancy restaurant" trick, but Fat Frank's (considered one of the top ten restaurants in North America) was closing, or so said the maître d'. We ended up at a café on Barrington Street where Joyce retold the evening's events in her most animated tones. "I know. I was there," said a young blond man from across the café. Dave Swick (later an editor with the *Halifax Daily News*) joined us for the post-mortem, and offered to walk us home.

The night was icy clear, floodlit by a full moon. "It's *way* too nice to go home yet. Let's go to the docks," I coaxed, still over-stimulated, leading them to the far end of Barrington Street, through the tunnel underneath the railroad tracks, and onto the waterfront. Directly before us, there loomed a shiny new freighter: the M/V *Zini* from Piraeus, Greece. "I bet if we go up the gangplank, they'll give us a tour," I said, climbing the steps. Joyce and Dave followed suit, too nervous to stay behind on a shadowy pier at midnight. And so the evening I met Irving Layton, I spent the night aboard a Greek freighter in Halifax Harbour, sipping Italian beer, nibbling feta cheese, and playing cards with the captain and his officers until dawn.

My pocket agenda notes February 16 as the "night of poets and Greeks." Surprisingly, I did not describe the evening in a journal entry. The only testament to the power of that night is that all subsequent journal entries down to end of term are in verse, not prose.

Joyce and I later approached Professors Klug and Monks to ask for an extension on a term paper, owing to having had Irving Layton read my poem at the Rebecca Cohn and then being guests of Greek officers aboard their ship. Klug shook his head at me and said, "And you said you didn't like Faulkner for *his* hard-to-believe stories!" The extension was granted.

Despite Layton's advice to the contrary, I quit school at the end of that term, unable to see myself spending another three years at Dalhousie to get a B.A. When finals came, I lit a cigarette and poured myself a coffee, leonine nonchalance oozing from every pore. Helen recalls my declaring it was just too nice a day to go write exams. Panic remained hidden behind the swirls of blue smoke filling our apartment's one sunny patch. Two months later, I was planting pine seedlings in granite-strewn ground near Pubnico, Nova Scotia, earning money for a plane ticket to Paris.

3: Europe and Other Not-So-Bad News

MY FINAL YEAR at Dalhousie had involved much malingering by the phone and waiting for mail from my erstwhile French lover, Vincent. However, correspondence is not the *mot juste*. Other than his first letter, wherein he wrote how happy he was to have met "la reine de l'Acadie" (the Queen of Acadia), he sent only cryptic drawings. I sent lavish epistles sprayed with Chanel No. 5, love-verse done up with grains of sand glued to rice paper. Girlish, yes, but intensely creative, nonetheless. Whatever mania my roommates witnessed, Vincent was *not* my objective; adventure and "living large" were. I was more in love with life's grand possibilities than any one man. To a certain extent, I was also performing for the benefit of my roommates. They gathered round, a chorus of gasps and guffaws, me feeding them tidbits on the heels of Vincent's creations. His casual letters sent me into overdrive, deciphering what messages I chose to find.

Had Vincent been a communications course, I'd have garnered an A plus plus, working my brain hours on end, linking images and colours with meaning, and crafting clever responses. It was escapism wrapped in the gush and rush of my stunted adolescence, obliterating all constraints. By the time I met the poet, my fuse was primed for that lit match of an encounter. Later, when Irving read me his aphorism "How to dominate reality? Love is one way; / imagination another."[1] I replied, "How can love exist *without* imagination?"

My urge to travel as a means of escaping the relentless war with my mother had been fermenting for years. By thirteen, I was announcing plans to leave Belleville, usually through clenched teeth, chin and lips quivering with frustration and perpetual hurt. Threats morphed into reality once I quit school. Money from the car-accident payout was to cover the plane ticket. At the money's release date, however, my parents signed it back into the bank without my knowledge. Their end-run failed, for it was exactly this sort of patronizing control that made me want to leave in the first place — that and a desire to go far and live big. Regardless of their motive, my rage and reason won out. They advanced the amount from their savings account.

I planted pine seedlings for three weeks after my final year in school, saying "Another ten minutes in France," with each tree planted in the granite-hard ground. The pines, incidentally, eventually grew visible from Highway 103 near Pubnico. Each time my father drove past the place, he looked for them, seeing me via the trees I had planted. It filled his heart with an emotion too bittersweet for words, close to what I feel now, picturing him looking for me in those pines — some of which will outlive me as they've outlived him.

I planned to seek out Hemingway's Paris, roam the Left Bank for traces of Baudelaire, Camus, Picasso, Modigliani, Beckett, et al.; have a whirlwind romance with Vincent; and see Europe. Aboard the night flight to Paris I was truly on my own for the first time. At midnight, with Elton John's "Daniel" playing in my mind, I splurged on a small bottle of champagne — another first — toasting these auspicious beginnings.

Vincent picked me up in Paris, but the whirlwind romance I had imagined degenerated into an awkward month in Metz. Vincent had moved his grandmother to his parents' house so that he and I had a place of our own. Our love-nest lasted about a day, as Vincent waited until my arrival to mention his divorcée lover and speak of "the need to decompose the movements of the dance." He slept on a daybed in the living room, occasionally spending the night with his lady-friend, leaving me to contemplate the floral wallpaper covering every inch of his grandmother's bedroom. It was a blow whose elegance I quite admired, and absorbed like a cushioned punch. I was twenty-one years old and determined to parse out my traveller's cheques for as long as possible. Vincent thought me far too inexperienced to travel Europe alone, but I was eager to get going.

After only six days in Metz, a fifty-five-year-old man approached me in a bar where I had stopped to write in my journal. The bartender's stage whispered "He's a sadist" did not deter me from leaving with the man. Whether I lacked the gene for fear, or had an innate ability to distinguish killers from normals, I got into the man's funny little van. We toured near the Maginot Line, seeing mouths of old bunker emplacements begging to be explored. He drove me up Mont Saint-Quentin to the ruined Bismarck Tower. The place seemed alive with ghostly soldiers. So began the assault on my youthful ignorance. And so, too began my introduction to high culture. Vincent's mother, perhaps out of pity for the lost Acadian pilgrim in their midst, later took me to a Berlioz concert in Metz Cathedral. At that point, I still was unclear whether it was Bizet's *Carmen* or Carmen's *Bizet*.

Pamplona beckoned; Moire, an intrepid Dalhousie-days friend, was leaving Turkey for the San Fermin Festival there. Despite Vincent's misgivings, I took a practice solo run to Luxembourg on my third weekend in Metz. Aside from breaking a clarinetist's instrument by accident, it went well. Layton's distilled vision of civilized Europe's gore and glory was still beyond my intellectual reach. The death camps and "aesthetic cruelty"[2] forming the bas-relief of his work, was still barely discernible to me.

Quite understandably, for most twenty-somethings Europe was a vast playground. So for one memorable year, I backpacked through France, Luxembourg, Spain, Italy, Greece, Belgium, Holland — crisscrossing Europe at least twice, hitchhiking alone in eighteen-wheeler trucks where all that was expected, more or less, was that I tell stories in three languages as needed, sing, and keep the drivers awake. In return, a ride and always a meal. Other times, I slept on overnight trains, or outside in olive groves. In Pamplona, I slept directly on the filth-crusted sidewalks, with fireworks exploding at my feet, drunken crowds surging all around. On Calle Estafeta I accepted a bull's severed hoof as a love token, all the more potent for its caked blood and mud. In the port of Rotterdam I spent a night slumped over the steering wheel of a Scania truck, waking to the sight of hundreds of ships, sun-struck at dawn in Vermeer's own light.

After Metz, Luxembourg, Pamplona, and three weeks in Mondragon, Spain, with a Basque family, I travelled with a Mexican girl and her Basque boyfriend from the north of Spain to Corfu, Greece, in the back of a two-horsepower Citroën. Chambermaid jobs were easy to come by. As long as I had sixty dollars in reserve, I was flush. This would buy an Athens–Paris Magic Bus ticket. My first night in Athens cost two dollars and was spent on a stone rooftop, the day's heat radiating through a straw mat someone had left behind. There, weightless in the night air, the Acropolis, awash in honey-coloured moonlight against a dark purple sky, struck me dumb with its beauty. After chambermaiding for four months, I learned to speak and read rudimentary Greek, a language I still use from time to time.

In Athens there were highlights and lowlights, such as going into a pharmacy to ask in broken Greek if they had a cure for "micro zoë" (small life) my term for lice. This after walking from Lycavittos Hill to Omonia, streets eerily empty due to lethal smog levels, me a sweating Gulliver to the "small life" hatching and dropping down from my bangs in the heat. Nor shall we mention visiting an Athenian doctor for an internal checkup. He charged a special low price for travelling girls, and then withdrew my IUD device without my consent or knowledge. Girls were not supposed to have that kind of freedom. Malicious bastard.

Greece's mythic aura peeked out from the jammed streets and noisy Hellenes. Was I doing this right? More than ever, Layton seemed to colour almost everything I looked at. He had walked these streets, picking up inspiration the way others pick up coins in the gutter. I did not own any of his books, but carried the sound of his voice in my head. He loomed larger than the statue of Zeus, being for me a living example of a poet who could wring poems from thin air. How? What was his trick? I felt my own senses quickening, committing my excitement to my journal, but not quite able or willing to shape thoughts into poems. I searched the Plaka's cobblestones and souvlaki joints, the tavernas and museums, looking for whatever it was that had so entranced Layton. Europe had a bloody past, but with all the local colour, I felt compelled to inform the poet that Europe was not all bad news. So, I wrote him a postcard that spilled over into a letter. Not only was Europe a pretty good place by my reckoning, but, I hinted, it would be marvellous if I'd get to the American Express *Poste Restante* in Syntagma Square to find a letter from him. Would he even get my letter? No matter. The mere act of writing to the poet and hinting that he respond via American Express was, to my mind, something Hemingway-esque.

In the fall I shot up to Metz again for a quick visit with Vincent. A Scottish girl hitched with me as far as Paris. We wanted to pick grapes, but missed the entire season. Dejected and broke by the time we reached Paris, my companion decided to return home to Edinburgh. Vincent was impressed that I was still at large, and let me rest up for a week in his rooms in an old stone farmhouse he now leased. I rested, made stew with the leeks and soup bones he provided, playing Oscar Peterson in the dank, unheated air. In the cobblestone courtyard it was easy to imagine the German soldiers who once occupied the place. I paid for my keep by painting his living room; slate blue, fluorescent fuchsia trim. His divorcée girlfriend invited me to spend a day with her. Call it a practice run for negotiating Irving's cast of female characters.

I hitched back to Greece, quickly finding a chambermaid job at the Hotel Alma just off Omonia Square in the groin of Athens. Working for six dollars a day meant living close to the bone, but exploring the city was free. I sauntered to Syntagma Square to look for mail at the *Poste Restante*, bracing myself in case they refused to serve me. My traveller's cheques had been stolen in Pamplona, their numbers stolen in Alsace.

Predictably, the surly faced Greek clerk shooed me away. "You are not an American Express client." Just behind her, the "P" cubbyhole was crammed with mail. My heart began racing. One of those letters was for me. I was sure of it. Retreating for a moment, I approached the desk again. She didn't bother looking up, dismissing me with a flick of her hand. Withdrawing to the low bench, I sat down heavily, gathering resolve, and dug in my bag for the flimsy carbon copy of the Spanish police report documenting my stolen cheques. I put the document before her, pleading, begging her to look through the letters. Eye roll, tongue click, heavy sigh; she flipped through the entire stack with maddening deliberateness. Not only was there a letter from home containing one hundred dollars in birthday money, but, to my delight,

two hundred dollars for the winning poem in Dalhousie University's
W.H. Dennis Memorial Prize competition.

There was one more letter for me, this one on Famous Players' letter-
head, from Irving Layton. My knees gave way and I sank to the bench,
staring at the envelope. It was a moment I knew I would savour for years
to come. So I looked at it front, back, sideways, and edgewise too. I took
forever to open that letter, sensing it held powerful indications as to how
the rest of my life would unfold. It would ultimately become part of the
Layton Collection at Concordia, but that morning, I knew only that it
was more important to me than my passport; it *was* my passport.

His letter, dated September 29, 1981, came from an apartment on
Toronto's Bathurst Street. I would learn later that his wife left him and
had taken their child — a bitter ferment that would become *The Gucci
Bag*. Still, in the midst of it all, he found the time to write:

Dear Annette Pottier:

There's no date on your letter, so I've no idea how long it's
been chasing me. It arrived today and along with the autumn
leaves put me into a fine melancholy; remembering my days
in Greece, the sunlight on sand and stone. Of course I gave
you that piece of advice because I recognized at once your
independence of spirit and knew you would reject it. What
I didn't know was that your rejection would take you all the
way to the Aegean and transform you into a chambermaid.
Next time I shall be more prudent when offering young
people rejectable advice. I don't want to have someone going
off to the Hebrides. However, Greece is another matter. It
can only do you a world of good — if you keep your eyes
and ears open, meet some of the poets, swim as often as you
can, drink lots of *retsina* and stay sober. Be very selective
about Greek lovers. If my poems don't tell you what I saw in
Greece, no letter of mine will be able to tell you either. But
maybe it wasn't the country that turned me on, but that I was

on my holidays and could spend days doing what I like best: drink wine, make love, dream, and write poetry.

Wherever you go in Europe, keep remembering that natives regard you as fair game and have no scruples about relieving you of whatever money or valuables you may possess. I've been cheated and robbed in every European country I've been to, no matter how hard I try to stay alert and on my guard. If we ever do get together over a bottle of wine, I'll have some amusing stories to tell you in exchange for yours. The only advice I can offer you now is keep on writing, if not poems, then a journal of some sort, a diary. Don't let yourself become discouraged until you're eighty; even then, try to hang on for another decade or so.... I'm sorry but I must admit that I can't remember what your face looks like. Are you beautiful? Tall and blonde or short and dark? Snubnosed and freckled or classical Greek? What makes you think you're a poet, except your defiance of advice? After all, you weren't born circumcised as I was! What, if any, were the heavenly signs when you dropped out from between your mother's bleeding legs?

Well, give my love to Constitution Square. I can actually see you going up the steps to the Am. Express, and as you ascend, I am looking at your trim feet and ankles. Ah, the poet's imagination.... Stay well, and good luck go with you always wherever you go or whatever bad similes you perpetrate.

Avanti / Irving Layton[3]

Neatly typed, the letter had seven manual corrections and his signature at the bottom. "If ever we do get together.... " Well, of course we would! *Fortuna et cupidas.* Luck and appetite. Poets make lucky things happen.

I rounded out my European year with two fellow travellers, Caroline and Tracey from Wales. After less than stellar chambermaid work in Athens, we spent ten weeks in Naples working in a waterfront bar, dancing for a pittance plus whatever tokens we earned for the rum-less cokes and warm Spumante men bought us. I deemed it being a "call girl that doesn't answer" — a line Irving later used in his poem "Aristocrats."

Europe yielded fistfuls of meaty stories. It was now May 1982. Before the year was over, I would be living with Layton, drawing on these stories to Scheherazade him through the worst of his troubled days and sleepless nights.

4: From Cabin-on-the-Lake to Niagara-on-the-Lake

RETURNING TO BELLEVILLE was like a death. I came back a conquering hero in no one's mind but my own. Soon as my pack touched the kitchen floor, a chapter ended. I would never be that free again. Only a few people, models of caution and circumspection, dared ask about the trip. My grandfather, for instance, trying not to imagine what I had gotten up to, asked where I had slept. To my blithe "Oh, sometimes outside, sometimes while taking a night train," he turned away in disgust: "Pas mieux qu'ain negg." (No better than a [negro] hobo). Down came the pedestal, shattered to its very plinth. How could my adventure have provoked such a decent man to speak so out of turn? He died shortly thereafter, and was spared contemplating my going to stay with a Jewish poet — one, moreover, old enough to be my grandfather.

I had no skills, no degree, and owed money to the bar owner in Naples (rumoured to be Lucky Luciano's nephew) who had fronted me for an emergency root canal. The future stared back with blank eyes.

Staving off the depression that set in after a week, if not a few days, I fled to Mavillette Beach, fifty kilometres north of Yarmouth along the Bay of Fundy. There, I walked the empty sand, ankle deep in glacial waters, and pondered why home was a foreign place. Sunlight on the waves lifted my spirits as I walked moodily, yearning for a way out, yearning for a nameless kind of glory with a force as elemental as the famous Fundy tides.

This yearning, a fierce ache for success and significance, was painful in its intensity. No one around me could imagine what it meant to drink retsina in a Greek taverna while flirting with handsome bouzouki players; or to walk into a crowded Pamplona bar, prouder than Ava Gardner, with a severed bull's hoof hooked over my shoulder and the smell of feces and death in my flaring nostrils. Belleville and I were never a perfect fit, but now the desire to escape became almost mad-making. So I kept to myself, recovering, plotting the next move. Much as my blood coursed with salt water more redemptive than any church, Belleville could neither spark nor sustain me as a writer. Irving Layton, however, knew the what, where, and how of such intangibles. All I had to do was ask.

My parents stayed in Digby County during the week where my father was overseeing the building of a dam. I found a summer job painting fences and low-income homes in Yarmouth, earning barely enough to keep me in gas and cigarettes. I slept at our cabin across the road and down by Eel Lake, swimming every night at dusk, gliding tirelessly through the day's last sunlit water. Afterward, I worked on poems and jotted down ideas for short stories. The poems, not surprisingly, surge with tremulous erotic romanticism. I can be forgiven for not being the next Edna St. Vincent Millay, but I matched her breath for breath with my innate desire to express all that I felt, saw, and touched. I shared my poems with Joyce Rankin and Dave Swick, to whom I sent a love poem he inspired, but it did not lead to the imagined eating ice cream in the rain and kissing.

My parents, bless them, were relieved to have me home, and baited their sweet trap, saying, "You can stay here as long as you like rent-free and write all you want." It was death on a plate, even if offered with their best-wrought love.

By July, I felt good enough to write "Summer Classic," a poem about Yarmouth's "long-legged boys" whistling at "slack-jawed girls slumping past / jaws working double-time / on bubble-gum." Irving later helped parse it down to its essence. Renamed "Yarmouth, NS: Small Town Summer," it became my second published poem, though *Poetry Canada Review* lopped off the subtitle and first stanza (see Appendix 1).

My journal repeats Irving's advice like a mantra: "Write something every day, if not a poem, then a story." Yes. It was time to send him another letter. Audaciously, I wrote asking would he not come down and be my guest. On a television interview I saw around this time, he seemed troubled, agitated. The Nova Scotia salt air would do him good. In exchange for his literary counsel: tranquillity and companionship. Vague as this notion was, it felt utterly natural. Though sharply aware of his stature and my utter lack thereof, I retained the sense of being goddess to his god, nervously sending along "Decadence" and one or two other poems.

By the end of July, days before turning twenty-three, my journal entry opens with "Cabin-on-the-Lake, Nova Scotia: perhaps my next trip will be to Ontario to find Layton." I wrote, anxious that he might not be able to make it to Nova Scotia. The entry concludes, "But I still sense the positive conviction that I will indeed sit face to face with him one day. It will happen."

My routine that summer never varied; after a hot day of scraping, painting, or working on asphalt-shingled roofs, I made supper at the house, then rushed down to the cabin to swim, write, and sleep. Each day was the same: work, supper, swim, and write. I merged with the heavy, summer-scented evening, fearless of the glassy black water. Out in the lake, I was but one more creature. Loons called out mournfully as I sliced through the warm salt water, oblivious to the thousands of jellyfish mulling life a mere two metres below the surface. Day followed day: work, supper, swim, and write, usually with Greek or Italian pop songs on the cassette player.

However, on August 2, my twenty-third birthday, something broke the routine. Inexplicably, I could not leave the house. I ate quickly and wanted to head to the lake, but something kept me back. Instead of rushing down for my restorative swim, I paced restlessly from room to room, picked up magazines and threw them down. Television on. Television off. From the front windows I could see my lake's velvety black calm. It beckoned; yet I stayed, pacing nervously. Dusk. Sunset. Dark night invaded the entire house. Suddenly, at 10:00 p.m. the newly installed telephone rang. Its loud bell shattered the stillness, making me leap out of my skin.

Must be someone calling Dad about work. "Hallo?" I asked hesitantly, unused to speaking on the phone. A man's voice, English, with a tinny yet deep-sounding tone, said he wanted to speak with Annette Pottier. "Yes, that's me," I said, suddenly realizing that I was on the phone with the poet. Irving Layton. *He* called *me*. The voice came at me in a flood of half-remembered vocables, their distinctive rhythm rising and swerving.

"I tried to look up your number, but directory assistance found nothing," he said. Reverse look-up matched the Pottier name with my address. I was beguiled! The poet had looked for and found me. My cheeks flamed up. How embarrassing, here was the man I had decided would become my mate, and I didn't even have my own apartment or phone number.

He had received my letter, he continued, "but I'm involved in litigation and can't make it down." I was unsure what "litigation" meant, surmising it had to do with that ugly divorce. In any case, he could not get away to Nova Scotia. My heart was pounding, mind racing. Failure was not an option, but failure to what? Failure to make a lasting impression, to make luck happen. Gut instinct took over. It was imperative I remain natural as possible. If I could manage the high-wire walk between cheeky-breezy bravado and an unfazed, warm, highly intelligent, non-neurotic, affectionate, discerning woman, surely I would pique his curiosity. Somehow, I needed to harpoon myself into his world without damaging it, or blunting my own individuality.

He was calling to decline my invitation and suggest I be his welcome guest for "an unlimited amount of time at his large house in Niagara-on-the-Lake where," he continued, I "would have plenty of room to write." He liked my poems, especially "Decadence." Also, he would help me get a manuscript together. I was to bring my portfolio, for he could "help me get unblocked" vis-à-vis my short stories — this said in a gruff, playful tone — and offered to pick me up in Toronto. My journal entry for that night opens with, "Oh the elation," and closes with an unpunctuated, "Must get some sleep there is too much to dream about."

Instinct told me that trying to tamp down or ignore the fierce desire simmering within me could only end in catastrophe. On August 6, I note Hiroshima's anniversary in my journal, having dropped "a little bomb tonight. Told Mom I'd decided to quit my job and was heading out to Ontario." I considered Ontario more foreign than Yugoslavia. "It would be so easy and safe to just curl up here forever ... Could this actually be my beginning? I'm scared. Very, very scared."

Within days, I experienced a classic anxiety attack. There were screeching banshee-like noises in my head each time I neared a mirror; I was certain the reflection would show my face — my self — fractured into a thousand jagged shards. Even then, I was my own best psychiatrist; I talked myself away from the brink of madness. Creativity being the best balm, I snapped out of it noting how the mechanics of going insane would make a good short story.

I quit my job on Friday, August 13, 1982, and spent the rest of the month breathing in all that Belleville meant to me. The sunlight on Eel Lake, spruce balsam and baked earth smells, salt breezes, the soft light, softer air, and how the sun rolled like an orange in the silvery summer bowl that was my village. All of it. I visited old childhood haunts and buffeted waves of nostalgia, almost tangible, so bittersweet they made me weep. Home could not hold me, and I was leaving its collective memories behind. Call it premonition, conviction, mad desire made manifest, but I knew I would not live there again.

Dad blanched at the sight of my yellow backpack, flap open, filled to bursting yet again. Europe was somewhat comprehensible, but *Toronto?* To visit that poet character whose divorce was making national headlines? No. My parents were anxious, unsupportive, but wise enough to not try changing my mind. When my father noticed me packing winter clothes, he grew even more distraught. I tried to mollify him, saying it was for maybe three weeks, three months. Finally, all I could carry was packed. My Smith-Corona manual typewriter came too. The sight of me, typewriter in hand, made him wince with embarrassment and disbelief. If there was a crumb of admiration anywhere within him, it stayed well hidden.

My imaginary world of drinking wine with Baudelaire, prowling foreign streets with Hemingway, clearly could not withstand another season in Belleville. I can easily recall how perplexed and powerless my parents felt. Any chance for accommodation passed and would never come again. Not when I was committing thoughts like these to paper:

Decadence

Ah decadence
sweaty lint in the navel of the mind,
bloodied grit
baked
under the fingernails of the soul
rusty tin can lid
for a plate
I feast
on your banquet of scum
and other carnal delights

Which Irving changed to:

Decadence

Sweaty lint
in the navel of the mind,
Bloodied grit
baked
under the fingernails of the soul.
I feast
on your banquet
of scum
and other carnal delights.

After an early morning flight to Toronto, I splurged on a limo (well, a minivan), as I didn't want Irving to drive all the way to Toronto to pick me up, and was dropped off at the St. Catharines Holiday Inn, where we had arranged to meet. I couldn't see him anywhere. Then again, more than a year had passed since that night in Halifax, and I was not sure I would remember what he looked like.

5: At His Invitation

A SHORT MAN WITH silver hair, reading glasses perched on his nose, flew past me in a brown blur. Was that him? I wasn't sure. Unaware whether poets in this part of the country wore velveteen track suits or not, I stood bolted in place, perspiration turning to haloing steam. Ignorant of how hot and humid southern Ontario was in late summer, I was wearing a massive woollen sweater, two shirts, and hiking boots, which had enabled me to cram more into my backpack. Feeling fainter by the minute, I noticed that man again. He had a clutch of correspondence in his hand, and appeared to be reading the letters. Must be Layton. I marvelled that he was so busy that he had to be reading his mail while coming to collect a visitor.

Presently, he got up and walked quickly toward the bar, and then back into the lobby, shooting covert glances at me over the rim of his reading glasses. At last he pivoted and approached. "You must be Annette," he said jovially.

My heart thumped a double-beat as we shook hands, me groping for an insouciant but urbane, "Irving Layton, I presume." It was indeed the poet-man.

"Well, why don't we have a drink?" We proceeded to the empty bar. He ordered a Labatt Blue, me a glass of house red. Later on he confessed, somewhat sheepishly, that the sight of me towering and aglow from the heat, bulky and burdened in my East Coast clothes, made his heart sink a little. "You looked like Bertolt Brecht's Mother Courage."

I was not altogether sure what that implied, but "courage" felt complimentary. I might have said I'd wished he'd been a bit taller, or perhaps younger, but said nothing. Not then, not ever.

The waiter brought our drinks, and after small talk about the trip, Irving looked squarely at me and fired off this question. "Do you think it's possible to have sex with someone without being in love with them?"

After a quick flashback to recent escapades in Europe, my answer came without hesitation. "Of course!"

He leaned slightly closer, a very mischievous smile on his surprisingly boyish face and continued, "Do you think it is possible to be in love with someone and *not* make love with them?"

"Absolutely not!"

"Right answer!" his blue eyes alive with Puckish delight.

With that, we collected my things, got into his small red Datsun Citation, and headed for Niagara-on-the-Lake. I was very nervous still, being in such close proximity, bereft of conversation, and dreading that I might fail to maintain his interest. He had the radio tuned to CBC. An opera played loudly. I had not really listened to much opera before, and found myself almost in a state of vertigo. I was miles from the ocean and felt disorientated, unsure what direction we were headed in, and dismayed at the featureless, bland countryside. This was Canada, not Tuscany — yet there were all these preposterous vineyards. The flat light and flatter land seemed a ridiculous setting for any poet.

We motored along, me trying not to notice how inattentively he drove. I would later learn that getting into a car with Irving Layton was a test of courage and friendship.

Just then, a cantilever bridge ahead of us was going up to let a Great Lakes freighter pass along the canal. My spirits sank commensurate with the rising bridge. We'd be parked for ages, and I was still tongue-tied. "Why on earth," I blurted, "are you living in this part of the world?" A place he just told me people went to rehearse what is was like to be dead.

He explained that it had been his estranged wife Harriet's idea. She had insisted so vehemently on wanting to be a writer that he agreed to buy a beautiful old house on Castlereagh Road. He did so to provide her with a peaceful retreat in which to write. Over time, he would confide intimate details of his relationship with Harriet, but then he gave me only an overview — how it began, her showing him mediocre poems, her exclaiming that she was about to have a mundane but acutely embarrassing operation, and how that made him take pity and accept her into his writing workshop. How she pursued him, eventually convincing him she truly wanted a home and a family. Alas, no sooner were they ensconced in the marital home than she grew bored, irritated even, by his relentless creativity. By the time the bridge came down, I felt almost completely at ease, as if we knew each other already, and very much his welcome guest.

The house was indeed beautiful. Sparkling white exterior, black roof, complete with a white fence and ramshackle garden out back under huge hardwoods and spruce trees. He hefted my pack up to the guest room and introduced me to Joanne B., his housekeeper. She was an English teacher who taught at a community college in nearby St. Catharines. Irving had hired her as a housekeeper when Harriet decamped. He enjoyed her as one of the few people in town who could handle discussions about literature and politics. She enjoyed the extra money the job brought and having a quiet place to write. Joanne was brisk in her mannerisms, smelled of patchouli, and welcomed me without fuss.

Irving suggested I might wish to shower and make myself comfortable. The upstairs bath had a Victorian claw-foot tub with a daffodil-yellow shower curtain and an old-fashioned latch on the door to lock it from the inside. I turned on the water, stepped into the tub, and drew the shower curtain closed. Irving's voice called from the other side of the door, asking if I needed anything. "I'm fine thanks!" I breezed.

That is when my eyes fixed on the brass doorknob. It was turning. My heart stopped for a second, horrified that after all my imaginings, yearnings, the insanely risky travail to get here, maybe — just maybe — he would turn out to be an ordinary man. Men of a certain age had lusted after me all across Europe. They were a dime a dozen, and woefully mundane. The latch held. The knob stopped turning. There was no further attempt to breach the bathroom door. Had he entered, I was fully prepared to be worldly and matter-of-fact about it. Still, I desperately needed him to be anything but ordinary.

I came down to a splendid meal, wine in a silver goblet, and conversation as airy and redolent as the Drum tobacco smoke that floated above the dinner dishes. I was in heaven.

After dinner, Joanne retired upstairs to do some writing; Irving ushered me into the beautifully appointed living room where we sat on a yellow-gold-burnt-orange sofa. The tall windows, their curtains gone, gave the living room an unsettling forlorn atmosphere. Lighting his pipe, Irving explained between puffs how a compliant Harriet and her spiteful mother had ripped the curtains down. Harriet's mother, Mrs. Bernstein, an opera singer who had given it all up to raise two children and who would go into lavish fits of weeping each time she listened to female sopranos, he described as even more vengeful than Harriet. "We are going to bleed you white!" she had hissed at him as they shoved past, curtains clawed into a ball.

Despite his raconteur style, he was clearly pained and distressed. Harriet had convinced Irving to give her a baby a couple of years before the agreed-upon time. He had wanted her to be sure she wanted a baby more than the writing career she had once spoken of so effusively. He knew the worm had turned when his father-in-law, Jack Bernstein, invited them to a private screening of *Popeye*. Afterward, over dinner, Irving explained why the movie would be a flop. Jack, high on the Famous Players' Toronto totem pole, was adamant it would be a hit. Harriet, Irving noted, took her father's side. He knew the marriage would not last much longer.

Irving shook his head, recalling Harriet's jumping the marital ship almost as soon as she had the baby. "I'm a pensioner in my seventies and they are trying to leave me without a penny for my old age!" he exclaimed, his voice pinched with fear.

The evening took more pleasant turns, playing out like an unfinished scene from an old movie: when his pipe refused to draw, he rolled us some Drum tobacco smokes, made us a nightcap, and rather tenderly advised that we should not sit too closely on the sofa. He confided that Harriet might have a private investigator outside, waiting to photograph him with a woman. What I took from the novelty of it all was that he was being protective of me. "I don't want you named as a co-respondent," he said in a low voice. I had landed in the midst of his war with the Bernsteins. It was a war he could not win — unlike Irving, they had ample wealth to waste on lawyers — except via the written word.

The next day, we took a long walk around the town, sitting in a park near the George Bernard Shaw Theatre. Irving spoke at length about his current situation, including the agony of having limited access to Samantha, still a toddler. Putting aside his worst fears, he asked me all about myself.

The following days flowed like a river as we talked non-stop, or sat on lounge chairs in the backyard, me reading a book between smokes and smooth spurts of conversation. He looked at my poems and brought his expertise to bear, and this in the most generous, kindest way imaginable. He took me seriously as a nascent poet, or certainly made me feel that I had talent worth developing. The Harriet fiasco kept resurfacing, no matter the topic at hand.

"All Harriet did once we moved here was look bored and flip through magazines while I wrote poem after poem, gave readings all across the country, and taught. How in hell did she not know who I was after all that time she pursued and finally got me to agree to marry her?" he demanded. Despite pouring his rage into the writing of *The Gucci Bag*, there was still a vast store of hurt and anger within. It would take more than a year of talk before the pain subsided to bearable levels.

In my journal that last summer before life with Irving, I soliloquize about two young men. To my consternation, they lacked the sense to return my affection, presumably too shallow to forgive my slight weight problem, and reinforcing in me the idea that a conventional love life was not in the cards. I deflected the sting of rejection by concluding I was far too spirited and rambunctious for the average swain. Irving was quite another matter. We talked for hours on end — I could make him laugh, pique his physical as well as spiritual and intellectual interests. It felt as if we belonged together. He had me firing on all pistons as never before, the excitement obliterating thoughts of other men.

That said, even with my notion of "touching face" and being part of his life, time was not ripe for my moving in. For the moment, I was still his guest, his life too busy to allow for any new commit-ments. Irving's day-planner for September 1982 notes appointments or calls from Shaindel Ross, a married Jewish lady who owned a career woman's clothing boutique in Toronto; Elspeth Cameron, his would-be biographer; Venie, a former student who lived in Montreal; third ex-wife Aviva; Samantha, his baby daughter whom he was fighting to see and would soon be denied access to; Ellen MacDonald, his divorce lawyer; Joycey-Woycey, an old friend he'd helped escape a bad marriage years earlier; Lucinda Vardey, his literary agent; and Karen from Sault Ste. Marie, the passionately devoted fan who produced the record *Layton Reads Layton*. There were also appointments with David O'Rourke, who would later turn his interviews into the source-material Irving drew upon to write his autobiography, among others whom I would later come to know.

I had arrived in Niagara-on-the-Lake on a Wednesday. Early impressions of me must have been good, for by Friday Irving brought me along to meet Shaindel in Toronto. By Saturday, my journal shows me in full social-minded fervour, taking up arms against *our* enemies; the middle class, philistines, and WASPy southern Ontario. I note in high-minded socio-political tones that, without workers, there would be no "flux," no tension. Irving and his housekeeper engaged in impassioned discussions about life, literature, and politics, which I soaked up like the proverbial sponge.

From the outset, it felt as if Irving and I had known each other our whole lives, or even longer. That is how comfortable, welcome, and equal he made me feel. By the third night, certain boundaries were breached in the most pleasant, altogether natural way. Those first weeks, my future was as alluringly empty as the days were languid. Two things were certain: I would write and I would live with Irving. This feeling was so powerful that I needed no plan; "how" didn't matter.

After six days in Niagara-on-the-Lake, I write of having come far and, while my disposition remained unchanged, I would never be the same. Seven days in, I was using "Uncle Irv's" pen to write in my journal:

> He is beside me here now, basking in the summer's last hot rays. A new book on the little cedar table. What a wonderful spirit he is. Above the soil, yet made of not much more than

that. He intones arias and operettas. I don't know if they are
real or glorious snippets composed by his devilish mind. How
I want to conquer his same mountains. Though he has suffered and suffers still, a part of him has remained untouched,
ever-capable of reaching out and embracing new things. His
spirit is my reminder. If it were not such a mistaken thing to
even dream about, I think I could abandon myself completely to his triumphant soul. Ah, who can love the wind with its
myriad balmy breezes and holocostic [sic] tempests.

This passage, while painfully high-pitched thirty years on, hints
at one of the reasons why he and I made a successful union. To wit:
I sensed he was an ordinary man in some respects, but also a self-
contained entity or force of nature whom no one could possess. Ergo,
if he was his own revolving planet belonging to the world, jealousy was
ludicrous. What is not yours per se cannot be lost. That insight won
me his enduring gratitude, and dagger-eyes from many angry women
— not because he wanted to stray, but because his appetite for life, for
extracting poems from people, could flourish without diminishing me
by one iota. The more exuberant and productive he was the more my
own contentment and pride grew.

One afternoon toward the end of that first week, I was happily
reading a book from his library. He held his red clipboard chest high
and sat beside me writing, half-singing, half-muttering phrases under
his breath. Without warning, he sat up and handed me the final draft of
the poem he had been working on.

To my utter delight, I read it. "Tragedy" for Annette Pottier. The
first poem he had written for me. Simple, a mere three verses long, but
in it, the core of our connection. I am young, but do not feel particularly gorgeous, he is seventy and plagued by memories, the arthritis
only there for effect. Irving is not old or blind but alive, with unending
vigor and curiosity and joy. I set him alight, as he did me. I knew it, and
now knew he did as well. The poet's alchemy now cast its magic onto
me. Simple words again changed by thought and emotion into a lasting
thing. Only years later would I appreciate what is meant by tragedy;

how Irving distilled what is suggested by Oedipus and King Lear; and how astonishingly apt the implications.[1]

Unbeknownst to Irving, as he wrote "Tragedy" I had drawn a sketch of him. Clearly, it is an older man's face, but his energy and spirit made the creased lines irrelevant. Only now do I realize there are no eyes behind the reading glasses.

6: Chance and Appetite

THE SECOND WEEK flowed much like the first. Aware I was still a houseguest, and despite Irving's offer to stay as long as I wanted, pride and common sense indicated one can not simply arrive and never leave. My summer's wages running out, I voiced the need to find a job. By the end of those fourteen days that shook my world, Irving tactfully spread the *Globe and Mail*'s Classifieds on the breakfast table.

With my abbreviated education and limited work experience, all I could hope for were nanny or housekeeping jobs. Irving suggested I would be very good at TESL (Teaching English as a Second Language), and urged me to look into it. I packed up and Irving gave me a lift to Jarvis and Queen in downtown Toronto. He pulled my yellow backpack from the trunk and wished me well with an embrace and a kiss. Irving sensed I would be fine, and said he, too, wanted us to stay in touch. He remained in my thoughts, but I needed to find a job before doing anything else.

It was sink or swim time. My traveller's instinct came flooding back on a wave of pure adrenaline. I had assured Irving I'd be fine, that I had a friend's number, and would stay in touch. In reality, I was alone in a foreign city with no real place to go, no job, and very little money left. All around me, dark shapes, alone or in small clumps, moved slightly or lay perfectly still in the grassy park. The difference between their homelessness and mine was but a question of time. Wanting to wring everything I could from this galvanizing situation, I took a room at the YWCA. The writer in me craved such moments. That night, I started a poem called "The Priests of Jarvis and Queen" — priests being those lost men scattered about like warning signs. Helen from Dalhousie days had grown up in Toronto. She put me in touch with her childhood friend Joanne G., a Polish-Canadian girl who lived near Roncesvalles just west of downtown. I stayed there a few days, soon finding work as a companion for an elderly woman way up in Willowdale, near Bayview and Steeles, north of the city. It was light, if mindless work. She actually subscribed to *The National Enquirer*. The poor dear was wheelchair-bound; my duties included packing her into her Delta 88 for ice cream runs and helping her down to the indoor pool. There are few things more sobering than being twenty-three years old, in a steamy shower room filled with geriatric ladies, all of them nude. Irving was about their age, but he was not old. Not like that. I called to tell him of my job and give him my new phone number.

On free nights, I amused myself exploring the Danforth, Toronto's Greek neighbourhood. It was almost like being in Greece; I even became the favourite *koritsi* (girl) whom everyone at The Strouga restaurant loved to tease, flirt with, and pretend to protect. The flirting never went far, done more out of boredom than lust. There was a hard edge to these Canadianized Greeks. A coldness. Another favourite haunt was the Thesperides Coffee House where my friend Moire and I sang one night. My main hangout, however, became the Free Times Café on Spadina. True fact: the very first alcoholic beverage they served was my drink, Pernod with water, with which I toasted myself in honour of Paris and its literary ghosts who, in my mind, applauded my plucky fumblings.

Was it there I saw a poster announcing Irving's reading, or had he called to tell me? In any case, it had been some two weeks since we parted on Jarvis Street. I settled my elderly charge for the night and took the subway for Spadina. Dressed in black — as that is how Irving was accustomed to seeing me — with a glittery jewel on my right sleeve and my hair swept up to the side, I waited, looking relaxed, feeling terribly nervous, five feet from the stage and four hours early.

The Free Times' small performance space grew packed and electric with anticipation. At last, Irving arrived with a blonde in a hot pink cotton dress that seemed more appropriate for a summer BBQ than a poetry reading. He did not notice me, not even after shaking hands with a man at my table. About thirty minutes into the reading, in full flight, he looked up and scanned the room. Seeing my face, he neither missed a beat nor looked at me again for the entire reading. Whatever crossed his mind, nothing distracted him from giving a fiery, polished performance. The blonde lady leaned heavily against the far wall. What puzzled me was how dismal she looked, her face blank except for the ennui draped over the Slavic cheekbones like a mask. How could anyone lucky enough to accompany the poet look so nonplussed? It was none of my affair. Venie, it turned out, was a Montreal woman and former student of Irving's who had known him since the 1960s. She and I did not meet that night, but would later clash. Several times.

With the reading over, I jostled past the photographers snapping pics of Irving and the broadsheet he had printed up in defiance of the biased "wet fart WASP judge." It listed the harrowing costs of having married Harriet. The crowd swallowed Irving whole. I suddenly felt ill at being so near, yet so far. Fate seemed unwilling to nudge me toward Irving or him toward me. I needed air, needed to leave and continue my miserable life as best I could until fate would throw us together again. Handing the cashier a traveller's cheque to pay my tab, she shook her head doubtfully. I nodded toward Irving, now busily signing books. "Irving knows who I am," I said, trying for Lauren Bacall nonchalance. It worked. Irving then glimpsed me, excused himself from autograph-seekers, and rose to embrace me. It was a modified déjà vu from the Halifax encounter. What I said next is long-forgotten, but I recall struggling to keep my composure, launching thought-missiles at him, desperately hoping he'd pick up on how I ached to be with him again. At least he seemed pleased to see me. Walking in the cold rain to the subway, I was both elated and dejected.

Our next encounter was via a phone call. An editor and I were having dinner at his place. He cooked while Leonard Cohen sang from the hi-fi, and I tried not to say or do anything gauche on this dinner date with my literary host. Leonard's record over, my date played the superb *Layton Reads Layton* album. Barely a few minutes into the first poem, the phone rang. It was Irving. I must have phoned him after seeing him at the Free Times reading and mentioned that I would be dining with the editor, though perhaps Irving wanted to discuss an upcoming interview with the man. In any case, the editor handed me the phone and Irving asked me out, though I recall no date coming of it, as I was obliged to work while Irving was passing through Toronto on his way to an engagement in Montreal.

Not long after that dinner, my journal entry for an undated Tuesday in October gushes with "Ecstasy, waltzes of joy, unabashed delight. He's back [from Montreal where he attended a book launch[1]], he called, he wrote another [poem] with me in the back of his mind." Very likely, the poem is "The Flaming Maple."

"We should get together sometime," he said cheerily over the phone, later. I was standing in the kitchen, having tidied up after giving my elderly ward her supper. When Irving said those words, a black pit opened in the linoleum floor. This was it. "Well, let's do it," I said, "let's not just say it and not do it!" trying to modulate the urgency in my voice.

Off I went that weekend, trundling down the highway in the back of a Greyhound bus to visit Irving. No longer strangers, we took up exactly where we had left off, just as I sensed we would. His company was as invigorating as ever. That Saturday, Irving was house-hunting and invited me along. The air was rich with the smell of apples and burning leaves. Wistfully, girlishly even, I couldn't help wishing he and I were already a bona fide couple, looking for a house of our own. Wisely, I kept the fantasy to myself. None of the houses suited him. He and I spent the rest of the weekend enjoying hearty meals, talk, wine, and each other. When he drove me to the bus depot for my return trip, he handed me a copy of his *Collected Poems*, published in 1971, inscribed as "something to hurl at the world when the going gets tough." I took my seat and hugged the book close as the bus began to pull away. Irving walked briskly to his car without looking back, unaware of the tears rolling down my face.

The naked truth is that there was no person or activity anywhere nearly as exciting as he was. George Brown College had interviewed me, then rejected my application. So, almost by default, and very conscious of the slight theatricality of it all, I leaned ever closer to the edge of the Irving cliff. There was nowhere else for me to go. Toronto was as far from my imaginary Paris as I was from being a world-class writer.

It would take more than just fierce wishing to become one. I slumped against bus, subway, and trolley windows, watching the grey monster of a city slide past. At least there was Kensington Market, the Free Times Café, and some authentic grit here and there, but Toronto would never let me in, not this Belleville girl without a dime, much less a B.A., to her name. *Blacken pages*. I needed to blacken pages, as Irving called it, and trust destiny. After all, Irving Layton believed in me.

As luck would have it, in the first week of November, my elderly charge fell out of bed, dislocating her hip for which she required hospital care. She kindly let me finish out the month at her place while I looked for work. I could think of no better tonic than spending another weekend with Irving before starting my job search anew.

Irving continued to look for a home near Toronto to be closer to his daughter Samantha. He had become increasingly distraught at how Harriet kept quashing the agreed-upon visits. Time after time, she would let him drive all the way from Niagara-on-the-Lake to Toronto, only to have the babysitter close the door in his face, claiming Samantha had a cold. With Joanne the housekeeper accompanying us, or rather me along for the ride, we met Irving's friend Shaindel in Oakville, a suburb of Toronto. Her many talents included expert home evaluation, apparently, for she began slapping at the doorjambs and stomping her slender foot, looking for dry rot. With a final hard little stomp, she declared the house on Lakeshore Road sound enough for purchase.

At that point, Irving thought Joanne would stay on as housekeeper, though I suspect she sensed Irving and I were getting along so well that she might soon be redundant. On November 8, a clear Monday morning, we came down to breakfast, after which Irving was to give me a lift back into Toronto where I would resume my job search. There was a note on the kitchen table; Joanne asking if Irving could take care of her cat, as the apartments she was looking at did not allow pets. He took it to be her letter of resignation.

"Well," he said, looking at me intently, before pausing. Then: "Looks like you're the new housekeeper!"

In the fraction of a second it took to respond, I knew with eerie certainty that my life was about to change — spectacularly and permanently.

This was not to be a brief stint at playing house with a celebrity. This was *it:* destiny. My heart was pounding, my thoughts racing, awed at seeing my premonition that night in Halifax now coming true.

"Yep," I answered. Irving made the coffee, I made breakfast, and that was how we began to live together. To mark the day, he gave me a blank hardcover book meant to be my reading journal. I designed its title page, named it "The Books Book," and listed myself as the author, Annette M. Pottier. It is one of the last times I would go by that name, as the whirlwind was already underway.

7: Meshing

BY NOVEMBER 17, fully ensconced at Niagara-on-the-Lake, I began recording my life with Irving Layton in the "Blue Book," a thick journal I had begun in Athens. The days were peaceful, mellow; they allowed us time to mesh our lives together; this idyll would serve us well when it came time to face the onslaught that followed moving to Oakville.

One afternoon I left him in his study, already stripped of most of its books in preparation for the move, to do a grocery run. Returning as he finished some correspondence, I brought him a glass of wine and retreated unseen, returning later with the bottle of Chianti and my glass.

Sitting on the thickly carpeted floor, I propped myself against a stack of boxes. He was barefoot, raked back in his chair. The autumn sun lit my face. We joked, bantered, and then he read me a letter from *Who's Who in Canada*, requesting approval on his listing.

"Don't let it go to your head," I countered, "my Uncle Vincent was in the *Who's Who* from 1945 until about 1977."

"Just wanted to gauge your reaction," he laughed, testing me, relishing the back-sass. "So, how do you think you'll like living with a genius?" he asked. I answered by smiling at him over the rim of my glass and taking another sip of wine, fully prepared to join myself to what I imagined his life to be.

Irving glanced over the assorted papers on his desk, sighing heavily. Harriet's angry exit had left him raw, pained, and still, over a year later, very frustrated. He mused at how he could have let it all happen.

"The poet's need for chaos?" I asked.

"Women. There are three types of women: itches, witches, and bitches. The confusion comes in trying to tell which is which. Now see, Harriet was an itch who changed into a bitch. Aviva was all three in one. You, you are an itch and a witch, but not a bitch ... " The conversation turned to sex and we talked as candidly as two teenagers just learning about the mysteries of the body. He liked my being as earthy as himself — earthy, but not vulgar. I marvelled that he could still be awed by sex having, well, lived for so long.

It was during this conversation he assured me that he was neither arrogant nor vain, that he was a very humble man, citing Voltaire's quip that he'd have a bigger turnout for his execution than for his return from exile. He encouraged me to make notes about what he said, not because he was vainglorious, but because people would want to know.

"Put down any wise thing or witticism I say. All this will be primary material for those who want to know what the man is really like. Gossip," he continued, "that's what people will want to know. People want to know what the man is like. Look at the great novels. Nothing but gossip. *Madame Bovary* [which he called Madame Ovary], *Anna Karenina*, nothing but an account of a series of adulterous affairs."

Anyone watching us in those early days would have been struck not so much by the age difference or our appearance, but by how naturally we interacted. My desire to learn, to fill the gaps in my reading, was so pronounced it was almost painful. Irving recognized this straight away, calibrating his comments like the superb teacher he was. The more I apprehended, the more complex he could permit himself to be. If there was a Pygmalion-like aspect of creating his ideal companion, he took care not to make me feel like an Eliza Doolittle. That said, I recall teasing remarks when we later watched *My Fair Lady*. He not only urged me to read, but also to write. Likening my storytelling ability to that of Colette, hinting at how her husband resorted to locking her in her study, forcing her to write in spite of her procrastination or laziness.

Among the very first books Irving put in my hands: Nadezhda Mandelstam's *Hope Against Hope*; D.H. Lawrence's *Sons and Lovers*; Edward H. Flannery's *The Anguish of the Jews*; *The Poems of Catullus*, edited by J. Michie; Françoise Gilot's *Life With Picasso*; *The Life of Dylan Thomas* by Constantine Fitzgibbon; Colette's *My Apprenticeships, and Music-Hall Sidelights*; R.J. Hollingdale's *Nietzsche*; and E. Hamilton's *Plato: Collected Dialogues*. Even if I managed to read only the Gilot book in its entirety, the books' distilled essence filtered through in our daily conversations. What I could not read for lack of time, I absorbed through my skin while marinating in pools of ideas and thoughts.

The remaining days in Niagara-on-the-Lake padded by like softly muted footsteps on carpet or forest floor. Oakville — I braced myself — would mean total immersion into his maelstrom. I worried about not knowing how to entertain and cook. When I confessed my fear of losing his interest for my lack of experience, background, and education, he quickly assured me he liked me just the way I was, adding, "You know, I don't think I ever want another woman under my roof." It was not the blank slate aspect that attracted him; it was my eagerness to fill the slate with my own markings. What clinched it for him was learning that I was born in 1959, the year his mother died. Half-jokingly, but with a wistful catch in his voice, he surmised her spirit had entered mine at birth. Keine Lazarovitch had sent me to look after her son. The notion sat easily with me; with other people, not so much. Three skeptics called in the space of a week, each insisting on seeing Irving alone. His son Max; his ex, Aviva; and that Shaindel woman all wanted to know what Irving — or, more accurately what I — was up to. He and I, already intertwined on so many levels, ignored their "concern" as mere piffle and meddling jealousy.

"You can't make me happy," Irving pointed out, "because I'm already happy." For my part, I felt he could not make me great, as I already was. Nor did my ego need his validation. Would it be an easy road? No, certainly not. I was keenly aware that I was about to devote the best years of my life to a man forty-eight years my senior as his "chatelaine." The term, "keeper of the keys," appealed for its quaintness. After only two weeks together, this is how I described a typical evening in my journal:

> Tonight after an ample and satisfying meal, after biscuits
> with butter and jam, I go and make myself a cup of cocoa,
> loading it with honey, vanilla, and salt, fully intending to

let it turn to fudge while I scurried upstairs to change the sheets and start considering the laundry. Irving was sitting at the kitchen table, still engrossed in Albert Memmi's *The Liberation of the Jew*. He watched, with sidelong glances and furtive but deadly peers over the top of his reading glasses, saying nary a word as I filled my face with the gooey brown syrup, the cup held through a kitchen towel. The radio ceased its classical music and Chekov's *Three Sisters* began. He put down his book, fumbled for the volume dial and said, "Listen to this!" then ahhhed his approval at the naming of one of the actresses. After but a few minutes, no, even less than that, he sat back, frustrated. "It's lost on me. I have to see it." It is painful for me, who has known him only this short length, to see time begin to make itself known.

Homemade chocolate goo indicates that I was under stress, as that was how I self-medicated. A few days later, I would be packing up the entire house without a clue as to how one did this. The last Monday of November 1982 was Irving's last night in Niagara-on-the-Lake. He dumped a box of Harriet's business cards in the garbage, salvaging a pair of black wool slacks he took to return to her. For me, she would never be more than a ghost. The house had expunged itself of her smell. All that remained were her recipe collections and a couple of photo albums she had assembled. We kept the posh Famous Players and Barrich Productions stationery for their luxurious feel. Everything else — the chintz kitchen curtains, spices, décor — spoke of the bride who once made her home with Irving. The kitchen, as evidenced by a Polaroid photo, had echoed with Samantha's cries: there was Irving at the kitchen table holding a tiny, diapered Samantha on his lap, his face looking stunned and unsure.

This had been their home, and for two heady months, it was where I enjoyed the start of my life with Irving. For him, that last night was about endings, empty rooms, and echoes he'd as soon forget. It was all over but the shouting, as he was fond of saying. The one redeeming thought, aside from having helped create Samantha Clara Layton, was that he had recorded it all in *The Gucci Bag*. The Mosaic Press limited edition was slated for publication in March 1983.

"I don't know where I'd be if I'd not written *The Gucci Bag*," he told me. "This time last year, I was in a small apartment on Bathurst Street. When I think of the depths of anguish — not despair, I never despair ... *Amor fati* has always been my motto. Love your fate."

No matter how intemperate he could become when discussing Harriet, he always ended on a note of pity, usually abject, sometimes with a sour edge. "These poems are going to live on for decades, if not centuries. Judas, at least, had the good sense to hang himself! Oh, I don't envy her. I, of course, won't be around, but you make it a point to see her ten, fifteen years from now, and you'll see a fat, miserable, mediocre..."

What irked him the most, he said, was the not "the shabby way in which she left," but that "she could betray me as a teacher. The two things I pride myself on most are being a poet and a teacher. How could she have heard me say over and over again for seven years that the poet always has the last word? She heard me tell of what Byron had written about Castlereagh, the British PM who ordered shots fired into the crowd of striking mill workers. After Castlereagh's death, Byron wrote a scathing eight-line satirical poem where he pisses on Castlereagh's grave. She heard me when I talked about Archilochus who, upon being jilted, drove the girl's entire family to suicide. And those poems have been around two thousand years! She also knew about Catullus and he's been around for three thousand years! Her father, I can excuse because he is a lout, but she knew ... "

Most unpardonable of all was the betrayal of her handing his love letters and poems over to her divorce lawyer. In his first post-breakup letter, he praised her for having the courage to leave once the marriage no longer satisfied her, declaring he'd not have left her, just as he'd not left Aviva. "The bond had been made and I could not leave them. Thank God they left me," he laughed, protective humour returning.

So he took one last look at the home, addressing the malingering ghosts that *The Gucci Bag* was written to serve as an example, to teach

Ids [his term for philistine Jews] an unforgettable lesson so that no one after this should have the misfortune to suffer as he had.

As moving day approached, I helped Joanne lug her entire library out, loading it into her friend's van, naively expecting she would reciprocate. No such luck. My curses echoed in the empty house as I packed everything, including furniture and oddments from all his previous unions. Irving had gone ahead to Oakville, staying at Howard Aster's home and attending to yet more divorce proceedings. Howard, a former Montrealer whom Irving had taught at Herzliah High School, now taught Political Science at McMaster University and ran Mosaic Press. He was one of Irving's spiritual sons.

Fallen leaves blew into the open door faster than I could sweep them out as the movers hurried around me. "Are you sure you're moving today?" the boss asked. I was a few months into my twenty-third year, and so green that I'd not had the appliances unhooked. He shook his head incredulously and set about those tasks.

As to the actual Gucci bag, Irving told me it was a gift Harriet had given him after a trip to Italy with her parents. I can still see the bewildered expression on his face wondering what Harriet was thinking buying him a designer man-purse. I helped Irving nail it to the wall by the back door as a talisman to ward off bourgeois philistinism. For Irving, the bag represented Harriet's colossal miscalculation of what the poet and teacher was all about. Howard asked to use it for the cover of the Mosaic Press edition. It has since disappeared, as did the last traces of Irving's presence in Niagara-on-the-Lake. Nine Castlereagh, someone once told me, was later razed to the ground.

PART TWO:

A BROAD INNOCENCE

8: Oakville

OUR NEW HOME AT 395 Lakeshore Drive East was a sumptuous, ten-room, two-storey, white stuccoed affair, complete with a huge backyard, trees, a veranda out front, and a sunroom that Irving called the Florida room. Its tongue-and-groove wainscoting, restful blue-flowered wallpaper, and pine-trimmed kitchen put it somewhere between an English cottage and a Canadian farm-style house, minus the farm. I arrived from the bus depot to find Irving helping direct the movers amid boxes and commotion. Darkness fell as the movers drove off. We were ravenous. Before I could go get a pizza from up the street, however, Shaindel arrived.

Despite Irving's circumspect manner, Shaindel seemed to imagine there was more to their relationship. Nothing scandalous transpired between them far as I knew. I was glad she helped Irving with practical things during post-Harriet days. *The Gucci Bag*'s "New Shining Worlds" is for her, ending with the less than erotic lines, " ... only from rot / are new shining worlds begot."[1] Irving permitted Shaindel to act as if she was in charge, indulging her ruse of bringing him tins of Chock Full 'O Nuts coffee, as if there was none in Niagara-on-the-Lake. It was her excuse for showing up at least once a month. Now that we were living even closer, I suspected she would turn up more often. She was one of several women less than pleased with Irving's newfound happiness. If I wanted "wifely companion" status, I would have to fight for it.

So, on our first night in Oakville, Shaindel strode in, dug out the set of cheap-looking dishes she bought, and spread a BBQ chicken meal on the table.

"You *seeee*, Irving," she cooed smugly, "I *told* you I'd get you dinner the first night in your new home!" So much for our honey-time together. Real life was officially underway and Shaindel's presumptuousness had me bristling. What fantasy was *she* living, her with a husband at home, that she felt it pivotal to usurp my desire to provide the first meal? I ate, jaw muscles twitching, eyes glaring, taking stock of her, noting how she kept brushing close to Irving as she leaned in, repeatedly, to serve him like a Jewish June Cleaver. She treated me as though I ranked no higher than a random teenager. Wolfing down the grub, I was too hungry and too polite to voice my dismay. Later that night, Irving agreed she had overstepped the bounds, and that he had failed to correct her. His somewhat off-kilter sense of chivalry was set on "Indulge the Guest," even if it meant offending the mate. Was this wrong of him? Yes, many times it was. His saving grace? My certainty that he never intended to cause me displeasure.

The *Toronto Star* announced Irving's move to Oakville and his shiny new twenty-three-year-old companion. Normally, one works decades to obtain life's tangible and intangible fruits — things like a national presence, a fully paid-for home, and a steady pension; there was a car in the driveway, PoetPuss the cat on my lap, four ready-made children (albeit two of them older than myself), and a stimulating life. True, I had produced only gossipy titterings as yet, but without doubt had landed into what Irving called a *schmaltz grieb* (a Yiddish term Irving used to mean bed of insanely good luck). What more could any twenty-three-year-old want?

A new house in a new town came with a new name, one bestowed on me by Irving a few weeks earlier. "I can't stand the name 'Annette,'" he said, wincing a little. "You see, every time I say it, I think of the Annette who married my nephew Bill." Bill was four years younger than Irving, and they had been very close growing up in Montreal. When Irving warned Bill that perhaps this European lady was not so much in love with Bill but with getting her foot through the immigration door, Bill was outraged. Bill married Annette. They had a son, and she soon absconded with the baby, leaving Bill for an American doctor in Buffalo. Bill and Irving's friendship survived, but the name "Annette" had to go. "Do you mind if I call you Anna?" It felt alright, like Anna Magnani, I thought.

Barely settled into our new home, Irving spent the holidays in Montreal visiting the circle of friends whom I was too new to meet. While he left for what I called the Forbidden City, I boarded a train to Nova Scotia, experimenting boldly with an old silver Chai necklace that he had given me, even wearing it outside my clothes on the way back home. Returning to WASP territory as a Jewess almost by virtue of wearing it, I felt as if people looked at me differently, as if it emanated fierce powers, that wearing it was akin to looking for a fight. "But of course!" Irving exclaimed, "You're wearing five thousand years of Jewish history around your neck!" In deference to my parents' sensitivities, or lack thereof, I kept the Chai out of sight while in their presence.

To no one's surprise, home was still fraught with me-versus-them moments. Only now, back in those familiar surroundings, could I truly appreciate how much I had grown in a mere four months. Breathless and excited, I nonetheless kept up the pretense I was just a housekeeper. Irving's phoning me on New Year's Eve thus took some explaining. My parents were not amused.

Nor was Irving's ex-student Venie, the woman in the pink dress at the Free Times reading, as it turned out. She was recovering from her own nasty divorce, and Irving was staying in the basement guest room of the house she shared with her parents in Montreal. A few months earlier, not long before I moved in with Irving, he had been in Montreal for the launch of *CIV/n*, a collection of previously published essays, edited by Aileen Collins. On that trip, he wrote "Thank You Veneranda," poem 92, the fourth from last poem in the Mosaic Press limited edition of *The Gucci Bag*. I had no doubt he was grateful for being shown that Kali was still extant, and "the phallus a fiery brand plucked from hell." Nor did I have a problem with that. They had known each other since the 1960s; he and I were not a couple yet.

By New Year's Eve, however, Irving and I were two months into our relationship. Venie was hosting a party at Biddles, a popular Montreal jazz bar that she loved, and was displeased that Irving, her prized friend, slipped away to call me. Their relationship is best described by Irving in poem 52, "Seventeen Lines and Three Kisses." That poem, written in September 1981, describes the poet alone in a mundane breakfast setting. He reads a book, while she dreams of the perfect existential lover. He notes how she had suffered from love and men. Grateful for her capacity for laughter and sensuality, he "tiptoes into her bedroom / and leaves three sincere kisses on her pillow." Not on her mouth, I noted. Intuitively, I knew not to be bothered by the suggestive closing lines in "New Year's Poem for Veneranda," written on December 31, 1982, wherein his "denuded stalk" will turn into a "sunflower in her hand." It appears as poem 110 in the Mosaic Press paperback edition, published in 1984. Not only did he discuss the poem with me, I helped type the drafts. Recalling her expression from that night at the Free Times, there was no reason to be upset. His recovery from the Harriet fiasco was all to the good. Poets are not ordinary men, I was not the average female. Ultimately, though she and I would clash, there is no denying the role her friendship played in Irving's recovery, and for that we can only be grateful.

I can't be certain what Irving told his Montreal friends about us on his 1982 Christmas visit as he made the rounds, gallantly flitting from one social obligation to the next. I say "obligation," a term that would no doubt dismay his female acquaintances. Later, as I came to know many of these ladies, it seemed that he had little in common with them beyond the shared Montreal memories of his teaching days at Sir George (later merged with Loyola College to become Concordia University). Some had inspired poems or enjoyed brief trysts; many others were simply long-time acquaintances.

Women, he declared, were far more complex than men, and thus much more interesting — for the poems they could inspire, not for bed-romp banalities. His poem "Vampire," written in 1973, served as fair warning. In it, Layton discloses his intentions. The poet lusts for truth, not breasts or thighs, warning his love that her youthful blood risks being drained to feed his immortality. Once a subject had yielded their "quota" of poems, the poet's interest dwindles to nothing.

Men, on the other hand, were generally wary of him and kept their distance. He confided over one of our breakfast confabulations how he felt lonely for the company of men. Not finding it, aside from a handful of spiritual sons and a *rara avis* like Leonard Cohen, there was always a surplus of women on the periphery — Dorothy Rath, a devoted fan who became a lifelong friend, being, as he said, "The best and purest of all." Perhaps it is just as well that an early conception of his memoir *Waiting for the Messiah* never materialized. In early 1983, its working title was *While Waiting for the Messiah*. In it, he considered talking about women just as he had spoken to me one day, comparing them on a spiritual scale. "Aviva fell short," he mused, "because it all boils down to having to *love* poetry to stay with me." If that was his main criterion, I was sure of passing with flying colours. When he read "Vampire" aloud to test my reaction, I must have given the right smart-aleck response and simply kept evolving in a continuous arc, thus de-fanging the vampire and holding on to whatever beauty and truth I commanded.

Whatever the basis for these friendships, he had known some of them longer than I had been alive. Here again, jealousy on my part would have been absurd. I showed no possessive insecurity for one reason: I had none. Irving chose me, after all; or, more precisely, we chose each other. Venie was now fully aware of my existence, but unwilling to believe I was more than an awkward — and temporary — housekeeper. Whether out of cowardice, misplaced chivalry, or a dread of ugly scenes, Irving let Venie think what she wanted as she shuttled him around Montreal. In any case, he returned from Montreal with new poems in hand and eager to see the Mosaic Press edition of *The Gucci Bag* through to publication.

I spent much of my visit home rigid with anxiety and anger, on the defensive at all times. No matter how my parents pressured, I had no plans to ever return to Nova Scotia. This did not sit well, especially with my mother. Nothing I did could elicit so much as an approving nod. It had been so since childhood. As a young boy, my brother piously crafted crucifixes as gifts for my mother. She lovingly inscribed the date in pen on the back and saved them in her lingerie drawer. Once, hoping to please her, I gave her a lovely piece of driftwood. It sat on the window ledge for a few days. Then, I watched in pained silence as she used my gift as kindling to light the kitchen stove. To this day, I cannot read D.H. Lawrence's *Sons and Lovers* without glancing over my shoulder as chills of recognition chase one another up and down my spine.

There are other such examples of my mother's dislike for me, too painful and plentiful to mention here. Suffice to say that, by the age of thirteen, seeing how my being a female had upset her world — that my being attractive and exploding with a superbly active imagination caused a mother such displeasure — I knew I would not risk having children. My receiving only a few sprinklings of mother-love had, I felt, left me unable to give love to a child. During my adolescence and early womanhood, I feared becoming a potential child-abuser; that I would avenge what my mother did by hurting my baby. So, by the time of my first period, I vowed never to bring a child into the world. Irving's unconditional love would later banish this decade-long misconception, freeing me of its grip.

My mother tried to understand what I was up to by picturing herself in my shoes, only to panic at the strangeness and crippling embarrassment she imagined on my behalf at being with this old Jewish man. Unable to perceive how I coped with a life she could barely discern, she singed me with rebukes and withering put-downs. This would go on throughout my entire time with Irving; she could barely bring herself to say his name, spitting out only "ton vieux" (your old man), with heavy emphasis on *old*. Nor did my parents ever visit me, meet him, or even venture to phone me more than three times in nearly fourteen years. Her excuse, as feeble as it was poignant, was always, "Oh, I don't want to disturb you." In fact, she was terrified Irving might answer the phone. She did not know how to address him — or that "Hello" would have been fine.

Still, for all her misgivings, and this I shall always recall with a burning and misshapen fondness, we drove to Yarmouth and wandered into R.H. Davis, my favourite stationery store. An enormous ledger-style record book caught my eye. I hefted it, fanned the pages to generate that clean paper smell, and put it back. Thirty dollars was beyond my means. Mom promptly bought it for me. Although she did not know, approve of, nor understand what I was doing with my life, if this massive blank book compelled me to fill its pages to help me become a writer, so be it. It would come to hold verbatim conversations between Irving and me, even the description of my slight nervous collapse upon realizing the enormity of what my choices entailed.

The holiday, rocky and bittersweet, ended. I left Belleville with relief, eager to return to Oakville where the Minch, *mein mensch*, was waiting for me — as was everything else life with Irving held in store.

9: Buckle Up

CALL IT INTUITION, call it reading the handwriting on the wall, but I sensed Oakville would not be our home for long. For starters, it was in the very heart of WASP Canada. Irving could never feel at ease there any more than the statuettes of Ezekiel and Jeremiah in the church of Notre Dame, to whom he'd once brought his "hot Hebrew heart," standing with them awhile in "aching confraternity."[1]

For confraternity in Oakville there was Howard Aster, soon to bring out a limited edition of *The Gucci Bag,* as well as four leather-bound copies of the same. Irving and Howard talked politics like seasoned pundits, discussing world events through clouds of pipe smoke. Irving and I were always welcome at the Asters', enjoying the distinctly European ambiance emanating from antique Spanish furniture, art, classical music, and ever-present pipe smoke paired with warming glasses of cognac.

Howard had ventured into the book trade in the seventies, publishing a lavishly slip-covered edition of Irving's *The Uncollected Poems: 1936–1959* (1976) and carrying on through until their last project together, *Final Reckoning: Poems 1982–1986* (1987). Irving could pitch a manuscript and have it accepted virtually straightaway. This did not always sit well with Lucinda Vardey, Irving's literary agent, who had to run interference with Irving's other publisher, McClelland & Stewart. Mosaic occasionally dismayed Irving with typos, always more egregious in poems than prose. In early 1990, Lucinda sternly ordered

Irving to withdraw a later Mosaic Press project. *Onion Rings*,[2] a volume of new and selected poems, was duly withdrawn, as McClelland & Stewart owned the rights to many of the poems. Lucinda shepherded subsequent editions of Irving's books through to McClelland & Stewart, various overseas publishers, and McGill-Queens University Press.

As with all of his spiritual sons, Irving's friendship with Howard never waned or faltered. McClelland & Stewart had published Irving since the 1970s, helping Jack McClelland raise his company's profile by participating in promotional stunts guaranteed to interest a broader public. Lucinda kept watch over Irving's rights and contracts so efficiently, and Irving seeming unconcerned with such details, that I never quite mastered Irving's publication rights dossier. I did, nonetheless, notice how McClelland & Stewart sent detailed royalty statements, unlike the less formal Mosaic Press. Italian publishers, such as Einaudi, sold out the entire print run, but monies never materialized. Nor were other Italian publishers good at following through with advances, royalties, and sales figures.

As for me, even without a history of excoriating WASPs, I felt equally out of place in Oakville. Outmatched by the locals' bank accounts and fine clothes, we made a game of annoying them. Come summer, for example, I was grimly fond of walking barefoot up Lakeshore Road wearing nothing but a flimsy sundress, defiantly queuing up alongside the Crabtree & Evelyn set at the Toronto-Dominion bank. Once, while lunching at a local restaurant, exasperated with diners ratcheting their chairs to eavesdrop but never deigning to say hello, Irving looked at me with an especial glint in his eye, and started ad libbing about how thrilled he was at being invited to Prince William's christening. Not missing a beat, I too made like an ecstatic monarchist. We guffawed all the way home at how the eavesdroppers bought it — even if only for moment. At the annual street fair, Irving danced the cancan with a bevy of Irish nannies. Oakvillians snapped photos left and right, likely assuming he had fondled, if not bedded, each one. Whether performing for crowds or needling his critics, Irving had an instinct for what was expected of him and how rumours start. Playing to the crowd, he linked arms with Oakville's bodacious nannies (friends of

the Aster family nanny), kicking higher, laughing rakishly, giving tit-
illated townsfolk exactly what they wanted. Not surprisingly, Oakville
threw us a farewell party when we left.

When invited to a party or event, Irving generally excelled at performing as a poet — that is, being witty, informed, jocular, an exciting
conversationalist, and an even better listener. It was expected; he delivered. We threw very few parties, in part due to my lack of hostess
expertise, but also because, more often than not, Irving preferred being
home, reading or watching a movie on TV. Regardless of the alleged
megalomania, Irving was never keen on forced social intercourse. It
taxed his patience and energies, and he loathed being trotted out as a
pet celebrity for the amusement of a certain hostess's bourgeois friends.
One such ambush, where he'd been led to believe it would be just the
lady and her husband rather than a full-on party, provoked heated
words and his berating her afterwards for pulling that trick once too
often. It earned the hostess a poem about a bourgeoise hating her reflection in a mirror that stays too expensive to smash. Social occasions
brought his usual modus operandi into play, i.e., asking people about
themselves and listening intently for any revelatory crumb that might
spark a poem. For self-preservation, when conversation waned and
boredom loomed, he either soliloquized or vituperated, depending on
his frame of mind.

My Christmas trip to Nova Scotia confirmed "home" meant "trap"
and that my family was from a different planet. With Belleville no longer my home and Oakville sanctuary more for Lake Ontario ducks than
for us, it was critical we continue to build an unshakeable bond. One
of the first challenges we faced was having Moire MacLeod, my friend
from Dal who had travelled a bit of Europe with me, as a boarder. On
some level, I wondered if the feminist in her would disapprove of the
way I took care of Irving. Perhaps more pointedly, would her being
single and free make me question my non-single, non-free life?

Moire — a willowy redhead who looked and moved like a model in
her Persian lamb coat, her blue-green eyes set off by delicate freckles and
a milky smooth complexion — had landed a job as a guide at Toronto's
CN Tower and rented our guest bedroom for a couple of months. Her

presence was not overly disruptive, but did raise the town's collective eyebrow as they noted not one, but now *two* young women living with the supposed Lothario. I welcomed her company. It would be nearly the last time I would have a friend my age within sight or sound.

In early February Irving was eager to take in the William Blake exhibition at the Art Gallery of Ontario, a half-hour's drive east of Oakville. No one objected when I got behind the wheel. Irving sat up front, Moire just as happy in the back seat of the little red Datsun. We made it to downtown Toronto without incident. On a broad staircase leading down into the Art Gallery, we met a strange-looking little man coming up, almost troll-like, with bulbous eyes protruding from his washboard face. "Milton!" Irving cried, clasping the wee forlorn-looking man in a bear hug. It was Milton Acorn. I gasped, taken aback not only by the look of him, but at meeting him in the flesh. He was the Maritime poet who had once been married to that other tragic poet, Gwendolyn MacEwen.

Life had not been kind to Milton, and it showed. Irving, a longtime admirer of Acorn's work, later told us how, in 1969, he'd been outraged that Milton's book, *I've Tasted My Blood,* was overlooked for the Governor General's Literary Award in favour of George Bowering's *Rocky Mountain Foot.* The injustice of it drove Irving to enlist the help of Eli Mandel, a literary critic, poet, and fellow York University professor, with whom he sent a letter of protest to the Governor General's Award committee. He then sought support from others, such as Al Purdy and Margaret Atwood, to create the first People's Poet Award, its presentation ceremony held at the aptly rough-edged Grossman's Tavern. Occasionally, mention of the event appeared in print or on radio. Irving's role was either obfuscated, minimized, or left out completely. His championing of Milton Acorn did not jive with Toronto's preferred image. In their eyes, despite facts to the contrary, no self-aggrandizer like Layton could possibly be supportive of another poet.

Introductions were made and Milton chatted briefly with us. Still bowled over from the exhibition, he was happy that we too were to see it. With that, he continued on his way. This would be their last encounter. Milton died three years later.

After William Blake's dazzlingly coloured illustrations, Toronto looked all the greyer under leaden clouds. It was late afternoon and growing darker by the minute. Nearing home, I cut through Oakville and pulled up at the corner of Reynolds and Lakeshore Road. On the green light, I pulled into the intersection only to see a pick-up truck headed straight into us with a bang.

The truck essentially bounced off my face and came to rest on the far side of the intersection. Irving sat motionless, looking disgruntled and bewildered. Moire alternately groaned and laughed while slowly picking herself up off the floor. We were all okay, though shattered glass and cold wind sent me right back to my first car accident. In a robotic voice and seized with a terrible thirst, I began repeating that I'd "seen this before." Irving sustained only a deep bruise on the left side of his chest. I had a very sore right wrist, so presumably my arm had swung out violently and collided with him. Irving heatedly refused to go to the hospital, thereby minimizing the effect of being reminded how vulnerable we are, how fragile. Hospitals meant sickness and death; he wanted no part of either. Moire and I were X-rayed and held several hours for observation. She had blood in her urine; I had a mild concussion and was instructed to stay awake that night. We limped home to find the wrecked car in the driveway and Irving sitting up in bed, quite pale, reading a book. Moire and I stayed with him for a while, making light of our brush with disaster. Irving never bought another car, though once in Montreal we did not really need one. Twenty-five years elapsed before I drove again.

What stands out vividly about those early days is how Irving and I smoothed out various bumps and misunderstandings. Had I been older, more set in my ways, or more mature, perhaps, our coming together might not have happened. My journal entries record a highly developed sense of self in terms of being a serious would-be writer, but I neither saw nor thought of myself as a woman. I *existed*, yes, but not as an adult female. Aside from my mother, I had no role model from which to pattern how to live with a man, particularly a much older, very active public figure. My mother epitomized dedication to her home and family. She strove to make our lives comfortable despite limited means. "No matter how poor you are, you can always afford soap," she would say, proud of her spotless house, her clean well-behaved children, and putting supper on the table every night at 5:30 p.m. If Dad came home late, she was to place his supper in the oven and he would eat whenever he arrived, regardless how spoiled, and he was not to utter one complaint. Her homemaking skills added to her stature, and I took that as my cue: make the man providing for you as comfortable as possible, because that is your part of the bargain. Irving laboured much harder than I did working on a poem, giving readings, and so why should I balk at doing household chores?

Regardless of my curious mix of wisdom and ignorance, instinct told me that flexibility was paramount. In a cryptic note written around that time, I describe the poet's persona coming to the surface — though it is not clear whether I am referring to myself or to Irving recovering from the Harriet fiasco. Perhaps I meant both of us, for it says *we* don't need to be conscious of being "normal" as we rise to poetical heights and flights of fancy to the point of almost "non-being." In other words, reality and convention were of no importance. Being sustained by poetic ether, however, mattered very much. Somewhere on an imaginary Mount Olympus of Poetry, Irving and I merged easily beyond constraints of age, time, or social convention. My friend Moire, the first feminist I met until observing Betty Friedan throwing back vodka tonics while edging real close to Irving at a PEN International function, took a hard line with what she saw. Moire wondered whether I should be so dedicated to a man — *any* man. Though she and I were of the same generation, my Acadian upbringing formed me as if in an earlier time. With deliberate awareness, I let him be the driving force. To balk would be to break, and I had no intention of breaking.

Irving never expected me to be "just" a housekeeper. From the outset, he sought my opinion on a multitude of things; a word or line in a poem, the title of his memoir, what I thought of his friends as we dissected them to their very marrow. My responses interested him and he never condescended to nor patronized me. What I recall with tremendous affection, and this confirmed by numerous journal entries, was that the teacher in him exhorted me to read, to work on a poem or the journal entries he delighted in. "Go! Finish your drink and go write in your journal. Fifteen minutes and you'll feel better. *Schreiben!* (Write!)," he'd say, slapping his open hand down on the table, his eyes bright with equal measures of challenge and encouragement. Other times, he'd craft little aperçus and reel me back from the laundry room with, "Now, put this down in your journal," bursting to explain a poem or relate tidbits such as how, years ago, he'd predicted Leonard Cohen would never write another book of poems, despite his super-abundance of talent. "He's cut the cord," unlike Henry Moscovitch, who'd gone crazy and stopped writing for years, "but Henry never cut the cord! I look how unique [Henry's] poems are. Magnificent poems, stark and stripped-down. Not like the rest of the stuff in Canada, that non-poetry."[3]

Many of Irving's comments struck me as worthy of being noted verbatim. For example, his rhetorical question whether Aviva would write another novel after her roman à clef *Nobody's Daughter.* "Unless she wrote the truth, now *that* would be a tour de force! She is too narcissistic, much too subjective. That's alright for a poet — " Many times, he shared his dismal prognosis on the state of Canadian poetry, pained by the godawful stuff being churned out. I grabbed pen and paper to catch as many of his observations as possible. Afterwards, I would disappear into my study to work on poems before the entire literary enterprise imploded.

Early mornings were a favourite time of day. We took our first cup of coffee in the large, light-filled country kitchen, each cocooned in silence. Irving was often distant in those early days, preoccupied with things such as a troublesome line in his latest poem; news out of the Middle East; Quebec politics and how they affected Venie's teaching career (she constantly bemoaned the uncertainty brought about by political unrest); or the ongoing battle for visitation rights to see Samantha. I sat quietly across from him, observing his movements, gestures, and the way he fixed that laser-beam stare on whatever befell his eye. Without a word passing between us, I formulated thoughtful questions for later and mapped out my day. By the second cup of coffee, he shifted gears as we lolled at the sun-warmed table, luxuriating in hours of talk, pausing only for the news. We pounced on the morning mail like two mastiff pups tearing into whatever the postman forced through the slot. Blue smoke from roll-your-own Drum cigarettes clouded the air. Almost daily, letters triggered stories about the sender. Letter by letter, story by story, I learned of his acquaintances and their place in his life.

Amid this writerly unfolding of days, there were foibles such as his missing the ashtray with errant flicks of his cigarette, his cursing at misplaced glasses, or throwing the cigarette fixings down in frustration when his thick fingers rolled one too tight to draw. This always tore little pieces of my heart as I commiserated, blaming the cheap gadget while rolling him a fresh cigarette. I ascribed these foibles to outward signs of genius. He was busy with big things, I reasoned, little things could slide. Such as his habit of over-writing my plans for the day.

From a budding poet's perspective, dropping everything in order to help transcribe poems was incalculably educational. Everything I did to help Irving lent my life significance I could never garner working in some office. Serving as his amanuensis was my choice, as was deciding it was wiser to bend than protest. Clearly, his being a poet mattered to me. It was as redeeming as it was magical. Increasingly, all I wanted to do other than write was to engulf Irving in limitless understanding and warmth.

The writer's life, alas, cannot exist in a vacuum. Nor should it if the writer hopes to be relevant for more than a season or two. In our case, perhaps the most uncomfortable moment in our entire relationship came early on, during that year in Oakville.[4] One day, wracked with a bad case of PMS, incensed that my Nova Scotia medical insurance objected to paying my hospital bills, and frustrated at my meagre poetic output, I grew petulant about wanting to do exactly what Irving was doing — going upstairs to write. Instead, there was a never-ending pile of dishes and cleaning to do.

That morning, in an effort to help me prioritize, Irving listed chores that needed doing. Rather than hopping to it, I dawdled and moaned the morning away. Perhaps wanting to forestall my petulance at having wasted time, he just as insistently urged I *forget* the chores and read and write for the rest of the afternoon. That is, until he remembered the cat needed medical attention, so *that* superseded my writing. I may have ventured an eye roll or a testy remark because, to my utter shock, he went off on me with the absurd question, "What were you doing when I was holding down five jobs and writing poetry on top of that?" I hunkered by the phone table in the little alcove off the kitchen, biting my tongue. He knew perfectly well I was not yet born at that time. "You've come along when I've practically retired. I could easily say *fuck this*, turn my back on the whole thing, go to Hawaii, get myself a native girl, and become a beachcomber! Do you think I *like* to do all that correspondence? Sure, there are lots of things I don't like to do, but I do them anyway. *Grow up!* It's time you learn there are certain things in life that we have to do."

I looked at him sulkily, stung at the unprecedented sharpness in tone, and silently proceeded to ready PoetPuss for a trip to the vet. A few minutes later, having wrangled a disgruntled cat into my shopping basket, Irving came up beside me, took my hot face in his hands, and said, "That's what I like about you!"

"What, that I carry on so?" referring to my earlier rant against Maritime Medical Insurance.

"Yes. Shows you've got temperament; proves you're not a WASP." Truth is, he was very easy-going about the housework. *I* was the one putting pressure on myself and becoming increasingly irritable. I threw my arms around his neck, kissing him my promise I would try to do better with the chores and that no, I did not want him to go to Hawaii.

Perhaps his outburst was a vestigial blow-up from previous relationships. Fact is, as he says in one of his poems, he had four mares shot out from under him. At his age, he had neither the appetite nor the stamina for another catastrophe, confiding that sometimes at night he watched me sleep, worrying some stranger would come steal me away from him. Numerous times, he prodded me as to whether I genuinely preferred his company to that of young men. My reply was always the same: I had spent a whole year in Europe getting my fill of young men, and they bored me stiff. Irving, on the other hand, was a genius and, I assured him, I felt privileged to be in his company. Two things not in doubt: he faced encroaching old age and always fared poorly as a bachelor.

Without warning, on February 24, 1983, he sat me down and presented me with this typed note:

I, Irving Layton, agree to pay Anna Pottier the sum of three thousand ($3,000) per annum for every year that she is employed by me as my housekeeper.

The sum of money so accumulated as wages is to be paid to Ms. Pottier as a claim against my house, owned by me at 395 Lakeshore Road East, only at my death and [or] when the house is sold.

Any moneys paid to Ms. Pottier will be deducted from the sum owing to her at the end of her service.

Below it, his typed name along with "Witness." He called Moire in, asking her to witness his signature. I was puzzled, particularly since he never formally hired me as a housekeeper or anything else. Beyond saying it "looked like [I was] the new housekeeper," we had no contract or agreement of any kind. I began living with him on November 2, 1982, but drew no salary. It wouldn't be until several years later, when his income threatened to put him in a higher tax bracket, that Irving's accountant set up a payroll schedule (thereby lowering his taxable income) and I actually drew a "wage." Sums identified as "salary" were used as household money for groceries, bills, and sundry items — not as wages for me.

In 1983, reading this odd promissory note, I was unsure how to react, unable to grasp its semi-legalese language or the ramifications of the phrase "at my death and/or when the house is sold." Was he in effect buying my, what, my "services"? How did my being his devoted partner and companion now have "wages" attached? Any other woman in my place would have sat him down before a notary or lawyer and solidified a plan regarding her financial well-being. My Acadian roots, however, made such a conversation abhorrent. I was giving him my labour, body, heart, and soul. Asking for money was distasteful as it was unthinkable. Naive? Not if you were me, at that time, sharing a bed and home with the man whom I loved and cared for with all my being.

Clearly, Irving's memo was perplexing, especially as I had told him — and would tell him repeatedly over the years — I was with him because I loved him and because his was a genius that I wanted to "serve" (for lack of a better term), and would do so for nothing. If I pride my-self on any one thing, it is for being scrupulously honest, now as then.

In retrospect, holding the original note in my hand as I write this, I surmise he used the term "housekeeper" to lend respectability to my living with him. It was too early to call us husband and wife, particu-larly as his divorce from Harriet had not yet come through. To the squeamish, such as my parents, the term cued them as to what to tell the neighbours. Irving's rationale behind the promissory note was that few working people manage to put aside twelve hundred dollars per year in savings. My being with him removed me from the workaday world, freeing me from time-clock drudgery. To compensate for a lack of regular earnings, he promised me three thousand dollars per year, equivalent to ample savings, without my having to scrimp and slave in some office. Furthermore, I was free to leave him at any time, upon which I would be entitled to collect on this promise. It was his way of doing right by me. The explanation made sense, dissipating the initial feeling that I was a "bought" commodity. Signed and duly witnessed, Irving happily put the note in the green steel cashbox he kept in the upper-left drawer of his desk.

Before Moire left, after three months or so of observing our home life, she quietly urged me to marry Irving. Cohabitation and love alone were no way to protect one's interests, she pointed out. Her wisdom, alas, failed to dissolve my blithe, trusting outlook. For good or ill, I felt fully committed to Irving, and had no desire to be other than who I was, or was on the way to becoming.

10: Coming Out

MY FIRST MAJOR glitterary event was novelist Morley Callaghan's eightieth birthday party. Howard Aster drove us to Cowan's Bottom Line, an upscale restaurant on Toronto's Yorkville Avenue. I had no idea what to wear — in fact, I had nothing remotely appropriate. Oakville's one edgy boutique had a black ankle-length cotton-rayon dress with an empire waist, bell sleeves, and antique Afghani embroidery on the yoke. This became my "ethnic number," worn with grey leather boots and a necklace of black discs, coloured beads, and with an imposing brass ball that hung close around my neck. Oh, and a midnight-blue scarf shot with Lurex, and small brass balls on either end holding the tassels together which, so help me, I wore as a turban à la Simone de Beauvoir. To complete the look: an abundance of black eyeliner with dark indigo and gold eyeshadow; magenta lips pressed into a cryptic little smile. On the drive into Toronto, I worried about the unruly turban. It kept trying to slide off my head as if embarrassed, while the question "What on *earth* am I doing here?" buzzed in my mind like a neon sign.

Not that I wanted to be anywhere else, but compared to Irving's life-long experience with such events, I was a bit of a wreck. However, one must not let nerves show. Irving took my arm and we glided up the steps into a sea of black-tie men and elegant women's faces, flashbulbs, news cameras, journalists, and le tout literary Toronto. Out of the din, Barry Callaghan's deep, ringing voice welcomed us just as a tray of champagne flutes floated mercifully within range. One had but to hold the glass, sip, cast sidelong glances into the crowd as if one had done this a hundred times, and imagine there was a friend just beyond the lights waiting to rush up and greet you. Irving told me I needn't be worried. "Remember, an 'interesting person' is one who asks questions of the person they are speaking with. Just ask questions." Still, here were tables set with sparkling dinnerware for Morley Callaghan, a writer who had known Ernest Hemingway, F. Scott Fitzgerald, James Joyce ... he'd probably glimpsed Picasso on the streets of Paris for all I knew, and rubbed elbows with men who helped define an era. How could I not be struck dumb? Being ignorant of which fork to use was nerve-wracking enough; but making conversation with this crowd would take a bit more champagne.

My eyes grew accustomed to the dim light, prompting a wave of queasiness. No one else was wearing headgear, and all the ladies seemed to be hovering about in low-cut taffeta gowns instead of ethnic numbers. Over there, newscaster Knowlton Nash stood next to his wife Lorraine Thomson, pre-eminent television host, as she mingled, cool as a breeze. She held out her hand and, in her matchless contralto voice, said, "Hello. I'm Lorraine Thomson." That's all you had to do. Slowly, I got the hang of it, extending my hand like a pale meat cleaver, tomahawking my way nervously through the crowd.

Irving was hailed on all sides. Suddenly, I became aware of a lull and that all eyes were on me as he chatted with a towering lady, her bosom undulating like the decks of aircraft carriers on a heaving sea — the socialist or socialite (I wasn't sure which) Barbara Amiel. The crowd seemed to hope I would hurl dagger-looks at her, which, to their disappointment, did not happen. My mind was fixated on locating the ladies' room. Pushing apologetically through the guests, I spotted a vaguely familiar-looking woman standing by herself near the back wall. That she was heavy-set, had large glasses, and wore a decidedly ethnic caftan-type dress, drew me toward her. The poor thing looked as uncomfortable as I felt. "Excuse me," I said flatly, "do you know where the toilet is?" She did not flinch at my deliberate use of "toilet," intuiting perhaps my need to let some helium out of the high-society balloon. She pointed the way and sent me off with a wan smile. I crept along gratefully, then stopped in my tracks: Margaret Laurence had just helped me find the bathroom.

Back at Irving's side, he continued introducing me to faces in the crowd. Here was Harold Town, the celebrated artist whose sketch of Irving in a fireman's hat hung in our home. In contrast to the drawing's flowing lines, Town seemed prickly as a bottlebrush under wiry white hair blending into an equally stiff beard. His small eyes pecked around the room like an angry bird's. I put him down as aloof and unpleasant, until he loosened up and began shouting comments to Barry who was nervously trying to emcee the evening.

Suddenly, Irving turned to a lady he'd been speaking with, Anna Porter, if memory serves, and said that he hadn't bought a present for Morley, but perhaps he could bestow a titty-feel upon him. Yes, this was excruciatingly cringe-worthy, particularly since he was offering up one of my breasts, not his. "*Oh!* I have to watch this from a distance!" she shrieked, adding she thought Morley still too Irish Catholic to appreciate the gesture. She followed along in our wake, Irving leading me by the hand. I was mortified but willing. It would become one of those anecdotes, I thought to myself. Yes! My breast would one day enter whisky-fuelled conversations about that night at Morley's birthday party, taking on a life of its own as the damnedest offering of all. Well, the proffered gift failed to set off any sparks, lascivious or otherwise.

Morley met Irving's troublemaking smile with a terse one of his own, politely but firmly rejecting the offer. "There is a place for everything, and to do such a thing in a public place would take away from it, would reduce it to simple burlesque." For someone who would soon publish a book titled *A Wild Old Man on the Road,* it could easily have degenerated into scandal.

Only many years later, watching a CBC Digital Archives clip of a 1959 *Fighting Words* episode, did I understand what might have provoked Irving to make such an outlandish gesture. The program's question up for debate centred on James Joyce's prowess: was he a better novelist or poet? In the film clip, Morley jabs at Irving repeatedly. Whether for colour or from personal antipathy, he snipes away, taking snide potshots as if Irving was too obtuse to understand: Jews like him were not welcome in the poetry club, and that he was too jarring to be worthy of being called a poet. Irving remained surprisingly

self-contained, letting Morley continue in this vein. Then, with a box-
er's grace, Irving made his point, declaring, "Poetry is the finer breath
of knowledge," and Joyce's *Ulysses* was "*the* epic poem of the twentieth
century." By unanimous decision, the poet scored one over the scrappy,
patronizing novelist.

My awkward moment at Morley's table peaked and passed quickly. Guests pressed in close around us, including Margaret Atwood,
who, to my surprise, remembered me from an earlier McClelland &
Stewart gathering. She and Irving seemed to be enjoying an uneasy
truce, though they had got off to the wrong foot many years earlier
when Irving attended one of her first readings where he had infamously fallen asleep and snored his way through her poems. When Irving
described the incident to me, he swore it had not been deliberate; rather, the combined effects of his being very tired, a stuffy room, and her
monotone delivery had caused him to drift off. As to Atwood saying
he did the same to Gwendolyn MacEwen, all I can say is that whenever
Irving spoke of Gwendolyn, he did so with utmost respect. By 2012,
Atwood had yet to forget the incident, invoking it as part of her talk
at the Layton Centenary in Toronto. She opened with, "Irving was a
naughty old scamp," leaving little doubt as to her preference for the
poet over the man.

With Atwood, as with most other literary luminaries, Irving was
cordial but wary. To this day, Irving is a sort of Rorschach test in that
people ascribe apocryphal events to him — often derogatory, some
more humorous.[1] What I witnessed from 1982 onwards was Irving
being unfailingly civil with whomever he encountered. If he wrote
withering letters to the editor or to individuals, it was in reaction to
being provoked.

That night at Morley's birthday, Senator Paul Martin told me he
knew Senator Ernest Cottreau, my former school principal, and there
I was, mingling with Mordecai Richler, Jack McClelland — ever the
silvery fox who flirted as if by rote — the serene and impossibly graceful Alice Munro, and June Callwood. Venerable television personality
Gordon Sinclair, in his trademark plaid jacket, had a little of June's
crustiness, but without apparent warmth, as if he expected opposition

served up like haggis. What a setting for my debut performance. I could now pretend along with the best of them that I too was expert at the game of controlled charm and tightly bridled wit, howsoever rustic my charms.

As for the other literati at Morley's party, I cannot recall one instance where we socialized or visited their homes. There was a distance, as illustrated by Ralph Gustafson's comment at a later University of Toronto event. Irving and Al Purdy were present. Afterward, the very tall Ralph put his arm around the equally tall Purdy, who put his arm across the much shorter Irving. While someone asked Irving a question from the edge of the stage, I heard Ralph say to Al, "Well, we're still looking down on him!" The two laughed, then looked slightly sheepish. Irving had a very warm regard for Barry Callaghan, admiring his flair and dedication to literature. He gave Mavis Gallant the edge over Munro's short stories, and was, like everyone else, quite awestruck at poet P.K. Page's beauty, and thought her poem "The Stenographer," bordered on the sublime.

There was no choice but to hit the ground running in my new life with Irving. At about the same time as this first public foray, I threw our first private dinner party. Our guests were both people whom we met through Howard. Rena Paul, a social worker, was an older, Polish-born Jewish lady with beautifully coiffed white hair and a stately, sophisticated air in her black dress and presumably genuine pearls. Howard's friend, a book-trade colleague named John, was flying in from London and Rena was to be his date. Oh, that awful gaping cluelessness! I had no idea how one received such elegant guests, and barely knew how to boil water, literally. Nor had I ever cooked beyond throwing dubious concoctions together, never for more than two persons, and never for people outside my social class. Saturday night supper? I once served beans from a can and boiled wieners, which Irving shot down. Not that he was a gourmet, but it reminded him of poverty and desperation and he quietly forbade me to serve the meal ever again. Moreover, I grew up in a dry household and knew nothing about wine, much less wine-and-food pairings. My anxiety level shot through the roof. There was nothing to do but bull my way through.

In one of Harriet's old cooking scrapbooks, I found a recipe for Dover sole amandine. That and mashed potatoes, steamed veggies, and homemade chocolate chip cookies for dessert seemed adequate for the event. Irving was all for it, and tried to get me to calm down. By the time the guests arrived, I was beyond frazzled and striving to keep my nervousness hidden. John was like a figure straight out of Masterpiece Theatre. With sleek silver hair, the most crisp, most blindingly white, and the blackest shade of black I'd ever seen in a man's suit, he was as impressive as he was imposing.

Despite our guest's stature, I set the table beautifully, yes, but not the elegant parson's table with its pale velvet-covered chairs in the formal dining room. No. We were in the kitchen, not three feet from the built-in Coppertone Brown stove. Flanking the chrome dining set, Irving's Harvest Gold fridge stood next to the portable dishwasher in Avocado, a gift from Shaindel. If I could do it over, there would be candles and a centrepiece, and we would have enjoyed the dining room with its William Morris-y blue-and-white flowered wallpaper and dark-blue wainscotting. We didn't use the proper room because the table was covered with drafts of poems as well as notes that would be turned into *Waiting for the Messiah*, all fanning out from Irving's Smith-Corona typewriter. He had a beautiful study, complete with floor-to-ceiling bookcases and a non-functioning fireplace, but the long table, bathed in glorious sunlight, drew him into the dining room more often than not.

Rena and John likely noted my dabbing the sweat coursing off my brow and upper lip as I hauled the fish out of the oven (which was none-too clean), politely allowing me to writhe in my discomfort as if unseen. One makes do. The sole, to my dismay, was a bit on the crunchy side. Rena pronounced it "wonderful," albeit though closed lips while chewing with great care. I noted to myself: graciousness means complimenting the chef, even while worried about one's dental work. Despite it all, conversation sparkled more brightly than the wine, and everyone seemed to be enjoying the literary talk and repartee.

Alas, there had been no time to bake cookies. To make up for this failure, and given that my guests were somewhat older, I thought, brilliantly, to warm the store-bought cookies in the oven. Their aroma would

add a nice touch, and they would be nicely softened. Having run out
of foil, I hit upon using the foil wrapper from a large Sarotti chocolate
bar. Briefly, the kitchen smelled of baked cookies. Then, suddenly, burnt
sugar. I flung the oven door open to see the foil's paper lining in flames,
along with the cookies. My guests saw it all. "Cookies flambé, everyone!"
I managed, putting the fire out with the damp dishtowel, and then sliding
charred cookie remains onto a plate for my poor guests.

While writing this chapter, I contacted Howard who informed me
that "John" had been John Calder, *the* John Calder of Calder Publishing,
the man who published Henry Miller's *Tropic of Cancer* in the United
Kingdom, who introduced Marguérite Duras to English readers, who
was a close personal friend of Samuel Beckett's, and who'd won several
famous obscenity cases. Good thing I was unaware at the time, otherwise dinner would have been a catastrophe.

Rena Paul became my fairy godmother, inviting me to dine at
her place. The evening was a crash-course in etiquette and elegancy. I
quickly sensed that dinner was a ruse, and absorbed every nuance as
best I could. Unlike other females in Irving's periphery, she wanted me
to be at my best when attending champagne receptions, mingling with
ambassadors, consuls-general, and dignitaries. The Junior Ma Kettle
exterior would have to go, as would the rayon elastic-waist skirt with
the fringed hem and tinkly bells on the drawstring.

Rena's apartment, a glamorous feminine space awash in apricot, per-
simmon, creams, and gold, was magazine-perfect. Each step — welcoming me, taking my jacket, having me sit, offering a drink — was performed
with deliberate care, showing me how it was done. At the table, she gently
unravelled the mysteries of which fork to use, as well as the bread plate's
mystique and the trick of buttering only the piece you will eat as against
my inclination to use the butter as dip. We ate steak, the utensils held as
Europeans do, conversing as Rena maintained a delicate balance between
instructing without humiliating, for which I am ever grateful.

After dinner, again with superb tact and charity, she made much of
outfits that "simply didn't fit her anymore," beseeching me to help her
make room in her closet. Oh, and what did I think of this eyeshadow?
She applied some under the guise of asking my opinion, while showing

me how to highlight my features. I went home with an armful of classic Italian-made skirt-and-vest sets of fine wool; *two* pair of Amalfi shoes; a long, ultra-suede Halston coat in bottle green; and some Helena Rubinstein makeup. I soon lost touch with Rena, fearing perhaps she might begin to see me as a second daughter. I had no time to socialize with Rena or anyone else in the coming weeks, months, or years.

11: Telegram Written on Water

THE NEXT BIG SOCIAL EVENT was the launch party for *The Gucci Bag* in March 1983. Irving had mentioned to me, vaguely, that Venie would be sort of planning or hosting. After the burnt cookie disaster, naïveté still largely intact, I felt her help would be a good thing. But then, a month before the party, Irving announced to me that Venie was definitely planning the launch, and oh, uh, would I agree to let her think she was still a special friend as they had been before my arrival? In plain English: would I pretend — for the sake of not upsetting her — that I was his housekeeper, and would I agree to sleep downstairs?

Venie had been lurking in the background like a mako shark. If Irving was hedging his bets or comparing us, she was much closer to him in age and shared many memories with him. I had youth, energy, and unbridled enthusiasm on my side. Still, Irving questioned whether my youth carried with it volatility — and if so, would it cause me to move on. How long would I stay before needing to experience life solo, not filtered through his prism? Despite my assurances to the contrary, one can hardly blame him for wondering.

If ever I needed to rise to the occasion, to test my mettle, this was it. Refraining from undue possessiveness was relatively easy because I still saw myself as a would-be writer rather than an adult woman, and I knew how deeply Irving cared for me. I was committed to our relationship and expected that he, too (artistic licence aside), would not colour outside the lines. Still, after nearly five months of sharing Irving's bed and board, would I allow another female to take my place, even for a weekend? Artistic licence be damned. It was a monstrous proposal. I could understand *Venie* wanting to push my buttons while clinging to a fast-fading fantasy, but Irving? What motive could he possibly have for such an egregious lapse in judgment?

The answer became clear once I got a bead on Venie. She demanded a surplus of attention, even going as far as grabbing Irving's pocket calendar to highlight her birthday. Fail to call on that date and there was hell to pay. A high-school drama teacher for many years, life was a play subject to her direction. If you dared confront or challenge her, she could turn on you with vindictive fury. Fascinating to watch, yes; less so when you were the target. Irving remembered her as a bright, earthy, somewhat brazen student decades earlier when he taught at Sir George. She had written her master's thesis, "Love and Loathing," on Irving's work. Postcards, letters, and brief visits had kept their friendship from sputtering out over the years. By tiptoeing around the nature of our union, however, Irving painted himself into a nasty little corner. Her train ticket was booked and she expected to be on his arm at the reading, and then be his hostess at the party here in our home. My home.

Venie's frankly sensual side and Latvian charms had inspired several poems, including fairly recent ones. On that same trip to Montreal in October 1982, he also wrote "The Flaming Maple," poem 84 in Mosaic's limited edition. It was written after Irving stayed with Venie at her parents' place on his visit to Montreal, while I was still living in Toronto. I seem to appear in the last line, rather than Venie. In it, a man waits on the platform as a train chuffs in, sounding like an old bull roaring with pain, a god being slain. The bull roaring image alludes to the poet's fate, his straddling that razor's edge between pleasure and pain. In contrast to the human pleasure/pain nexus, nature is mindlessly dying as per the season. Building to a crescendo, he identifies with a flaming maple tree, its bright colours mocking nature's death throes. The man defies old age and death by "obsessively imagining a young girl's limbs, her passion-moist nest."

That my passion-moist nest landed itself in a poem was a tad embarrassing. Looking back as from a hundred years in the future, however, my "nest" would still be warm and alive on the page long after my death. Likewise, "The Hairy Monster" in poem 86. Here, a Greek girl in Piraeus watches her grandfather slaughter a pig. It is a story taken almost verbatim from one of my childhood tales. The bloodletting and white enamel basin are from a scene I took part in as a young girl, recounted to Irving during one of our pillow talks. Seeing pieces of my stories dressed up and becoming part of Irving's work thrilled me no end. Surely, *this* was the writer's life, and I was living it from the inside out. Naturally, there can be no glory without sacrifice.

Thus, with some misgivings, I agreed to cede my place in our conjugal bed to sleep a night or two on the altar stone of art. If he *was* hedging his bets, comparing the older friend against the younger companion, fine. Let the comparisons begin. My agreeing to participate in this scenario actually drew us closer together as co-conspirators. I further rationalized it as a spectacular opportunity to show how game, how free I was from estrogen-fuelled jealousy. In retrospect, he should not have asked, nor should I have acquiesced. Venie's victory, however, was as hollow as it was short lived.

The night of the party, we had to number and sign the entire Mosaic Press edition. After supper, I stacked all 429 copies on the kitchen table, opened each one to the signature page, handed it to Irving, and re-boxed them assembly-line fashion. He paused early on to inscribe copies to various people, such as John Metcalf. I hoped one of these early volumes would be for me, but after nearly two hundred copies, the edition number getting further and further away from the coveted Number One book, I wondered aloud which was mine. Startled at the oversight, he apologized and made amends, writing "The Bumless Wonder, with love for Anna Pottier, Oakville, Ont., March 16, 1983" in copy 188.

"The Bumless Wonder" was one of several pet names I had for him; owing to his dismayingly flat posterior. I sometimes went by Poupeleh (Yiddish for "little doll"), Poupski, Hanneleh, or Anna-Panna. In any case, it was our language and only we needed to know its intent. For my part, such endearments helped winnow the legend from the man. He was my "Minch," and the one that became a favourite, "Biscuit Boy," later, "Irving Rabenu" and "PincuVing," made him somehow easier to manage. We said them with giddy affection, always infused with respect.

The launch party started with a reading at an art gallery in downtown Oakville. I had cleaned the house, made sure to remove all traces of my presence from our bedroom, shopped for and helped prepare party foods, and laid in the wine and spirits. I was grateful for Venie's help in setting everything out. With great effort, I tried to keep my anxiety hidden while fighting the urge to disappear into my study. The reading drew a good audience and went extremely well. I hung back and blended with the crowd, taking it all in. Venie wanted to be seen as his date, and so I played along.

Our guests included former students, Dorothy Rath, and several others whose faces blur together. Singer-songwriter Eric Andersen stood out for his star-power, though it was much later I learned of his iconic stature on the folk music scene. "Eric! You are the only one who never hit on Aviva, nor asked me for money!" Irving hailed the handsome poet-songwriter. Eric told me of his very first meeting with Irving. He had arrived at Irving and Aviva's place, pixilated, and had managed to take out his guitar when the room began to spin. Irving or Aviva caught his guitar as it slipped from his hands while he made a desperate crawl toward the fireplace, the only safe place to upchuck. To his astonishment, they called the next day — not to berate him, but to ask how he was feeling. The friendship endured until Irving's passing.

The launch party went off without a hitch. People mingled, ate, drank, and kept up lively conversations in almost every downstairs room. Despite leaning on Venie for help, my first literary party was a success.

As the evening tapered down, guests began trickling out as Irving thanked everyone and made his way upstairs. Venie followed suit, leaving me to help retrieve coats and tidy up. As Eric and his companions were in the hallway about to depart, Venie came halfway down the staircase. Lit from below, her face took on sinister contours as she paused before asking me, loudly, whether I had any candles.

Everyone froze as I gathered myself from the blow she had just landed between my eyes. "Gee. I'm not sure, Venie. I think there might be some in the junk drawer. Let me go look." I replied brightly through gritted teeth, returning empty-handed with a feigned Stepin Fetchit simplicity. Everyone had read the papers or heard Irving and I were living together. How could she stoop to pretend she was still his lady-friend? More pointedly, why would Irving and I allow this shameful farce? Her attempt at humiliating me in front of Irving's friends backfired however. Irving heard what she asked of me and, naturally, picked up on the venom and sinister intonations. Their on-off intimate relationship ground to a close that night. The last word was perhaps mine as apparently, there in the candle-less dark, she fumed and bickered with Irving after finding a handful of hairpins on the night-stand. Blame my subconscious mind for the oversight, for I had not left them behind on purpose. How *could* I have been so careless? Next morning, egos a bit worse for wear, she played out the girlfriend role, joined us for breakfast in her billowy cotton dress, straddling the heating grate in a bad Marilyn Monroe impersonation.

Domestic details notwithstanding, *The Gucci Bag* was making its way into the world. That is what mattered, I told myself. Still, in the days that followed, swayed perhaps by Moire's dismay, I wondered how I could have abased myself — or given the appearance of self-abasing submissiveness. After Venie's departure, I fell into increasingly irritable moods. Dark, angry thoughts began troubling the surface of otherwise calm days. Irving gave this disturbing facet of my personality a name, likening the change in my demeanour to being possessed by a *dybbuk*, a malicious spirit that, according to ancient Yiddish folklore, clung to one until its bidding had been done.

A few weeks later, Irving left for a reading tour of Spain, England, and Scotland with his agent Lucinda Vardey. The Spanish leg was in celebration of *Poemas de Amor*, the bilingual Hiperión edition of *The Love Poems of Irving Layton*. By all accounts, it was a successful trip, despite Irving battling an ear infection and the rigours of a very demanding tour. I delighted in the postcard he sent of a wonky-looking bird by Joan Miró. Its message: *even if* [I] *looked like that bird,* [he'd] *still think of me as the most beautiful creature in the world.* He was also supposed to go on to Italy after Scotland, and sent me a telegram asking me to meet him in Rome.

A telegram! Word of his Nobel Prize nominations had come by telegram. All the great writers telegrammed their lovers and editors, had they not? It was terribly exciting, and dismaying. How was I going to get to Rome? I wasn't even sure how to get to the Toronto airport, never mind Rome. Meet him where in Rome? Mere details. Riding this wave of high romance was thrilling in and of itself. Nevertheless, I called his bluff, so to speak, and actually bought a plane ticket with the last of my savings. Fortunately, I was able to return it after his next telegram informed me he was on his way home.

I found out later he had also contacted Venie to meet him in Paris. This struck me as hilarious; a glittering European capital for each of us when *neither* rendezvous would transpire. Six years later in 1989, reading *Wild Gooseberries: The Selected Letters of Irving Layton*, I learned he'd written to Venie from Edinburgh describing how he'd given three magnificent readings, taken in an opera (Prokofiev's *The Gambler*), seduced five chambermaids, had tea with the Queen, and wished she were there with all her "delicious orifices." By then however, I long-since knew that such telegrams and letters had been written on water. They originated from and existed in a wellspring of good intentions meant to brighten the recipients' day.

As early as those Oakville days, however, I felt that what he said and wrote for me came from a different place, from earth, not water. I knew I was loved, and *that* was the reality I chose to inhabit. After the launch party, I realized with sobering clarity the enormity of what I was doing. From here on in, my life was bound to Irving's, inextricably so. Whatever "normalcy" might entail, be it having children, a career, camping trips, or cycling jaunts through Tuscany, I had now forsaken it all — with trepidation, yes — but without regret or second thoughts.

12: The Carved Nakedness

A WEEK BEFORE the launch party, after a fitful sleep, Irving had written a scathing letter to Harriet explaining the irony behind *The Gucci Bag*'s dedication to "Gypsy Jo, a wonderful flower child I used to know." Whatever pain the book might cause her, Irving warns, it is but a "tiny washbasin compared to the vast ocean of suffering which the shabby manner of [her] departure plunged [him] into."

Even so, Irving, in calmer moments, felt the book transcended their relationship. It was the story of the poet against the corrupt world. Harriet was not "Harriet," any more than he was "Irving." *The Gucci Bag* extrapolates her betrayal of the poet as representative of the whole world that had turned against the Jew, and by "Jew" he meant the creative force or spirit. He wanted people to realize the book encompassed much more than a man lashing out at his estranged wife. "It is the poet against the philistines," he said. "I am taking up the fight for Lawrence and Lowell and Oscar Wilde and Keats."

Poetry was more than a vocation for Irving: it superseded everything else. Had the Muse left him completely, he declared, he would have had no reason for living, "*That's* how important poetry is to me." During outbursts like that, I could overlook the sparks of rage flying from his mouth as from struck flint, but not for one instant could I disregard the white-hot embers at his very core. On such occasions, it was like watching a volcano erupt, from which he siphoned lava to fuel poems such as "The Carved Nakedness." Though

Irving married Harriet with foreboding, *knowing* it would end in catastrophe, he still felt betrayed.

"If you ask me would I do it over again, I would have to say yes," he told me. The poems themselves drove out their engendering pain. "These are poems only an older person could have written," he said. "See, if you look at Solway's[1] poems — and they are good — you know how I praise them for being so cool and classical, almost nineteenth century. They are about rocks, water, and things in nature, things that touch your sense of aesthetics, but they don't touch the heart. To touch the heart, your own heart has to have been touched, but he's getting there. Maybe he'll make something of his wrecked relationships. I am 'modern' because I use things from my own life, contrary to T.S. Eliot and the way he's influenced so many to stay away from personal material."

For the McClelland & Stewart paperback edition, released seven months after the Mosaic edition, he removed the nastier Harriet poems to help keep the reader on track regarding the book's true intent. *The Gucci Bag* was his song of experience detailing a descent into hell and the sweet triumph of overcoming, of returning to life via Eros, poetry, and love. Its message was not about Harriet at all — it was about creativity's supreme place in a world permanently stacked against it. Small wonder it galled him when his editor Ellen Seligman called to say Julian Porter, McClelland & Stewart's legal counsel, found some libellous poems and recommended their removal. "*What!?* That poem has nothing to do with the Bernsteins at all!" he protested. "Are they such megalomaniacs that they think they are the only scum I'm referring to?"

To fully appreciate *The Gucci Bag*, he explained, one must be aware of Jewish culture to appreciate the subtleties involved. "This story is an old, old one, where you had the cultured merchant prince oppressing the rabbis, poor people. He knew he was being a shit and was conscience-stricken, but continued his oppressing with even more vehemence to prove that he could in fact put them under his thumb."

Working alongside Irving, I typed final versions of poems and helped ensure they were in sequence. Sometimes, I would ask about a poem's meaning, other times he spontaneously offered explanations. Any serious poet or artist, he pointed out while sketching a spoked wheel, will express his vision in such a way that you can look at a his poems and, like spokes emanating from a hub, see how each poem originates from and leads back to the central vision. Recurring themes in a poet's body of work become easier to decode with each reading. My copy of the Mosaic Press limited edition of *The Gucci Bag* contains these notes, scribbled while trying to catch each explanation as he shared them with me.

In poem 18, "Dead Souls," the last stanza's green dragon symbolizes creativity. The man's lost connection with the sun refers to *Apocalypse*, D.H. Lawrence's final attempt at summing up man's inner struggle between emotion and instinct versus intellect and reason and how this conflict alienates man from the natural world. Here, the lady's soul is dying. So, too, the poet, because their love has evaporated. Love could not survive between them, the bourgeois being antithetical to salvation through Art.

Poem 77, "Bottles," dedicated to the Italian painter Giorgio Morandi, seems as whimsical as the bottles Morandi painted over and over again. We are all bottles, fragile and empty until sensuality, symbolized by "a wise old whore," philosophy, or death enters and restores our humanity.

By poem 79, "Blossom," the poet is well on his way to recovery. The sleeping kitten is indistinguishable from vegetable matter and looks like a blossom until it opens its eyes. Written in Niagara-on-the-Lake after a kitten in an apple tree had startled Irving, its green eyes amongst the blossoms reminded him again of the difference between plant and animal life, as well as the startling diversity in the world. The welcome shock prompts his return to a more sanguine, reverential frame of mind.

The next poem, "Saxophonist," again uses animal imagery, likening a jazz saxophone to a snake. The player sounds notes so sensual that they have the ability to deliver the musician from society's constraints and limitations. Man becomes a god when he frees himself. The struggle, however, invariably comes with great pain, great cost. Human experience comprises the pain of bifurcated ecstasy.

Irving clarified that "Youth and Age 1981," poem 82, does not patronize the young Italian idealists whatsoever, and that he was truly happy to be among them. In the seventh stanza, he identifies with them as far as he possibly can. That he "won't pass their way again" means someone else will have to pay for the battle between power and beauty.

"Darkening sky" represents approaching death, as he observes the eternal difference between youth and age.

In "Central Heating," poem 83, Irving drew my attention to the importance of tone, particularly in the last stanza. Tone can convey meaning sometimes as effectively as words. Here, the fire of love gives a hellishly hot heat. Using ambiguity and irony, he observes that it can be hard to distinguish whether love's passion stems from the Diabolical or the Divine. Clearly, love is Divine, and serves as the world's central heating.

The first stanza in poem 84, "The Flaming Maple," takes you back to "Saxophonist" and the inextricable link between pleasure and pain. "The Hairy Monster," poem 86, in which the wind howls all night long like a lost, decrepit satyr, again expresses the link between suffering and ecstasy.

In poem 90, "The Carillon," the opening stanza defines the relationship between the poet and the world. He *must* soak up evil until his head is ready to burst with it. Nor must he beg off from pursuing the truth about evil; he must experience it and know it (such as entering into a doomed marriage). The poet lives in a world of ambivalence and turmoil. If he carries it too far, however, his voice will no longer have the ring of truth. Redemption is via art, particularly the creative word. Truth, likened to a Platonic sun, is powerful enough to restore us to the wholeness and laughter of childhood, denoted by the gazelles' running and playing. To know evil, and speak truthfully about it, lends the poet a voice as clear and compelling as that of a carillon.

"The Winged Horse," poem 91, turns on the *p* words: poem, pain, Pow, and Pegasus. As compared to aggression in nature (i.e., the lizard killing a dragonfly), humans also inflict and endure pain (as in having four failed marriages), but the knowledge does not make him morbid (i.e., "Serious? Who, me?") On the contrary, because humans have the capacity for Art (hence the imagined flight on Pegasus), Art is again posited as the only way out of this cannibalistic nature.

Irving indicated poem 93, "The Garden," as being pivotal and similar in scope to "The Carillon." We are minuscule, but the suffering is huge. In the eighth stanza, "dark shadows" indicate approaching death; the web-trapped fly signals nature's relentless aggression. As against that, beauty and music bring joy, and are uplifting forces. The white butterfly symbolizes purity, art, and transcendence. The Garden is The World, shot through with pain and ecstasy, beauty and pain. The World/Garden survives because of poetry; the Artist is self-conscious life. Matter becomes conscious of itself through the mind of the Artist and this justifies The World. As to the Garden of Eden, paradise: there is none.

"First Violet," poem 94, is for Kim Yang Shik, a Korean poet who sometimes went by the name First Violet. The flower's prevailing glow suggests that Imagination always seeks out Love. The poem is in no way indicative of resignation, but rather a Dionysian acceptance of tragedy. Placed near the very end of the book, it further expresses Layton's triumph at overcoming the anguish contained in the opening poems.

Finally, in poem 95, "Letting Go," Layton gives us a hard-won affirmation of life. A "candid" love is one he is fully aware of, but not disillusioned by. If you make too much of pain, you become merely a misanthrope. Clearly, pain exists, but it must be used wisely.

Many of the poems included in the McClelland & Stewart edition were written or revised after the Mosaic edition launch party. Irving spent hours feverishly going over the manuscript, revising, adding, rearranging. You could almost see the energy crackling around him as he verified the sequence and double-checked the numbering. "Want to hear some poetry?" he asked one day as I returned from a grocery run. He read his three new ones: "Psychologists," "Klaus Englehart," and "The Immortals," which was inspired by F.R. Scott rising to greet him at the *CIV/n* party launch party in Montreal. He had shifted this latter one's position, placing it after poems extolling love and poetry. He asked what I thought each poem meant. As to "The Immortals," he hinted there were two things that were immortal.

"Well ... the lines of poetry," I said hesitantly.

"Right! And ... ?"

"Beauty?" guessing too quickly.

"Nooo. Think of my mother's eyebrows."

"Vanity!"

"Now you got it!" He went on to say how it highlights F.R. Scott's mortality, or, more precisely, poetry's immortality. Simmering with excitement, he showed me the final revisions to "The Immortals," changing the order of "half-dead, half-blind," adding that "Only a very delicate ear could see that." He changed "poet" to "amorist"; "gratified vanity" to "self-love." As on many other occasions, Irving fired a question at me: "Which do you think is better?" My first response was "gratified vanity." Why? He kept asking until I began to see why it was the wrong choice. "Self-love," he explained, "is, first of all, more unexpected; ties in with 'amorist'; and sounds better than 'vanity.'" The poem, he continued, is also a reflection on how Jews see the world and themselves. Unlike Christians, who deny this world and say there is something on the other side, and Hindus who say all this is unreal, "Jews *know* this is all shit but still strive to do something with it." The lesson ended with his making sure I noted how *The Gucci Bag* closes not with anger, but with love.

13: Showdown

ADJUSTING TO LIFE with a new partner can be a delicate matter for any couple. Irving had lived with four women, whereas I had never lived with a man. At times, the house and my dishevelled self looked like I was waiting for a mother to swoop in and put the place in order. In short, I was the one who had to do most adjusting and all of the growing into couple-hood. Irving was Irving; I was not quite *me* yet. Like waging war on three fronts, I continued striving to mature as a woman, be a better homemaker, and become a writer — frying my nerves in the process.

I was not without a certain gift for drama, especially when overwhelmed. Irving mistook my sputterings and increasingly black moods for ambivalence, prompting his request that I be continually happy around him at all times. This struck me as unfair, if not childish. His other bombshell scenario, moving to Montreal and living with or near his sister with me as a live-out housekeeper, also struck me as absurd. "Decide what you really want to do," he said, "I can't stand ambivalency. I always land on my feet. Nothing leaves me devastated. It never fails! Something invariably happens to women with whom I become intimate. They can't seem to take me. I've just about had it with women." He had also toyed with a nebulous scenario where Venie was to "look after" him and he would "care for" her daughter, again with me the live-out housekeeper, free to go any time. "You owe me nothing. I always land on my feet," he repeated.

Ambivalence? That was rich. Had I not just allowed Venie to usurp my place in our bed, proving my commitment? Whatever ambivalence existed came from him, not me. Clearly, Venie's visit set off a delayed depth charge, the resulting shock waves hitting us hard. Perhaps guilt drove Irving to call my dark mood "ambivalence," for his role in the Venie weekend was disgraceful. Understandably, anger flooded in after all my artistic acceptance.

Though I would never let another woman into our bed, Irving's less inappropriate gallantries were easy to deal with. Shaindel, however, was a special case. She had a propensity for irking me which, owing to my youth and Acadian DNA, I could not counter. When Howard sought Irving's input for *The Gucci Bag*'s cover design, Shaindel jumped in as if the book were hers. Howard, Irving, and I trooped behind her into Harry Rosen's, where she led Irving to the tie rack. He was to look at neckties for colours that appealed to him to use on the cover, where-upon she selected navy blue and burnt orange. Shaindel, moreover, knew a leather supplier and if Irving wanted a leather-bound copy, she could make that happen. Naturally he wanted one, Howard too. With one for Shaindel and possibly one for her daughter Lisa, that made an edition of four copies. I asked her to get leather to make one for me, to which Irving voiced his enthusiastic agreement. Instead, I received a coy smile and a, "Oh. I forgot to order yours."

For my twenty-fourth birthday, Irving asked Shaindel to pick out something from her boutique, trusting her expertise. It came into play all right, for she selected the worst possible item for me: an ul-tra-preppy, cable-knit pullover in pastel yellow. It clung to me like a sausage case. Irving called eagerly from the foot of the stairs for me to show him the gift. I did so, fighting back tears, looking like a simpleton out on a day pass. As Irving groped for something nice to say, Shaindel stood carefully outside his field of vision, arms crossed, head cocked, grinning.

Irving's final attempt at having Shaindel and me achieve friendly coexistence involved a disastrous shopping expedition. I needed pants — well, anything that would fit, really. Shaindel gaily volunteered, bringing me to a bargain store. I found some pants. Shaindel pounced to my side, grabbed them, folded them open and, thrusting her arms high for all to see, screeched, "Size *thirty-eight*?! Oh well. Try them on." I emerged from the fitting room heralded by Shaindel loudly asking, "And they're *tight* on you?!!" I never allowed her near me again.

Irving phoned her from time to time, just to say hello. "But why?" I asked. "Why do you call just when she's finally stopped bothering us so much?"

"Because it makes her happy and it's a mitzvah," he replied matter-of-factly. Shaindel had been perhaps his most reliable friend in his post–Harriet Rue Bathurst days. When Irving sought to protect a sum of money to prevent the Bernsteins from taking his last penny, his son Max had refused point-blank. Shaindel helped without reservation. He never forgot this about her. Nor about Max.

In truth, it pleased me that he felt free to indulge in such gallantries. Beauty is goodness and should be praised. To me, Irving complimenting someone no more meant he wanted to seduce them than one would a daffodil. No woman could unseat me. Let them show up at readings in see-through blouses and black bras, trying to press their phone numbers into Irving's palm like that huntress at Harbourfront. Such digs came with the territory. I would have to find the grace to accept them.

More upsetting than the Venie episode, however, and more so than anything Shaindel could throw at me, was the fear I might not be able to handle the demands ahead and thus might fail to become a writer. Fear became anger, turning me again into a brooding *dybbuk*. I listened to Irving's "ambivalency" ventilations with a calmness that surprised both of us, then shot back that first, mutual understanding and sensitivity should spring from common courtesy. Even if I *were* merely his housekeeper, he should still be considerate of my feelings. My intention from the outset was to be shoulder to shoulder as mate and partner, never to limit him in any way. His reasons for being bearish and ab-stracted, I pointed out, were not more legitimate, as his being a poet was irrelevant. Furthermore, my relative lack of bad experiences was no reason to dismiss *my* bouts of apparent unhappiness; and finally, my *dybbuk* had nothing to do with our becoming intimate.

Late one night, alone in my study, shaken by rage spiralling up and down of its own volition, I wondered if perhaps I had allowed Venie into my bed to see what would happen. Had I sought to confirm their potential for couple-hood? Irving sometimes teased me about my Greek and Italian boyfriends, though I had none. Occasionally, he still asked whether I was going to leave him. All I knew is that I cared very deeply about him, his work, and his well-being, and wanted to be an integral part of his harvest years. If he felt Venie was *truly* capable of loving him and plunging into this demanding time wholeheartedly, I could permit myself to consider leaving before extrication became impossible. Despite trusting the Fates that led me to him, I was not blind to the fact that joining my life to Irving's meant existing within a shadow, no matter how much I loved the man casting that shadow.

Becoming part of Irving's world left me powerless to control anything but the minutest aspects of my life. Irving met his commitments without complaint. Each reading, interview, or literary event, enhanced his visibility and were part of the game. If it seems there was domination or imbalance, that was not the case. Irving's agenda dominated *our* lives. The notion that *he* dominated *me* is false. Being central to his life pleased me immensely. My sense of accomplishment increased exponentially the more effective and useful I became. At the time, however, I was in turmoil.

The artist in me sensed danger in coupling with anyone, especially a poet of Irving's stature. Can a household ever contain enough oxygen for two artists? This question, still faint enough to ignore, would later take on the insistent throb of a drumbeat.

My new life meant absorbing stings, such as being rendered invisible by rude educated people, or seen as a brainwashed child-victim of some unspeakable perversion. Inside our home, I loomed large, was adored and constantly sought out by Irving. Others, however, saw only Irving's outsized personality, and decided I was a pleasant but possibly gold-digging or daddy-complexed girl. Reconciling reality and perceptions, at times, threatened to do my head in. I coped by writing imaginary scenarios. One such tableau looked at life without Irving. In it, I was somewhere in Europe, composing my suicide note. As laughable as the imagined note is, the anguish tearing through me was not. I struggled to confine such concerns to my journal, but hiding my dismay from Irving proved impossible. He had asked me to be happy, which I thought would be easy since that was my natural state. Stress grew exponentially. I began to slip, my face went haggard, eyes hollow, beseeching Irving to understand. His heart sank, fearing our intimacy had been a mistake. All my paradoxes surfaced and locked up, neutralizing me to the point of near-catatonia some days. On others, I would pace like a caged animal. In that state, anything — a harmless joke, a remembered slight — could send me into a frenzy, shuttling between wanting to be left alone or wanting to scream for help. It was as if the *dybbuk* snatched away my true self, replacing it with a malevolent entity.

Shortly after the launch party, between my fears of failing and Irving's live-out housekeeper scenario, my unresolved tensions became almost unbearable. If I were to continue life solo, this was the telling time. My soul froze as I pulled that yellow backpack out, leaned it up against the closet door, and called Irving into my study. He had his brown velveteen track pants on as usual and bounced in with customary boyish curiosity. "Got something for me to read?" he asked, unaware.

I pointed to the backpack and told him it would not take me long to fill it up and disappear. There was no mistaking the gravity of my declaration, "*If* you think Venie's the one who can be a good mate, handle everything, love you with all her being, fine. I'll give you my blessings, wish you well, and walk out of here. You won't see me again."

He listened with mouth agape, went ashen, and quickly hugged me to him assuring me *no one* could, nor ever would, take my place. I was to put the backpack away. And that, to my enormous relief, was that. Over the course of the next week, we talked for hours at a stretch, which helped enormously. Between talking and journalling to the point of exhaustion, the *dybbuk* was finally vanquished.

One day, after rising from a late-afternoon nap and sharing a meal of tomato soup, Irving asked if I was happy. Yes, I was. Again, he assured me that did care, that he loved me, and that he would always be there. Best of all, he told me my "nervous breakdown" would not be held against me, making it easy to move on.

After the backpack showdown, I blithely told Moire that, were all his former wives to meet, I would be his staunchest defender. "Well, I hope you do understand him, for your sake, because I certainly could never live with him." To which I merely smiled, pleased at my uniqueness.

In retrospect, the crisis was unavoidable. I wanted to write. At my side: one of the greatest poets in the English language. Humour was a saving grace, as I could and did tease him. When, for example, my name first appeared in print as his paramour, I waved the *Montreal Gazette* clipping in the air, declaring, "Look! I'm in all the papers! I'm in all the papers!" parodying Layton Triumphant. When he extolled my best qualities or praised my feisty character I lapped it up, sassing back that he'd better not forget it.

Being with him fired my imagination, setting off metaphors and lightning-quick aperçus like rockets bursting from everything I looked at. The tools of poetry lay in my hands, but I lacked the skill to use them properly. My frustration grew the more furiously I tried to write perfect first drafts. I wanted to be like him: disciplined, focused, and unstoppable, all while retaining my own distinct personality. Though the crisis would pass, my fears for my own creativity would always remain.

The backpack scene and its resolution left me and Irving inalterably grateful for each other and the rock-solid ground now beneath us. From my place at his side, I watched it all as a grand comic opera, sometimes funny, other times tragic, but of no consequence. Besides, there was too much to learn and do in the midst of Irving's — of our — whirlwind life.

In the kitchen colouring, early autumn, circa 1964.
(Photo by Mae Pottier)

My sketch of Irving as he, unbeknownst to me, wrote "Tragedy."
Oakville, September 8, 1982.

Iconic folk-singer and song-poet Eric Andersen visited Irving, then at
Maimonides, in 2000. Here, after playing songs and reading poetry, he
bids his friend a final farewell.
(Photo reproduced with kind permission of Carol Rothman)

Irving and me on our first holiday outing in Montreal, here at a friend of Venie's place in Montreal West, December 25, 1983.
(Photo reproduced with kind permission of Veneranda (Venie) Kreipans-Wilson)

In Rome's Piazza del Popolo, Irving pauses while editing my poem, "To The Broad-Hipped Italian Woman," August 21, 1983.

Boschka, Max's partner Stephanie Rayner, me, and Max saying goodbye to Boschka, September 1983.
(Photo by Irving Layton, from the author's personal collection)

On July 20, 1983, the great Arnaud Maggs set up his camera in our backyard and made time stand still. This is one of my favourite photos of us.
(Photo reproduced with kind permission of the Maggs Estate)

Musia Schwartz seeing how we were settling into our new home, Montreal's Monkland Avenue.
(Photo by Irving Layton, from the author's personal collection)

14: Italy, "Kakania," and Poetry 101

ON THE HEELS OF Irving's second Nobel Prize nomination by his Italian supporters, summer 1983 was all about poetry. A healthy sense of realism kept expectations in check. That fall, and virtually every fall thereafter, I bought champagne in case he won and in case he lost. Either way, we celebrated. Telegrams announcing both nominations were kept in a shiny frame in his study.

Historically speaking, many poets burned out or killed themselves before reaching their forties. Irving's productivity continued into his eighties, much to the dismay of his harshest critics. This uncommon feat owes something to his stubbornness, quite a bit to his aversion to drugs and drunkenness, and much to the intense joy that came with rendering ideas and emotions into memorable language. During nearly all of my time with him, Irving remained dynamic and bursting with *élan vital.*

Irving's vitality and what he deemed a European sensibility precluded his feeling at home in Canada. His books seemed to make certain reviewers grab for distorting filters like drowning men for life preservers. Previously published articles were often rehashed, the journalist never squeezing out an original thought. It was easy work, and it sold papers. This anti-Layton bias ultimately culminated in a dismal pseudo-biography called *Irving Layton: A Portrait.*

Ironically, the woman who was then writing this biography would shed not a candle's worth of light on Irving's uneasy relationship with Canadian literati. Irving had his suspicions that *A Portrait* was not going to be a flattering book, but he preferred to extend the benefit of the doubt to Cameron, and so remained co-operative and very cordial throughout ongoing interview process. That would change dramatically two years later when he learned of her book's contents. But that conflagration still lay in the future.

With *The Gucci Bag* still warm from the presses, Irving was writing poems for what became *Final Reckoning: Poems 1982–1986,* published by Mosaic Press in 1987. One morning in late May, I woke to the sound of him typing furiously. "Hello, Beautiful!" he said as I rolled groggily downstairs. "You know, Anna, the crisis has passed!" Could it be the lugubrious post-Harriet shadow had lifted? His jubilant mood was infectious. "Boy, do I feel different from yesterday," he marvelled

Irving had been wrestling with the poem "Kakania," for weeks, trying to fool his own ear, forcing the wrong words onto the page. The poem would not leave him be. I joined him with my coffee, imbibing his high-energy revelations. "You know," he said pensively, tapping his copy of *A Wild Peculiar Joy*, "I'd been rereading my poems, and got all inspired with a sense of power, then gotten bogged down by the shit. When you write a poem like this," he paused, "you see your whole life passing before your eyes. You see all the shit. But rereading this, I realized again that I'm like an angel, floating above this shit, above the swamp."

After some two hundred runs at "Kakania," he was again riding high and feeling unapologetically triumphant. The problem had been incorporating images with the right rhythm. In the poem, rife with hyperbole, he compares the world's daily massacres, even the singular horror of the Holocaust, to the outrage of having an Ontario WASP judge deny him his "child's lovely prattle." The judge draws Irving's rage for wrongly denying him access to Samantha. In his dreams, he imagines William Blake pissing into the judge's mouth, Samantha making kaka all over the errant judge. In the last stanza, the unreflective judge asks his secretary to bring him his testicles.[1] An earlier draft ended with the secretary snapping on the judge's balls. "I knew that wasn't right. That would have been a cheap shot," Irving explained. He transposed the scene to the middle of the poem to lessen the focus. "And now the rhythm is right. I owe that to my saintly mother and her curses," he said, blowing a skyward kiss. His mother Keine's flaming litanies and hammer-blow Yiddish curses left a lifelong mark on her youngest child. Somewhere between his mother's curses, Tennyson's verse, and the crisp logic of essays by Francis Bacon and William Hazlitt, lay the foundations of Irving's distinct poetic voice.

"You see," he continued, sounding me out to ensure I saw what poetry meant, how it was done, "now it all ties in with the innocence. It is Blakean. I knew I was being Blakean. You know he wrote the *Songs of Innocence,* and kneecapping, you know the Italian mafia does that to judges in particular. Ah! It's perfect now!" With that, he phoned Shaindel to do her a mitzvah, perhaps as thanks to the gods for permitting him to complete the poem.

"There. You see?" he asked, returning from his brief call. "I just made her very happy, and what does it cost? Nothing!" I shook my head in mock-reproach, upon which Irving offered me this parable, a scene he witnessed one very cold Montreal day many years before. On a train platform, he saw a drunk lying perilously close to the track. Three women, thinking at first he was an ordinary man, went over to pull him up and away from the track. Seeing he was a drunk, they left him right where he was. Years later, Irving living alone on Bathurst and in a dismal state, Aviva had phoned him every morning to make sure he was okay. Aviva's concern, Shaindel's kindness, and, later, Venie's friendship, had meant a lot. Now that he was fine again, he had no difficulty reaching out to someone in need. As long as those on the other end of the phone understood the dynamics, I could fault neither his logic nor sentiment.

His triumph over "Kakania" propelled him out of his prolonged bunker mode. Indeed, he was a changed man, suddenly open and exuberant again. I preferred seeing him like this rather the abstracted scribe who broached no interruption. Much as I admired Irving's powers of concentration, having my playful advances rebuffed was a bit ego-bruising at times. No matter how innocently I drew near to trail my fingers along his muscled forearm or embrace him from behind as he worked on a draft or dashed off a letter, my attentions were not always reciprocated. What was a coltish partner to do? He explained that it made him feel old when I pestered him too much, and joked about leaving me for an older woman. Apparently, my aptitude for living with a man was on par with my cooking skills. Of the books he had urged me to read, he again nudged me toward Françoise Gilot's *Life with Picasso*, as well as Nadezhda Mandelstam's *Hope Against Hope* to gain a better idea of what living with an artist entailed. Gilot's was the only one I found time to read. Without a big to-do, Irving also quietly suggested I observe our cat, PoetPuss. In so doing, I learned an excellent lesson in conjugal savoir-faire: make no advances and the cat, invariably, will come to you.

With the patience of a teacher, and a lover's tenderness, he always took care to discuss my work. Take my poem for Diego the Clown. I met Diego at the CN Tower one day while waiting for Moire. He was from Cadiz, short, middle-aged, sad-eyed, and all alone, trying to get rude children to smile and buy his balloon animals. The sight of this pear-shaped man, clinging to his dignity in front of bored children nearly as tall as he was, broke my heart. He asked if we could meet at his favourite tapas bar. Irving, then on a European reading tour, was all for it. Diego, imagining we were an item, or to impress his friends, brought me his mother's black lace mantilla, placing it over my head as if I were his lady. The experience was a one-off, and scrupulously platonic, worthy of a poem. All that came out was doggerel as I bawled over the clown's imagined plight. Irving let the worst of it pass — he *hated* women's tears because, to him, they held the echo of a primal ache, a dissatisfaction so profound that he felt utterly incapable of providing comfort — and urged me to keep trying.

"Even if I write a good poem, it would relieve *me*, but what of Diego?"

Irving replied softly, "Art is the consolation for injustice."

"Who said that?"

"I did."

A few months later, I tried writing a poem for Moire, who had left for a place of her own. Irving and I sprawled on lawn chairs in the backyard, amid fading Japanese irises. He tried to jump-start me by throwing out lines. "I need to think with a pen and paper," I growled impatiently, frustrated at my clumsy stabs while he waxed poetic, "... showing her teeth, small and perfect like pearls ... "

"No, no, *no*! That's a *cliché* Irving. It just won't work!" I snap-dragoned.

"They're just ideas, notations. Get me my clipboard and a pen." Within minutes, he had a complete little poem that he wanted to "give" to me. "After all, it was all your ideas." I refused, as signing my name to it would have been dishonest. "Hedges" remains buried amongst my early drafts; the lesson he imparted remains with me to this day.

"First the idea, the emotions, the feelings must flow," he began. "That's the main thing. So you write down all thoughts that occur to you about whatever idea you have and want to write about. The tone usually establishes itself at this stage. Then, those thoughts that are the sharpest stand out and those are taken to be shaped into a poem. In a sense, it dictates itself to you. Very quickly, the woman in the poem becomes Any Woman, so there is nothing personal about it. It's the *idea* behind it that's so important. You don't start out trying to write a poem to fit the idea, it's just the opposite."

Irving helped build my confidence and parsed life's existential abstractions down, while patiently coaxing my poems along. Everything was shit, he philosophized. This insight, he confided, coupled with his love of poetry, had kept him sane. His outlook easily became my own.

Later, upon completing "Juvenal Redivivus," he pushed back from his typewriter and spoke of "the danger that all poetry can be put in the wastepaper basket and labelled 'fine sentiments,' *unless* the poet shows that he's aware of all these evil forces, how menacing and powerful they are. Otherwise, he will not be listened to. Latin poets had a hard-boiled, tough attitude towards the world, so you don't find any sentimentality as in Edmund Spenser." He had worked hard on this latest poem, determined to say how Juvenal was the poet of our time. "This poem says something about marriage that hasn't been said before," he explained. "You have to be brutal and elegant. In the nineteenth century, they suffered from a facile optimism. Today, it's facile pessimism."

One rainy afternoon in late June, feeling turgid yet full of promise, just like my last days of high school, I looked up and asked, "Irving. What does 'The Bull Calf' *mean?*"

First, he explained, there are no absolute finite interpretations to a poem, only interesting ones. "The Bull Calf" is far more complex than a careless reading reveals. I had the poem between us on the table. "Why, in the last line, does the poet turn away and weep?" he asked. It is *not* because he feels sorry for the poor calf. It is *not* because he thinks the men are cruel and heartless. "Now, look at it again. Which word appears most often?"

"Pride." I said, counting three repetitions.

"The calf is born with it," he pointed out, "and with vitality, the 'promise of sovereignty.' But this is all *unearned* pride, not unlike Richard II's. Despite the calf's vigour, the capitalist farmer — see his name? — 'Free-man,' his freedom having been bought, decides to kill it."

He went on, prodding, "Does religion intervene?" Then he began decoding the symbolism. "No. Look at line fourteen. The sky is empty, devoid of a god, and the clergyman looks on impotently. So, the calf is struck dead. Line thirty-four shows it is 'bereft of pride and so beautiful now.' *Now*, in death the calf is beautiful, more so than when he was alive. In fact, he is '*perfectly* still.' Only death can bestow such beauty and perfection on someone or something, and it is *this* awesome realization that causes the poet to turn and weep."

I typed it all up in a letter to my high school English teacher, Mr. Meuse. Echoing other Laytonisms with an unintentionally pat line about how poetry can say in a few lines what pages of philosophy can't begin to say, and poetry being a powerful way of saying vital things for those who have the curiosity and the patience to go beyond the words themselves. Embarrassed by my elevated tone, the letter was never sent.

With each newly published volume of his, or upon completing a poem, Irving was compelled to reread the great poets he so admired, be it Shelley, Shakespeare, Catullus, Milton, Keats, Dante, etc. The timbre of his own work still resounding in his ear, he compared the masters' cadences and visions to his own. The exercise invariably left him humbled, pensive, and grateful for the gift that helped him produce his best work. On more late nights or early dawns than I can count, the man I saw across from me at the table or sitting quietly amongst his books was anything but the braggadocio caricature so often portrayed in the press.

When he was on fire with a poem or a letter he felt must be attended to immediately, I dropped everything to transcribe, type, get photocopies, or run to the post office, putting out the latest urgency. This was only fair, since he pushed everything aside whenever I had something to read to him.

One morning, I leapt out of bed, elated with the thrill of working on a new poem. Normally he was first up, often singing, and irritatingly full of energy. This time, he materialized in the kitchen doorway, tousle-haired, half-awake, and with the most disarming lost look on his face. He asked half-plaintively, half-reproachfully, "Where were you?"

"Right here!" I reassured him with a kiss. Breakfast made, I told Irving of a long poem I'd been working on. There was no greater degree of nakedness than showing him a draft riddled with clumsy errors.

He prompted, "Go on, read it to me. Read it out loud." Seeing me lose my nerve, he used applied psychology, reaching into a stack of mail and held up a poem sent by a persistent fan. It was on the death of her father. "See that? It has all the bare elements, not a word extra. *Images,* you have to use images! Capture the *essence,* don't *tell* a story." he insisted.

"You're not telling me anything new," I countered petulantly.

"Easier said than done," he cautioned. Teaching by example, he told me that a few years earlier the correspondent had been turning out exactly the same sort of bloated drafts. "The difference is that you *know* the difference." With that, he asked to look at my draft and, noting my exasperated eye rolls, said rather sharply, "Look, you want me to help you, or would you rather go and work on it some more by yourself? I'm just giving you some criticism as a teacher to any student."

I slid the yellow pad toward him, wingeing about first drafts never being good enough. He smiled that knowing little smile over the tops of his glasses and picked up his pen. "Now see, a poem shouldn't have things like this in it," circling offending words and phrases. The key image was proving very tricky to work in, I said, as it involved masturbation. Irving stopped with pen in mid-air, unsure as to what I was aiming at, and let out a long, slow, "Why?"

"Why not? " I retorted cheekily. "What you really mean is *how,* not *why,* don't you?"

Irving continued circling my errors, skinning meat from fluff to extract the good bits, finally drawing a box around the salvaged verses.

"Now, there you have it. All the essentials and the reader has something to work with. This," he said, flicking the original version away with his fingertips, "is narcissistic. You can make love by yourself, but it's not as satisfactory as when you do it with a partner. You have to make love with the reader. Don't exclude him, because that's what poetry is: an act of love. Put *that* in your journal. That's what people will want to know. This is a master poet at work and these are pearls that I'm telling you."

To which I protested, "But you say so many things!"

"So put it down! Every day!" If only I had been equal to the task.

The poem was an attempt at conveying my Catholic girlhood, hence my trying to wax poetic on sexuality and repression. He further suggested I add ten or fifteen more lines, get Jesus in there somehow, and have the girl in the poem be older, perhaps fourteen or so rather than six, since adolescents become aware of sexuality and religion at approximately the same time. "Now *that's* new, different, offensive," he declared, adding in disgusted tones how today's poets have absolutely nothing to say. "They fill pages with nothing at all! But this is something. A Catholic girl who has left all of that behind and comes out with a poem dealing with puberty, religion, and sexuality? That has not been said before. It's daring and *that's* what I like to see. Offend them! That's *your* material. You have something to say. You've left your Church, your home, you've embarked on a journey ... now go work on this poem!" For good or for ill, it remains languishing in my drafts folder.

Lesson over, he picked up a thesis manuscript about him by poet and creative writing professor Pat Keeney-Smith, reading aloud her passage about his "fellow-poets, Marx and Nietzsche," the Montreal streets where "he knew he could beat up anyone" and his "heroic vitalism." Here, the glasses came off and he shook his head in dismay at how she was stuck on that worn-out phrase of "heroic vitalism," how she'd misinterpreted his poems, and had not yet begun to look at his later work.

"If only she'd come to see me when I lived just around the corner from her on Bathurst and listened," he began. "Wynne Francis[2] was the same way. I had to teach her. Thumped her on the head again and again until she was tired of being thumped. And when I showed her the proofs of *The Gucci Bag* in Montreal, she said to me, 'Well, at least you got it out of your system.' God! If I had had a bucketful of piss water, I would have dumped it on her head. To think after all I'd taught her and to come out with a comment like that! *Feh*! For all their academic training, or precisely because of it, they can't understand. Unless you're talking to a poet, they'll never understand!"

Clearly, poets and academics were two different creatures. Reading further, he found he could compliment Keeney-Smith on the intelligent use she made of his metaphors. "See that?" he beamed, "I must admit it does give me some satisfaction to see metaphors that I have minted work their way into books, being used, talked about, studied by others — and this is just the beginning. She is just at the base of the mountain in the foothills of my poetry. Books and books will be written on my poetry, on my minted metaphors."

At face value, one could dismiss this as a woeful tendency to send himself chocolate-dipped valentines. However, listening to and watching him say such things, which he did from time to time, his tone was fulsome, yes, rambunctious even, but not that of a fool blowing hard on his own horn. Such remarks stemmed more from frustration, irony, and humour rather than anger. It was almost as if he had disassociated himself from the public figure, and was speaking as anyone might about a talented artist. Had critics and reviewers looked more closely at his work, or approached it with less personal animus, perhaps he would not have had to affirm his own worth as often as he did. Keeney-Smith's insights regarding Irving's belief that poetry, love, and friendship are the only things that matter also garnered praise, for she had rightly described all else — dynasties, civilizations, cultures — pales to nothingness in comparison, a theme running throughout his entire body of work.

That morning, putting Pat Keeney-Smith's manuscript aside, there was a long pause, as always, after one of his pronouncements.

"Well," I said, "I hope that one day, *one* day, people write about my *own* minted metaphors!"

Irving's face softened into an indulgent smile, as he asked ever so gently, "So, you want to mint metaphors? For that, you have to forge them on the anvil of your heart and soul."

"I know," I replied. Because I truly did know.

15: First Trip: Italy

ALFREDO RIZZARDI, chair of English studies at the University of Bologna and president of the Association for Canadian Studies, invited Irving to take part in the International Festival of Poets with readings at the University of Urbino and Rome's La Sapienza University in mid-August.

Rizzardi was instrumental in developing programs that introduced many Canadian authors to keenly interested Italian students. A tall, balding, bespectacled man, his ambling, laid-back-but-courtly demeanour made of him and Irving a pair of opposites. That is, until one shared an evening of, food, wine, and poetry with them. Poetry, and the ability to enjoy literature as much as life, drew them together in an enduring friendship. As a boy Alfredo had actually collected bottles for Morandi, the painter who painted bottles most of his life. He lived through the war and knew its terrors first hand. Neither death nor man's perfidy to man were abstractions, nor did Alfredo need prodding as to the Holocaust's significance. He could hear the deepest bass notes reverberating throughout Layton's work, so too the infinitely delicate tones woven into the lines in poems such as "Night Music." Alfredo had translated Ezra Pound and William Carlos Williams, among others, and Irving considered himself fortunate to have such an able translator. Together, they produced several bilingual editions, each prompting reading tours in Italy.

Another Italian friend, landscape painter Ettore de Conciliis, phoned, eager to have us stay with him. Ettore and Irving first met at a Toronto showing of Ettore's work organized by the Italian Cultural Institute. We would be his guests in Fiano Romano, forty-five kilometres outside of Rome, where he had a studio. Irving had written to Ettore about the "attractive housekeeper" who was twenty-three and "had the face and figure of a Greek goddess," mentioning also my absolute devotion, glorious meals, and that I gathered all his pearls of wisdom. With an introduction like that, small wonder I was made to feel welcome even before our arrival.

In those days, piecing a trip together began by calling or visiting a travel agency. We never owned a computer or even a word processor, and the Internet was non-existent. Logistics quickly became my department. I mapped out the itinerary, trying to make sure we had some down time, mindful that Irving was in his early seventies. Pre-trip preparation included counting the number of public appearances, listing the occasion, venue, hosts, noting whom to thank and clothes needed in anticipation of every need and potential emergency. Fortunately, Canada's Department of External Affairs usually helped with my travel fare, and I soon took over the task of drafting post-trip reports as per their requirements. We gave excellent value in return for those travel honoraria, agreeing to gruelling schedules, turning no one away, with Irving always available to meet professors, scholars, students, dignitaries, and journalists.

The departure date nearing, I focused on preparing for our first trip to Italy. Checklist in hand, I scurried downtown to the dry cleaner's, then to the shops to buy a sewing kit, band-aids, Alka-Seltzer, and various other things. Irving submersed himself in planning for the talks he'd give, selecting poems to read and deciding on their order in bouts of intense concentration. One day, I set about making lunch as Irving sat at the kitchen table, books and papers spread before him. I paid scant attention as he began writing madly for about twenty minutes, drawing near upon hearing his pen clatter to the table. He looked directly at me, his mouth alive with that familiar smile, and handed me the poem "I Take My Anna Everywhere."

As one can imagine, it took my breath away, even while sensing it contained a depth and scope that I was still too young, too inexperienced to appreciate. Triggered by my telling him I thought I would die young, this was truly *my* poem. My name was in the title. It commemorated "the proud thrust of my shoulder"; my gaze was "the unpitying gaze of a goddess." Death makes an appearance; Lear and Oedipus are in the last stanza; and there, permanently, was Irving among the men who, seeing me, now wanted "to live their wrecked lives forever." Even more pleasing was the insight that, were I to die, my name or some notion of me would endure. After a mere five or six months with Irving, I had attained immortality of sorts. The poem certainly denotes a milestone or division between the former "me" and a more rarefied sense of what I could become.

Ultimately, however, immortality by association can never be satisfying as that reached via one's own efforts. I read "I Take My Anna Everywhere" there in the kitchen as he enjoyed coffee and finished his cigarette. "Well, of *course!*" I deadpanned, "someone has to schlep the suitcases!" This became my favourite mock-response whenever the poem came up in conversation. I later suggested Irving place it last in *Dance with Desire,* his selected love poems brought out by Porcupine's Quill in 1992. It was unimaginable that any other love poem could surpass it any more than there could be a love beyond this one.

In late August, we were finally off. Boarding the plane, my eyes followed a middle-aged woman ahead of us. She wore loden green slacks, was impeccably groomed, and had a radiant Italian face. Something about her sparked my senses. No sooner did we take our seats, I began to write a poem, "To the Broad-Hipped Italian Woman." Seeing me in the grip of that incomparable rush pleased Irving tremendously. He settled in, ordered us gin and tonics and worked on "The Cyst," a poem about two growths that had been removed after a brief cancer scare. That poem prompted him to wake me several times between Rome and Calabria, reading drafts to me, discussing changes, until he deemed it complete.

Landing at Fiumicino, I had to pinch myself. Barely one year earlier, I had come through Rome as a nearly penniless hitchhiker, solitary, hungry, and barely distinguishable from millions of other backpackers. How very, very different for me now, stepping out into the Roman air, warm with oleander, refined perfumes, Marlboro cigarette smoke, and testosterone, on the arm of a poet who was soon to be received like a rock star. Canada? An illusion.

Ettore met us with his assistant, Janice, a young strawberry blonde woman from Seattle. She was Ettore's sometime interpreter who helped manage his American exhibitions and clients. We piled into his car and headed for Fiano.

Ettore's place was not just in the country, it was in the middle of a field. Next to it, a little road of brilliant white limestone bisected the rolling green expanse. He grew basil and other fragrant herbs out front in beds surrounded by pebbly white gravel. Cypresses and trees ripe with figs lined one side of the compound. Inside, there was a large, low-ceilinged living and dining area, all in white, with smooth terra cotta tiles underfoot. The only other colour came from his library off in its own alcove to the left and bright green gingham on the rattan sofa and chairs. A warm breeze blew lazily in from the field and ploughed earth. For a painter's home, the walls were surprisingly bare except for his painting of a crate of peaches hanging by the kitchen doorway. Its realism, down to the bright blue piece of plastic snagged on the crate, was mesmerizing.

Beyond the small, white-tiled kitchen, there was a well-stocked floor-to-ceiling wine rack, past that, a viewing area for private clients, and finally his studio. I went slack-jawed at the vast white expanse and all those brushes, all those paints, the pungent odor of oils and solvents. A stab of envy shot through me. He had an imposing studio easel on castors, sensuously splattered with paint, mostly green. On the ancient record player, a jazz — or was it blues — album, and some Joan Baez, with whom he'd been friends back in the day. This was heaven. Painting and writing need not be exclusive. I had always doodled and scribbled. Why not paint *and* write? It would be many years before I had a living room with one corner serving as a tiny studio of my own.

Irving loved Italy, and Italy loved him, even more so for his having a youthful companion. The pair of us made for them a living diorama on the theme of Truth and Beauty. Instead of hand wringing or rude whisperings vis-à-vis the age difference, Italians accepted it as the most

befitting thing in the world for a poet to have a young Muse. It gave the
men hope, and the women something aspire to. Better yet, I was teaching myself Italian hand over fist, which delighted everyone. In later
trips, I acted as a conduit helping nervous students approach Irving.
My being relatively close in age made for wonderful encounters, once
receiving roses as a thank-you, and I was even asked for an autograph
by grateful, life-hungry students in Udine.

Irving had visited Italy several times before, writing poems like
"Poet on the Square" and "Arcade" in Bologna. "Neo-Stalinist" was
begun in Rome after seeing a demented bag lady sitting on the edge of
the sidewalk café, raging unintelligibly at some unseen enemy. Her fury
illustrated what history has shown, albeit on a grander scale. Her obnoxious railings may have stemmed from a personal discomfort rather
than politics, just as fanatics may have frothed — not because state of
the world, but from personal shortcomings of their own.

Being anywhere with Irving was an adventure. In Europe especially,
he showed the world to me as through a giant kaleidoscope. His appetite for travel, for writerly pleasures like sitting in a café for hours with
book and pen, drinking the scene and people in with his espresso, was
insatiable. With each return to a place, he gave the kaleidoscope a mas-
terful shake and the entire city sparkled anew. He loved the stimulation
of being in foreign surroundings, watching for experiences unfolding
around him. We often sought out local synagogues, just to pay homage.
In Naples, he asked the young rabbi to bless me, and he did so, apolo-
gizing for not being able to shake my hand. It never took very long for
something to catch Irving's eye. Within moments, he then pared down
its essential meaning to begin a poem. A poet, he said, always seeks to
make sense out of chaos, always balancing between Apollonian reason
and Dionysian passion, as in his poem "The Birth of Tragedy." I don't
think Irving ever used a camera, not because he was technologically
challenged, which he was, but because poems were distilled experience. Photographs paled in comparison.

The first stop was the University of Urbino, an ancient school with
stone walls and archways might that have been sketched by its most
famous son, the painter Raphael. Ettore and Janice drove us there and

to all of our engagements. We could not have been in better hands. Ettore had a very refined palate and knew the best places to enjoy regional specialties. Rizzardi greeted us and walked us to our room in what had once been the nunnery, not without a few ribald comments passing between the two men.

In Urbino, as in every other Italian university, I witnessed something of a phenomenon. Clearly, the professors had delved into Irving's work and prepared their students well, for the moment he appeared before packed rooms, halls, or auditoriums, Irving was greeted with the raucous applause usually reserved for rock stars rather than poets. We could feel the excitement in the air on approaching the designated lecture room. Afterwards, we spent time with the students, the lowest on the academic totem pole, giving them a chance to say hello and ask questions.

Back in Rome, we made time for a long walk and a longer conversation about poetry, its future, my future, then, a stop at a fabulous little restaurant where he put "The Cyst" before me with the usual challenge. Could I tell him why this revision was better than the previous one? I was on target, but he pointed out the main difference was the distancing obtained by saying "each man's Dorian Gray" and cutting all the narrative out. My notes break off there, with Irving explaining how, "in this case, because of the effects of television and the media, everyone knows immediately — "

Perhaps I was too tired or too excited to continue writing everything down, for that same day, we continued our walk, stopping at a café by the Piazza del Popolo. Irving asked to see my poem about the broad-hipped Italian woman. As he searched for a few words, I took a photo of him in his bright red T-shirt. By adding that she "turned to wave farewell to her aging lover" and a marvellous closing line, the poem became startlingly alive.[1]

The next day, we were to fly south to Brindisi where Ettore would pick us up and drive westward to Alezio near Gallipoli. Despite appearances, these trips were the furthest thing from a vacation. There were always people that had to be entertained, and Irving was perhaps at his most active. His mind never stopped working, and since he shared everything, there was zero down time for me. On the flight to Brindisi, the Adriatic's waves became, to him, the "accordion skin of the water," likening it to an old woman's face. There was poetry in almost everything he saw.

Back in Rome, Irving took me on a pilgrimage to the Keats-Shelley Memorial House just by the Spanish Steps. We climbed the dim stairway, paid admission, and took in the rooms and relics that had once belonged to the two poets, as well as Byron, who had lived there for a time. We peered into a display case with a container said to hold some of Shelley's ashes. It was enough to just breathe the old air and imagine Byron himself bounding up the stairs any moment to join us. On subsequent trips to Rome, I could not help but note Irving's decline as measured with each pilgrimage. The next trip included a climb up the stairs, but not paying admission — partly out of budgetary concerns, partly because of fatigue. On the next visit, we made do with lingering in the foyer, only looking up the staircase and imagining those unholy boys trundling home to write or sleep. Later still, there was only a drive past the Spanish Steps, nodding our respects to the revered ghosts. Then nothing, no more trips to Rome.

16: Family Portrait

FROM THE MANY tell-all books by children of celebrities, it is easy to lump their stories into a tale of misunderstanding, unfulfilled wishes, and parents who short-changed their children, even when trying to be present. What child ever grows up free from hurt? What parent ever succeeds perfectly? Like everyone else, I can only imagine what it was like growing up and travelling the world with famous literary parents. All I know is what I observed when Irving spent time with his grown children.

Whether due to his obvious success, his self-sufficient way of life, or simply the clash of personalities, Irving's family relationships were strained at best, abysmal at worst. Aviva, his third ex-wife, mother of his exceptionally beautiful son David, was the first kin I met. In early 1983, Aviva was still living in what had once been their marital home in Toronto, sharing it with her new man, Leon Whiteson. They were in the process of selling and, with the market nicely inflated, realized enough profit to buy a home in Beverly Hills.

Irving and Aviva's rendezvous spot was the Varsity Restaurant on Bloor Street West, between Spadina and Madison. Max, Irving's son with his second wife, Betty, was to join us as well. I'm going to say this meeting took place in June, perhaps earlier. Irving and I took the train into town and stopped outside the Varsity while I gathered courage for this first "meet the family" trial. I had no mother- or father-in-law to impress, but Irving came with two ex-mates still on speaking terms, and three of four children in his life — two of them older than myself, and David mere five years my junior. I braced for a bumpy ride.

Irving pointed Aviva out. She had her back to the window, easily visible in a booth with her neat silver hair and petite frame. I had no clue as to how she would receive me. Worse still, Irving was in one of his high-mischief states. As my stomach began to churn, he insisted I go up to her and say, "The question arises, why are you a Pie-zes?" — the opening line of a family joke probably older than I was. There was only one answer: "The question is arisen, why are you a Pizen?"

I felt this was woefully inappropriate. "*Irving!* I can't say that to her! It's a family thing! She's going to hate me for using something from her time with you!" He chuckled some more, insisting it would amuse her and to go ahead. I approached Aviva's booth, deciding to go for the gusto despite feeling I was breaking protocol.

Poor Aviva glanced up at my rather oddly put-together self, grey fedora at the wrong angle, and was confused at this stranger posing the secret question. To her credit, she had the presence of mind to respond in kind. Irving never explained his reason for insisting on it. Perhaps he was giving Aviva a subconscious little pinch, letting her know that he'd not only moved on, but found someone with whom he could share everything, including obscure shards from his former life.

They chatted merrily while I mostly listened. She was a bit guarded, but to my relief, there were no rude questions, no catty left-hooks.

Memories of his Aviva years could still rouse feelings of frustration and exasperation in Irving. None of these outbursts lasted very long, for he quickly recalled her best traits and how close she had come to being his lifelong mate. He had found in Aviva a sort of mother figure whose presence was comforting, and took care of the boy in him. However, it also caused him to balk as irrationally as a stubborn boy. "Aviva's failure to understand that my interest in women was strictly a poetical one caused her to apply so much pressure to my system that I'd go out in search of more pleasant company," he confided, not at all happy to have arrived at these insights so late in the game. So, she had decamped; he had written the quota of poems that Aviva inspired. Rueful, bitter frustration aside, he retained a deep tenderness and love for Aviva.

Despite his reputation, he said he was most comfortable with monogamy. Though secular, the ethics prescribed by the Prophets remained at the core of his personal code. His heart and soul had remained with the spouse until the spouse had proven herself impossible to stay with. She pushed and pulled until one day, she had painted herself right out of the picture. One of the only true parts of Aviva's fictionalized book *Nobody's Daughter*, he said, was the part where he broke down and cried, pleading with her that he did not want them to be at odds nor to split up. At least she seemed to have found a certain amount of happiness with Leon, and Irving was glad for that, adding how he could but marvel at the fact that she never saw what I seem to intuit.

Soon, that day at lunch, a very handsome man strode past the window and into the Varsity. "Max! How are you, son?" Irving hailed him as Max slid into the booth across from me. He was striking, though his face and expression bore little resemblance to his Romanian-Jewish father's mischievous *punim*. This was as good as any Scottish lord might look. Chiselled cheekbones, honey-blond hair, piercing blue eyes, and a well-pressed twill shirt (he favoured stone, taupe, and concrete greys, which matched his personality, or blue to match his eyes) spelled handsome in any language.

The more he spoke, however, the more I cocked my ear. Something about his voice seemed odd, as though it were unnatural or stilted. Quite unlike Irving's mellifluous delivery, Max's phrases were expelled as if squeezed out in short, hesitant segments. Even more unusual, the sausage-link phrases were delivered with a Vincent Price tremolo. It was unsettling, especially as it was the polar opposite of Irving's voice. Strained. That's it. He spoke as if someone had him by the throat. It made me instantly wary, though I could not have known precisely why.

Their outlooks on life were as diametrically opposed as their facial features. Irving once described to me how he took ten-year-old Max on a visit to Montreal's poorest neighbourhood. He wanted his young son to see that others were less fortunate, that the world was unfair, and social injustice was something one should fight against. To his astonishment, Max took the grand tour in silence, noting the dilapidation and squalor. Afterwards, safely on his way back to their comfortable home, Max declared he would never live like *those people*. The coldness of it left Irving wanting to laugh at the exercise's ironic result, and cry that his son's heart was so different from his own.

Max and Aviva were pleasant toward me, convivial even. They had seen him with Harriet, and been witness to Irving's protracted misery. They could not wish another debacle on Irving, could they? Max's mother Betty was also from Nova Scotia, as was Irving's first wife Faye.[1] Perhaps the Maritimer in me eased Max's mind, helping him form an image of me as a stalwart and dependable. I hoped so. I had no desire to alienate the family phalanx. They had but to see me exactly as I was, and notice that Irving was smiling again.

Later that summer, we visited Max in the splendid apartment he shared with his partner Stephanie in a leafy Toronto neighbourhood. Her father and brother were both acclaimed artists, and she was a talented lithographer. She was the female version of Max, with a face like a Highland queen. The sculpted cheekbones, long blonde hair, and model's figure made her a standout. Unlike Max, she had a ready sense of humour and was not averse to belly laughs. Stephanie had travelled extensively, bringing back exotic objets d'art from places like Afghanistan. Max and Stephanie seemed unattached to their handsome bodies. Their conversation was so cerebral that their heads began expanding like floats in a Macy's parade, their tiny hands and torsos jerking for emphasis as they scored debate points.

Whenever Max was with Irving, he started heated, screaming debates about philosophy or politics. It was just as likely to happen with David around as well. One did not have to be a family psychiatrist to see that Plato and Aristotle were mere place-holders. There was no "debate" really. It was a verbal punch-up with the sons ventilated their long-held Oedipal grudges. Irving saw through the tiresome ruse, always letting them flail away at him, playing along as if they were college-trained debaters rather than angry, frustrated sons.

That evening at Max and Stephanie's was typical, with Irving, Max, and Stephanie going at it over films like *Blade Runner*, *Mad Max*, and muscled arguing about modern society, Babylon, and our place in the cosmos. Without such philological arrows in my quiver, I listened intently, unable to warm to Stephanie and Max's sense of intergalactic wonder,

their penchant for second-guessing God about outer space and other tes-
seracts. When all three paused for breath, I interjected that none of this
cosmic speculation held my interest or even mattered. To my mind, the
human being contains far more mystery and wonder than any star system.

My comment went over like a stone down a well, to Irving's amusement. Stephanie remained gracious. Perhaps because of the enormous
relief it produced, I can still recall her tasking me with making gravy,
which I had never made before. "Oh *Anna*! You're a natural gravy-mak-
er!" she exclaimed, praising my lump-free sauce. Irving seemed to be
enjoying himself, especially once dinner was served and the debating
let up enough to eat.

That night, it was with relief, if not a sense of triumph, that Max
bestowed a Russian-sounding name on me. His mother Betty had long-
since gone by the name Boschka, her tribute to the great Hieronymus
Bosch. At Max and Stephanie's dinner party, I became "Annoushka."
Max's friendly gesture permitted me to feel I was now a fully fledged
member of the Layton tribe. I was pleased, but still wary.

Near the end of summer, Boschka stayed with us for a week or so on
her cross-country drive from California to Nova Scotia. She brought with
her Naomi, her and Irving's daughter who suffered from a number of mental ills and was then living in the country north of Toronto. Given Boschka's
age, the trip had the trappings of a farewell journey. Only a homesick Nova
Scotian can know the pull that "down home" exerts on her exiled children.

Boschka's trusty green sedan, adorned with seashells all along the
front dashboard, was perfectly in tune with her diehard hippy-child self.
She told good stories, and was quite fun to have around despite a gruff
exterior. I wish she had told us more of her Big Sur days, for there were
surely stories there. What she did describe was how, at one point, she
grew envious of Irving's growing fame, took a lover, and left for California
with him. He was a poet whom Irving had spent hours helping with the
craft. It was a tetchy subject — taking their young daughter Naomi with
her over the U.S. border without Irving's permission had been a criminal
offence. As was the drunken first night in California, the tequila binge
which she described to me in vivid detail as if everyone drives across
the continent, puts a child in a motel room alone, and takes off for an

all-night party. Naomi later told me of that night as well, how terrified she was to be alone in a strange place, her mother and pals staggering home the next morning, under police escort.

These were some home truths that she was well aware of, but in her hippy-happy mind it was all in the past and meaningless now. Irving found two things impossible to understand or to forgive Boschka: selfishly pulling Naomi out of high school just before graduation so that she had a companion for her trip to India, and Boschka's refusal to let Irving's brother adopt Naomi. Hyman and his wife Ruth lived in Petaluma, California, where Hyman had been able to retire from his paint and flooring business at the age of forty. He longed for children of his own. After learning of Naomi's squalid flower-child home life, he begged to adopt her. Boschka refused. I asked Irving if this was because Boschka wanted to hang on to Naomi to assure the steady flow of money her way. He did not discount it. She took her reasons to her grave.

In the course of working on *Waiting for the Messiah*, or sometimes prompted by a letter from Naomi, Irving would tell me of how he had been completely smitten the moment he first met Boschka. So much so that his first words to her were that she and him were going to make beautiful children. He praised her artistic talent. Indeed, several of his early books feature covers and design by Boschka. They are as modern and striking now as the day they were made, still shimmering with the same kind of edgy vibe emanating from Greenwich Village in its heyday.

Enthralled by her talent, he built her a studio when they lived on Kildare Road in Montreal's Côte-Saint-Luc suburb. I still have the book on modern art he bought in order to be able to discuss her work on her terms. "But she never wanted to know a thing about my poetry," he said wistfully, his voice trailing off.

Her artistic potential was great. Keeping house held little interest for her as art came first. Irving was teaching at five different places, taking care of his dying mother, and fighting to bring stodgy Canadian literature into the twentieth century. To save Boschka from domestic concerns, he hired a mother's helper and had milk, bread, and groceries delivered. Absent-minded or just plain unconcerned, she would leave food out to spoil. Irving recalled summer nights where he'd "come home to find a line of green mould spreading from the rotting meat, milk, and bread, that had grown all the way from the fridge around the kitchen, along the counter and back to the fridge."

Ultimately, none of that seemed to have earned him any medals. Nor did his giving her every penny from the sale of their marital home, or his sending her a monthly cheque until the day she died in February 1984. She had left him and taken their child, so the courts would not have obliged him to support her, but he did to the extent we was capable of, sometimes receiving angry "where's the cheque?" letters from her.

Unlike Harriet, Boschka and Aviva both had at least respected the poet, but apparently found the man lacking. Who can really know what transpired? All we have are masterpieces like "Berry Picking," "Sacrament by the Water," "The Day Aviva Came to Paris," and "Night Music" as proof that a great, imperfect love existed at one time.

Boschka had another reason to be stopping with us in Oakville, namely the launch of her book of poems, prose, and drawings, *The Prodigal Sun* (Mosaic Press, 1982). There was a reading at Harbourfront hosted by Greg Gatenby, which was very well attended. I admired Boschka's courage in going onstage with her face disfigured by the paralysis of Bell's palsy. Despite it all, her personality shone through and her performance garnered much applause. In a rare double-bill, Irving read as well that night. It was the only reading Irving gave where Max and, I believe, David were present. Irving was very concerned about his voice that night, asking me if it was resonant. I suspect he was really asking whether it had broken at any point.

For a short time during that summer visit with Boschka and Naomi, we were a big happy family. There were odd moments, however. One evening I chanced upon a scene that I have not been able to shake all these years. Past Irving's study on the ground floor was the Florida Room. Other than my study, this was my favourite part of the house. Our yellow-gold sofa was there, fitting in perfectly with the pthalo-blue floor covering and robin's-egg-blue walls. A straight-backed chair stood by the door. There was a small coffee table, and a perpetually dying ficus tree in the corner. With windows all around and no curtains, it was as pleasant on moonlit nights and summer afternoons.

Boschka and I sat on either end of the sofa, talking about all and nothing. Naomi wandered in as dusk fell. To my surprise, she crawled onto her mother's lap, coiling her arms around Boschka's neck, nuzzling there like a toddler. Before I could pick myself up, borne away on a wave of intense discomfort, Naomi lapsed into an infantile voice, telling her mother how badly she wanted a car. "Ask Daddy, Naomi. Just ask Daddy. He's Santa Claus, you know! He'll get you *anything*. Anything you ask." Naomi was approximately thirty-three years old at the time.

When your step-daughter is nine years older than you, and she's being cradled by her mother, you don't interject. Nor can you ask the mother to cease from indulging her daughter with fantasies that can only end in disappointment. It was too intimate a scene, too sad for words. I left them to enjoy what would be one of their last moments together. Irving just shook his head sadly when I mentioned he might be asked to buy a car. Not only did he lack the means, more pointedly, Naomi whether on or off her lithium, was in no condition to drive.

The next time I met Naomi was at Max and Stephanie's place a few years later. She took no part in the fiery arguments over Plato's *Republic* or the existence of God or the meaning of the universe. Instead, she sat very quietly, face partially obscured by long wavy black hair parted down the middle, which she never attempted to brush away from her face. Naomi was like a pressed flower that still wanted to be part of someone's garden. Her subdued, slow-moving gait and the simplicity of her words and gestures, however, melted away when she picked up her classical guitar. Had the gods not played their malevolent joke, Naomi may well have gone on to become a concert guitarist. She was still gift-ed, had even studied in Spain with Segovia, but that was where her wheels fell off. She lived mainly in California, returning there after a brief time in Canada. Medicated and with a minuscule support system, Irving sending money whenever he could, she clung to her dreams if only by looking back at what might have been.

Her rendition of "Memories of the Alhambra" was Irving's fa-vourite. He asked her to play it that night, as he always did. She played gladly, pouring her entire being into the music and offering it as a gift, as though to distract from her damaged mind and body. Whenever

Irving saw his daughter's head bent in fierce concentration, as lost in the music as he was when writing a poem, it moved him even more than the haunting melody. This was Naomi, the little daughter who had run in the tall grasses by the river in "Song for Naomi." The poem, a lyrical meditation on the passage of time, compares nature's cyclical growth and rebirth against the child's linear growth. She wins out over the grass by summer's end, for it can only grow to a certain height. Vacation over, she is now taller than the grass. But humans too, with all their capacity for art and civilized existence, will one day fall to earth and must ultimately be folded back into nature's relentless cycle.

Soon Boschka was packed and about to depart. Naomi, Stephanie, and Irving all came out into the garden, now grown shaggy from neglect. We took pictures, everyone seeming happy to be together, Boschka had laughed at the sight of Irving and me arguing about making the coffee. He kept insisting that a man could make better coffee than a woman, garnering choice remarks from me. "You trying to make the leopard change his spots?" Boschka laughed, adding how nice it was to "hear two people bickering about the coffee and not have to worry about it."

That day, Irving was dressed for yet another meeting with his lawyer. He looked drawn, grey-faced and beyond sad. I could be mistaken, but I believe this was the day he was to argue one last time for visiting rights to Samantha. Now, the mother of his first two children was leaving, and it was extremely unlikely they would see each other again. The once-beautiful woman, who had startled him with her verve and a face that could have made her sister to Barbara Stanwyk and Ingrid Bergman, had changed, aged as he had. He read the poem "Divorce," which asks what is it about separation that permits their fingers to entwine and hold. I snapped the last photo of Boschka and Irving together, almost regretting it when I saw the ocean of sadness reflected in their faces.

David, Irving and Aviva's black-haired, green-eyed son, I knew from many photos as well as his appearance in the poem "Shakespeare." His child's mind likens rain to air crying, and his mother's nipples to drain plugs he wishes he could pull out, imagery taken as signs of early genius. David's precociousness prompts Irving to warn Shakespeare that one of his clan just might make it, might become the next cock-of-the-walk.

The adult David seemed to be keeping his talents hidden, like many of us who are afflicted with a fear of failure or of success.

We met properly at a brunch at Max at Stephanie's. David came in woefully late, keeping everyone waiting, sauntering in with his eyes barely open, yawning uncontrollably, with a sheen on his face as if he hadn't bothered to shower. Stumbling straight over to the low, white sofa where Aviva and I were sitting, he promptly collapsed full length with his face turned alarmingly downwards and pressed into Aviva's lap. His feet lodged against my leg, pushing me off the sofa. I clung on by pushing out one cramped leg, my buttocks clenched mightily to the sofa's edge. Irving dropped a sarcastic comment on how sorry he was that David had had to rise before noon.

At last we sat down to brunch. Irving was then in the midst of wrapping up a film shoot arranged through Joe Kertes, another former student and spiritual son. It was a small role in the made-for-TV film about Tom Longboat, an Onandaga marathon runner who had attained great fame and died in obscurity at the age of sixty-one. Irving's involvement in the film likely prompted him to prod David about filmmaking as a possible career. David, preferring his charming exterior to remain his best asset, did not welcome challenges, and threw his father off topic by launching into an appalling tirade, as bizarre as it was disgusting. After declaring everyone in the movie industry was neurotic, he ripped into his father. "You don't fucking know money!" he snarled at Irving. "You've never even seen money like *I've* seen at my friends' houses. *They* know what the fuck money is. *You'll* never fucking see that kind of money!" On and on he fulminated in this vein, calling his father stupid for failing to be rich like his friends' fathers.

Spellbound, I waited for Aviva to speak up. She did not. Irving did not let David's distemper spoil his meal, preferring to let his overheated son splutter out by himself. Max and Stephanie, even though it was their home, also kept their mouths shut. Naturally, if all of these family members were afraid to tell David to behave himself, the last thing I was going to do was shush him with a sharp reprimand. In a million years, I would never have dreamt of using such a tone or those belittling words against my father.

David then grew bored and returned to his game of "look at me, I'm so sleepy" while we carried on semblances of conversation, leaving the twenty-something to wallow in his self-inflicted drama. Afterwards, I asked Irving why he tolerated such rudeness. "Because," he said, his voice thick with sadness, "if I were ever to correct him, to tell him what I really thought of him, it would destroy him."

David never found the time to come out to any of his father's readings, except perhaps the one with Boschka, though I do not recall for sure if he was there. A few years later, he showed up at the NFB premier of the documentary *Poet: Irving Layton Observed*, emerging into the lobby afterwards, drunk, and pronouncing, "The film's a piece of shit, Dad, but you're okay." Irving, however, always had a soft spot for his second son. David, born to a Jewish mother, came into the world with what Irving called a Jewish heart. Irving was concerned David relied too much on his looks and charm. Many times, he exhorted me to always stay in touch with David, particularly as I was immune to his wiles. Irving hoped that perhaps, after his demise, David would have enough maturity and self-confidence to wean himself from his mother — enough to entertain other perspectives about his father. Whenever he expressed this wish, I replied it would be up to David. Aviva was his mother, and if he wanted to get to know me or learn new things about his father, I would *always* be available, but would never run after him. The last complete published poem Irving wrote, "Nest-Building," written on our last trip to Molivos, Greece, where I had arranged for David to join us, is dedicated to David.

As I write this, David has yet to contact me, nor did he at Irving's death. None of them have. As in a Greek tragedy, each hides their reasons for wishing I never came into Irving's life. That way, their views about Irving can remain intact, never to be challenged by an alternative perspective.

Irving often woke up at three in the morning, drenched in sweat, the mattress and pillow soaked through. As in a recurring nightmare, he would sit bolt upright in the dark, asking himself why he had brought children into the world. Sons, moreover, who could only resent their father's name and who, by all outward appearances, resented him for never being able to better it.

17: Montreal Awaits

IRVING ROUNDED OUT that year in Oakville with interviews for the *Oakville Beaver*; the *Toronto Star*'s book editor Ken Adachi; and the *Ottawa Citizen*'s Noel Taylor. He gave readings in Ottawa, Toronto, London, and Calgary, and did tapings at Sheridan College with Mike Walsh. There were three meetings with biographer Elspeth Cameron and at least two with David O'Rourke, who was interviewing Irving for his thesis. Irving also saw his divorce lawyer often, as well as his two dear spiritual sons, Joe Kertes and Ben Labovitch, who both taught at Humber College.

Through all this, though, there had been almost no further access to Samantha, including a seven-month period when Harriet prevented him from seeing her altogether. The disintegration of Irving's ties with his young daughter occurred during his last few visits with her. She began to express dislike, turning away from him as if coached. "Girls need to have a father in their lives and know how much their father loves them!" he'd exclaim, heart-heavy after an unsuccessful attempt at seeing her. Then, noting her changed demeanour, Irving realized they were weaning her from him, preparing to cut him out of her life. His greatest fear was that Harriet would stoop to accuse him of molesting Samantha. Obscene as the notion was, Harriet had already accused him of abuse when the babysitter alleged Irving had tried to use a rubber band to keep Samantha's jaw shut, misrepresenting a harmless game. If Harriet could go that low, Irving felt she would stop at nothing to defame him and divide Samantha's affections. Devastated, he grimly agreed to relinquish all parental and visitation rights. "At least she won't be forced to choose," he said, "and it wouldn't surprise me if they told her I was dead."

Howard Aster had done yeoman's work in bringing out *The Gucci Bag*, as well as the portfolio *Shadows on the Ground*. They had already begun to discuss *Final Reckoning*. Publishing concerns dealt with, and with Samantha off limits, there was no reason to stay in Oakville. *Waiting for the Messiah* was rapidly taking shape in Irving's mind, and the only place he felt could write this memoir was Montreal. My premonition about Oakville being a temporary home proved true almost to the day.

Howard hosted a private farewell party for us the same night Irving flew back from a reading in Calgary. We would miss Howard's rambunctious family, his generosity, and humour. Irving would never again have such an able interlocutor, someone with whom he could discuss and, indeed, resolve, world politics.

All in all, despite a wrecked car, dramas with Venie and Shaindel, and a showdown between me and Irving, it had been quite a year. I would never forget *The Gucci Bag* launch party, nor each initial encounter with Irving's family and friends. I had the rare chance to meet the late, great photographer Arnaud Maggs. He shot Irving and myself for his "mug-shot" series, and took what I hope were lovely semi-nudes of me for a series. I am told they are now in the National Archives, unseen. Before leaving, he very generously took photos of Irving and myself together, later sending me three prints. They remain the most intimate, accurate, and priceless mementoes I have of Irving and me in our early days.

Irving had written "I Take My Anna Everywhere," a poem already taking on more meaning for me as I grew in knowledge about poetry and life. We had shared splendid moments not only in the privacy of our home, but away in Italy, and, most importantly for me, I could look back and appreciate how far I had come, how well I had taken to the literary life. Already, some of my books and journals contained what I considered splashes of pure light, scribbled madly down as Layton illuminated Layton. He was doing it for me, but also "using" me in the best sense to diffuse his distilled knowledge out onto the larger world. My willingness to be his helpmate was utterly genuine, never rued nor regretted.

I had watched a master wordsmith working with such intensity that everything and everyone around him slipped into nothingness: driving himself to distraction at bad imagery, wrong sounds, words too crimped to convey the intended meaning. Then, final draft done, I had seen the bursts of joy, that unique kind of joy reserved for artists when their work seems to please the gods. Would I know that joy? Would I be able to negotiate my time, my space, so I could detach myself from Irving's world and plunge into my own? Of the challenges that lay ahead, I would need to mitigate those times when I'd be forced to leave pens and papers splayed on my desk, returning only after his and my own creative juices had cooled.

There was also that Cameron woman. We could only speculate what she was writing, for she kept every word of the biography about Irving to herself. Her inane question, fired at me that day in her car as she gave me a lift into Toronto, still rankled. Yes, Elspeth, I *would* think of marrying Irving. The mere thought of it had turned her entire face into a horrified grimace. Why on earth would I not want to be with one of the greatest poets in the world, particularly as he was not only my closest confidant, but also my lover and staunchest supporter — only a fool walks away from a man who loves the way Irving loved me.

If Oakville had been anything to go by, Montreal would be even more exciting, and much more exacting. Far down in a corner of my mind, and surely in Irving's mind too — he was going back to his boyhood city as one returns home to die. Before that, however, there were still a few supernova bursts of creativity and living to set off and savour. On the twenty-ninth of November, we boarded the first-class car on the train for Montreal.

PART THREE:

THE PROVING YEARS: LOVE, WORK, AND TRIUMPH

18: Montreal

MONTREAL WAS STILL the Forbidden City to me since, for the moment at least, it was still Venie's stomping grounds. The train brought Irving and me relentlessly closer, each mile confirming I was arriving as Irving's seasoned mate, no longer anyone's illusion. After a year or so at his side I showed no signs of decamping; certain parties needed to put their fantasies away.

Our first night in our new city was memorable for many reasons, not the least of which was meeting Musia Schwartz, star of the poem "For Musia's Grandchildren." Aside from Irving's immediate family, Musia and her husband, Leon, had known Irving perhaps the longest. They had met Irving in his English class immediately after the Second World War. Leon was from Byelorussia; she was from Poland. The Holocaust took her entire family save for one aunt who also lived in Montreal. Leon had been in the Russian tank brigade that captured Berlin, famously marking the beginning of the end of the war. They were unlike anyone I had met before, having layers of European sophistication, charm, and manners from another era. Neither Musia nor Leon suffered fools gladly. I would have to go on the charm offensive, and hope to pass their stringent tests.

The furniture had not yet arrived, so Musia and Leon welcomed us for the night at their home on Montclair, a few streets over from our house on Monkland Avenue in the Notre-Dame-de-Grâce (NDG) part of Montreal. Our neighbourhood was also home to Irving's nephew,

Bill Goodwin, his wife Sandra, and their two young sons, Danny and Jessie. For someone returning to the city of his youth, Irving could not have been better placed than NDG. Having his friends close by and all the amenities we could want made it ideal.

That first night, Musia served tongue. Beef tongue. A very large pink curling piece of meat that made my gorge rise so high I had to stand up to recapture it. Surely this was a test: *So you think you have what it takes to keep up with Eastern European Jews?* Irving had regaled Musia as to how adroitly I took to all things Jewish. Eating tongue and not heaving won me a slew of brownie points. Eating sprats (something with an unholy amount of pickled fish and dill) and cold borscht were other tests, all passed. My first taste of bagel and lox was at Musia's the night of the welcome back party she threw. Likewise with drinks, such as Kir Royale and Polish vodka, straight, always kept in the freezer. Passing the exotic food tests and using Yiddish words in the right places also garnered kudos. I was glad for the maternal warmth that permeated their home, and relieved that they accepted me into their circle. In time, I came to think of Musia and Leon as my surrogate Jewish parents.

The morning after our arrival, I saw for the first time what would be our last house. The movers were late, so I began ripping out the shag carpet and hallucinatory red-blotched wallpaper, throwing myself into it with bare-handed abandon. I looked past the thick layers of greasy cigarette smoke staining every square inch, deliriously happy with "my" home. There was no Shaindel to spoil our first night. Venie was waiting somewhere in the wings — in fact, she soon penned a letter to Irving after seeing how happy he was, vowing to "kick the chair of serenity out from under [his] ass" and choice remarks about me being little more than a "smiling petunia."[1] She tried to backpedal years later when I tweaked her about it — she claimed she merely wanted Irving to stay miserable in order to keep writing — the petunia in me smiled broadly, not buying a word of it.

The house was snug as an English cottage, complete with lead-paned windows, burnished oak trim, and oak floors throughout. There was a small sunroom on the second floor that jutted out into leafy tree branches. In the very private backyard, a tall spruce tree, surrounded here and there with honeysuckle, deep purple clematis, and an overgrown lilac bush. A tall hedge separated us from the Korean family who lived in the other half of the duplex. All along the hedge, spring brought out a pleasing blue froth of forget-me-nots waving up at us in the breeze. Out front, a scrub cedar that never did thrive, hyacinth, tiger lilies, and a scattering of tulips, mostly red. Best of all, the basement had a bathroom with a shower for guests, a working fireplace, and an entire wall of built-in bookshelves. The large laundry room was unfinished, but had its own door leading to the backyard and a quaint cold-storage room unchanged since the turn of the century.

The staircase, stripped of its offending carpet, was all oak and angled past a large stained glass window set with a red and green art deco tulip design. The bathroom, as per bygone days, had a separate commode room done in shiny wallpaper with gambolling corseted Victorian ladies. Later, I stripped the paper and painted the walls creamy brown. Our large sunlit bedroom overlooked Monkland Avenue. A shade tree out front obscured the view, but not bus 162's wheezing whines. The two other upstairs rooms suited us to a T. Irving took the front one with morning light and built-in bookshelves, glossy bright white against matte yellow gold. I took the other study overlooking the backyard. It remained mercifully cool all morning, enabling me to work without being distracted by the sun, which, when it streamed across my desk, made it nearly impossible to stay inside. Irving and I spent more hours there than any room other than the dining room, which is where we read the morning paper and mail, and where he dictated his memoirs to me. The entire house had double-hung windows, all in working order. At the first breath of spring, I flung them open, filling the house with mauve hyacinth perfumes and the smell of moist earth.

Seeing me in an apron, sliding a herb-covered chicken into the oven, or with a kerchief, sweating away polishing each leaded window pane, often prompted Irving to praise my *balabusta* ways (Yiddish for bustling, efficient homemaker). Far from a born *balabusta*, I learned to run a home as I learned everything else: by observing. I devoured the *Montreal Gazette*'s food and living sections for guidance, and milked experiences for knowledge. When, for example, the American writer Elizabeth Spencer, then teaching at Concordia, invited us for a buffet supper, I noted everything from the stack of napkins splayed for easy pick-up to how one laid silverware in groups to please guests with a table full of polished luxury. Elizabeth, the epitome of Southern charm, never knew how feverishly I took in every aspect of the buffet, including her grace and style.

Over those first few days I busied myself hanging paintings throughout the house. In Irving's study, he had one free wall for his diplomas and Nobel Prize nomination telegrams, seen by practically no one but us. Along his windowsill and on the side of the bookshelf, Irving carefully placed small black and white photos mounted on thick cardboard, an iconography of his closest, most dependable companions: D.H. Lawrence, Sigmund Freud, Nietzsche, Karl Marx, Walt Whitman, and Baudelaire. Despite thousands of acquaintances, he enjoyed a kinship with these and other great thinkers and writers. Each time an admired writer died, we watched the news reports, Irving mourning their passing. He read their obituaries with respect and care, often having me clip and place one in a copy of the writer's book.

Musia's daughter worked for the *Gazette,* so I suspect that is how stories about us wound their way into the paper from time to time. In fact, our arrival in Montreal coincided with Aislin's editorial cartoon tersely observing how Toronto got the Sun Life head offices as part of the second exodus of corporations fleeing Montreal's language wars, whereas Montreal got "Irving Layton." I clipped the cartoon meaning to have it photocopied, and set off to find a hardware store. When I tried to pay for my caulking compound and tape or whatever I was buying with a signed cheque Irving had given me, the clerk grimaced and shook her head. "But look," I said in French, "it's Irving Layton," only to be given an even blanker stare. I pulled the Aislin cartoon from my pocket and pushed it toward her on the counter. She accepted the cheque.

Montreal, no matter how politicians and demagogues try to destroy her, will always be the most beguiling city in Canada; spicier, more sensual, contradiction-filled — her ghostly personalities and long-gone beauty more alive than other cities' dull realities. Becoming part of her social history thrilled me. Someone with my roots could never become a Quebecker, nor even wish to, but a Montrealer? Yes, for that is altogether different. Irving treated me to a play at the venerable Monument-National Theatre where, as a child, he snuck in occasionally for matinees. Another night, we sashayed to Place des Arts, Montreal's premier arts venue, where we attended a play. In the audience, Musia's friends stared long and hard. One of them, the luminous Shirley Zimmerman, a former New York actress who had appeared on Broadway, called Musia the next day to ask, "Well, what's wrong with *this* one?" To which Musia replied that she could not find any fault, implying that she had looked closely for a false word, a bone-headed faux pas. I had long been aware of people staring surreptitiously at me, but this was Irving's hometown and the city would not forgive a single misstep on my part. I would soon have ample occasion to put its collective mind at ease.

While still content to make do with bits and pieces of furniture inherited from several ex-mates, I felt it was time to get some proper curtains. Musia let me go through the yellow pages, afterwards informing me how, *tsk*, I chose the most expensive curtain place and carpet-cleaning place in Montreal. Bill's wife, Sandra, kindly picked me up and showed me the best places to get vegetables, meat, fish, breads, bagels, and groceries, with my main go-to street being Somerled. Going "up Somerled" was like living in a small, pre-shopping-mall town, rather than a sophisticated city. I soon became a fixture there and on Monkland with its superb butcher shops (one French-Jewish, one Hungarian-Jewish), the Korean fruit and vegetable boutique for whatever Toscana's on Somerled lacked, the Polish florist, and, of course, Steinberg's for everything else. I walked everywhere. Over time, I felt my shoulder ligaments thickening and my arms bones lengthening from the almost daily grocery runs. The shops were just too close to justify taking cabs, and I had not realized I could have things delivered. Musia, Sandra, Bill, and even Venie clamoured for Irving to buy me a little car, but I refused. Not only was I still too rattled from our accident to drive, but we had a bus stop right on the corner. Eventually, after my shoulders could take no more and I had begun to lose sensation in my hands from the plastic bags cutting into my fingers, I bought a grocery cart.

Irving was ecstatic to be back in Montreal, having left in 1969 for a teaching position at Toronto's York University. The long hiatus was over.

Nephew Bill, a mere four years younger than Irving, shared a lifetime
of memories. He dropped by often, unannounced, never bothering to
knock. It never occurred to me to lock the door, perhaps for fear of offending him. I minded when he walked in and stood in the front hall
without announcing himself, eavesdropping, perhaps trying to catch
us in a set-to. It was human nature, after all, to look for flaws in other
people's lives. I wondered if he hoped to catch us *in flagrante* the time he
slipped in, paused, and came straight up the steps to find us in bed. I did
not care for that, nor did Irving. Mornings were often our busiest, most
pleasurable time and we did not care much for disruptions. Bill bounded
in one too many times saying he knew we were up because there was
no newspaper on the porch, which begat my little ruse of retrieving the
paper and leaving an old copy outside, just to buy a little privacy.

Bill's mother, Gertie, was still alive, as was Irving's other remaining sister, Dora. She was the one who had nursed Irving back to life
when he was young, after his accidental self-immolation candle-to-the-
nightgown-just-to-see-what-would-happen trick, leaving him badly
scarred over half his chest. Dora had us over for tea and homemade
honey-walnut cakes. Her small, questioning eyes and heart-shaped face
lit up when we met, and there was only welcoming affection in her embrace. I became part of the family straightaway, and with warm approval. Though still showing traces of her indefatigable energy, she would
soon begin that inevitable decline. Seeing her brother and me together
pleased her enormously. Clearly, Irving now had someone in his life
who understood and cared for him. He was loved and it showed. I still
have Dora's recipe for chicken soup. Meeting Dora as well as Gertie
gave an extra patina to the battered Lazarovitch family candelabra that
somehow ended up with Irving. I placed it on the glass-sided cabinet
where it dominated our dining room. Later, I would teach myself the
Friday night blessing, bringing it down to the gleaming Shabbat table.
Those Montreal days of fitting in, of making our home, were full of
excitement and innocence. Irving was perfectly content, and so was I.

Our first Montreal New Year's Eve was around the corner, and
since neither of us liked crowds, I envisioned *knoshies* and bubbly in
the basement, watching the ball-drop on TV in front of a crackling

fire. Instead, Irving got a phone call from an heiress who heard he was back in town. She either pretended he was single or had not heard that I was part of his life, and invited him to a swank party at her family's country manse. There would be a black-tie dinner, followed by dancing at the Montebello, a four-diamond resort partway between Montreal and Ottawa. He was to spend the night at the manse with several other high-profile guests. "Oh, but ... and so ... am I invited too?" I asked, unsure how she worded the invitation. "I don't know ... let me ask her." Irving said, as naively as me, and called her right back. No, I was not invited. Irving was to be her date, but noblesse oblige kicked in and the heiress allowed me to come along.

A limousine appeared at our door on New Year's Eve and delivered us to the snowy domain. The main fireplace at one end of the great-room was large enough to stand in, although our hostess was the one aflame with frustration. She asked what we would like to drink. Irving felt like a rum and Coke. I traversed the great-room to where she stood by the bar and ordered two "rums and coaxes." With Irving out of earshot, she sneered, "*Rum and Coke*? I didn't think anybody still drank that!"

My policy: play the innocent. We dressed for dinner, me in a bargain-bin sleeveless black sequined top and black rayon-cotton harem pants. I had nothing remotely formal to wear. Everyone else wore tuxedos and gowns. Irving had his white silk dinner jacket and black satin bow tie, at least. We survived a dinner where I kept trying to count the bottles of champagne, never having seen so many at one time other than in a liquor store. Afterward, a car took us to the Montebello where we danced for a bit. I was unprepared for the vulgarity of these high-powered lawyers and assorted bigwigs, one of whom drew me aside hoping to inveigle me into a discussion about hot lesbian sex. The hostess, regrettably, had stayed home, begging off due to being on her period, she said. The gown she had designed for the occasion, with its crotch-high slit, no doubt cast off and dejected as she was.

We woke early in a sumptuous guest room and, after making love to start the year on a good note, Irving rose up on his elbow before dawn, eager to articulate his latest revelation. The evening's festivities illustrated the difference between poets and non-poets. "Part of the reason for the tragedies and difficulties in my and any poet's life, have occurred because of my inability to see the world of non-poets as real." he said excitedly. The seriousness with which they described pure trivia and everyday banalities astounded him once more. He would have liked to sit them all down and get them to talk openly about themselves such as he had done at an earlier New Year's Eve party in his brasher days. Which — naturally — brought Pasolini to mind.

We had recently watched a film of his that featured a piano player. Between the film and the evening's tuxedo-clad crowd, Irving drew the disparate ends together. "The artist doesn't have to show us the whole truth, but the neglected truth. Once the civilities are dispensed with, the dark side is there. The piano player is the artist that provides the illusion of culture and normalcy, but she couldn't take it. The other Bocaccios," he continued, "took it all in their stride like the women at last night's party. They knew that men were made to rule the world and they were to accommodate themselves to the men in return for protection, security, and position."

After a revivifying country breakfast served by the hostess's sister and her beau, we disappeared into the waiting limo for the ride back home, perfectly primed for the coming year and our new Montreal life.

19: Ordinary Miracles

OUR PLACE AT 6879 Monkland Avenue was more than a house. It was be the entirety of my world for the next twelve years, filled with sunlight, activity, talk, love, music, cigarette smoke, and a stream of visitors. Distracting me in those first Montreal days was my friend Joyce Rankin, who needed a place to stay while juggling her plans. Joyce and I had kept up a correspondence since Dalhousie, redolent of our desire to become writers. She was our guest for the first three weeks of 1984. I wager she still remembers the day Irving decided to find out which of us was the heavier one. Joyce had an appetite for butter, which Irving and I marvelled at with round-eyed stares as she emptied the butter dish faster than I could refill it. It was part of her irrepressible charm.

So it was perhaps as a veiled hint regarding our waistlines that Irving took it upon himself to heft us to see which one weighed more. Joyce, shorter than my five-foot-seven frame, was no more a stick figure than I was. When I say "heft," I do not mean a quick bear hug lift off the floor. I mean he reached down, placed his hand squarely on our inner thigh about midway between knee and crotch, grabbed our upper arm, and hoisted us — each in turn — over his head and held us there, arms extended, for several moments before setting us down surely and gently. We were almost the same weight, he said. At the time, I weighed some 170 pounds. It was a pointless exercise, not remotely erotic, and bears noting as testament to Irving's unusual vitality.

Marvellous as it was for a seventy-two-year-old to be able to lift us over his head, his back was not pleased. It nearly gave out altogether. Irving's awareness of human nature precluded showing signs of weakness, so we kept his incapacity hidden as best we could. To this day, no one knows that for much of 1984 Irving was bedridden and could walk only short distances before excruciating pain forced him to sit or, preferably, to lie down with pillows under his knees. The floor could have provided better support, but even with sheets and pillows on the thick carpet, he absolutely refused to lie on the floor. The very thought conjured feelings of poverty and a complete loss of dignity. No matter how crippling the pain, he would not take to the floor.

Some days the pain subsided, only to flare up again. If he was unable to move around and guests were unavoidable, I helped him dress and limp downstairs where I propped him up at the dining room table. If books or materials were required, I had them at hand or ran upstairs to get them so that Irving could remain seated. On visitor-free days, I helped him to that huge velvet easy chair in our bedroom's corner, by the window. There, he read the morning paper or articles in *Commentary* (a gift subscription from someone) or *Encounter*. After that, he turned to a stack of books on the rickety chess table next to his chair. This could be anything from Frederick Exley, Byron, Shakespeare, Turgenev, Lawrence, to Tadeusz Borowski's *This Way to the Gas, Ladies and Gentlemen.* He read all morning, awash in the warming sun, trying to coax music from a transistor radio, often calling me in to read me a passage that had just fired his emotions.

I brought his meals up on a tray, having already cut the meat to make things easier, also to spare him the sight of having his food cut for him. Months passed. As the garden began to bloom, I added a fresh flower in a glass to cheer him up, always eating my meals sitting on the foot of the bed, which he appreciated enormously. This was our routine for many months. Eventually, he used his "sciatica flare-up" as an excuse to beg off certain social invitations. The pain finally drove him to seek medical treatment and gingerly allow his "physical terrorist" to provide therapy. He recovered, but it took a toll, particularly during our trip to Italy later that year. His muscle-relaxing pills included Robaxacet and another that began with *v*, which he dubbed "Rabelais" or "Rousseau and Voltaire".

Despite the trouble with his back, Irving pressed on as if compelled, and continued to give readings wherever they might be. Our first big undertaking of 1984 was a trip to California where Irving was to read at Berkeley, San Jose State, and Stanford, all arranged courtesy of Joyce Dawe-Friedman. Joycey-Woycey, as Irving dubbed her, was one of many high-energy gutsy women who had taken a shine to Irving's work. Years earlier, her fan letter had turned into a regular correspondence. Desperate to escape a bad marriage, she drew courage from Irving's Nietzschean outlook and one day turned up at his door with suitcases and four young daughters in tow. Aviva answered the knock and one can only guess at her surprise seeing Joycey-Woycey on the doorstep. They helped her get back on her feet. Joycey-Woycey eventually moved to San Jose, California, and married a trombonist who became the Chicago Symphony Orchestra's principal trombone player. Joyce's intelligence and warmth endeared her to me. She could and did make things happen, including arranging this reading tour. When Irving decided I was to join him, Joyce found a well-appointed cabin in San Jose that we rented for one month.

A day or so before we were set to fly to California, Max phoned with news of Boschka's death. Her heart gave out just before Valentine's Day. Irving seemed to take the news well. Hanging up the phone, he walked silently into the dining room and sat at the table. Old age. Time. A bad heart. Death always comes, always finds us. He sat quietly after telling me the news, then disappeared upstairs. Returning stiffly with a book of poems, Irving again took his seat across from me. In a quiet voice that seemed to electrify the still air, he read Edna St. Vincent Millay's "Dirge Without Music," his voice breaking as he tried to get through the last stanza. The reading tour was now a funeral trip.

We arrived in San Francisco where Max picked us up. Soon we were driving over the Golden Gate Bridge on our way to Goat Rock, a tiny hamlet near Guerneville high up the Sonoma coast where Boschka's cabin sat nestled in a hollow just behind a cliff overlooking the icy Pacific Ocean. We pulled up at a fair-sized cabin of weathered wood. Inside, there was an old-fashioned school desk, the square all-in-one kind, painted a bright enamel blue and perfect for writing or contemplating one's painting efforts. Boschka's narrow bed with its white coverlet stood in the corner opposite the front door. Across the bare wooden floor, her book-lined shelves on which — to my surprise — there, facing her bed, was a bust of Irving. It was a ten-inch tall copy of Esther Wertheimer's original bronze sculpture. Boschka's was one of several painted plaster copies that Irving had given to a few family members and close friends.

Even to a casual observer, the placement of that bust so that it was the last thing she saw at night and the first thing she saw every morning after decades of separation spoke to Boschka's lingering affection for Irving. The open floor plan and unpainted woodwork lent Boschka's last home a decidedly rustic air, but pleasing to a painter or writer. Many of her paintings were stacked in the studio area. Max took control of everything and, to my best recollection, chose not to offer Irving a single memento.

Boschka wanted her ashes spread around the base of a young apple tree on a grassy slope behind the home of two of Naomi's childhood friends, Boz and Cat. We gathered there on a morning in mid-February, me dressed all wrong, as always. Everyone else looked as though time stopped in 1972. My black pumps, charcoal sheath dress with elliptical black buttons angled all down one side, and crimson silk scarf all screamed Montreal chic. We made our way in the warm sunshine, my heels punching through soggy ground. I quickly changed into more casual clothes for the informal service. In the distance, geysers erupted in tall white plumes against the soft blue sky. There were birds in the blossoming apple trees. We formed a half-circle. Naomi kept herself together for a brief moment before recalling her mother and breaking into heaving sobs again and again, turning to her friends for comfort. Irving stood near her, silent and very sombre. Max held the box of his mother's ashes, and rightly commented on the incongruity of her bohemian self being somehow contained in a small square box of white cardboard. He gripped the box in his two hands and, holding it level with his solar plexus, eulogized his mother. I believe he spoke of her larger-than-life spirit, her heart, his warm boyhood memories of her. But his voice jarred me with its odd cadence and that tremolo.

It sounded more like the voice a car salesman or preacher in a loud suit would use — so incongruous that I sighed with relief when Irving stepped toward him and gently took the box. He spoke lovingly and very softly of Boschka, their love, and, bringing the box of her ashes to his lips, saluted her freedom with a farewell kiss.

Max struggled a bit to open the lid, flinching at the disheartening sight of a plastic bag. As far as containers go, it was practical but not remotely poetical. We lined up after Max, Irving, and Naomi, each reaching into the box for handfuls of ash, depositing them around the base of the apple tree. Its stiff, fragrant branches poked at our faces as if to push us away. Soon, a thin, whitish grey circle lay on the spring-fresh grass.

By the time it was over, Boz and Cat's young child, frightened at first by my strange appearance, now clung to me as if I alone understood its grunts and cries. Irving walked alongside me as we all headed back for the house, remarking how the ashes reminded him of popcorn. It was almost true. As with so many other things, the poet's eye transformed reality, in this case softening it with a freshly minted metaphor. I wondered whether a part of him simply could not accept the grim reality. Naomi needed sleep perhaps more than anything; Max, raw with emotion, busied himself in another part of the house. Irving withdrew to a quiet corner and began to write "Popcorn." I can only begin to imagine his thoughts as he stood next to his two children, holding a handful of their mother's charred remains.

The next day, he wrote "Boschka Layton 1921–1984." Its lines were all the more moving considering he alone knew the pain of her infidelities, how she had left, the way Naomi had fallen through cracks and how that might possibly have been prevented, and how he only seemed to annoy her, even during their good years. In the poem, he chooses to remember her not as she was at the end of her life, nor of the crabbed insolences that marked the end of their marriage, but as the beautiful woman with whom he had made handsome children. She wanted to have her ashes spread around that apple tree. Irving pays homage to the miracle that will permit her ashes to return to the earth so that her essence blossoms forth year after year, circumventing death.[1]

Our cabin in San Jose was the in-law suite detached from a sprawling ranch house somewhere off Story Road. It was perched on a cliff so steep that I hoped it would not rain, under trees whose names and foliage were foreign to me. Everything was intriguingly unfamiliar: the strip malls, faux Hispanic stuccoed houses in every shade of pastel, bungalows seen only in TV shows such as *The Partridge Family*, the soft light, and San Francisco's old, far-away forgotten charm. All of it sent odd shivers down my spine. My never-vu sense of nostalgia for a long-ago America reached apoplectic levels when Joycey-Woycey drove us into the Haight-Ashbury district, pausing by the famous street signs and on to City Lights Bookstore where Lawrence Ferlinghetti himself greeted us. He and Irving chatted a bit, light conversation, nothing earth shattering, but appropriate for icons who both understood what time does to young ambitious men in love with words.

Mornings had Irving resting his back on the sofa back at the cabin, reading Graham Greene, complaining about Graham Greene never rising to desired heights. Joycey-Woycey kept us stocked with groceries and gin — one bottle saw us through the month — and delivered a large envelope of mail sent along from Montreal. There were so many letters to answer that she rented a typewriter and brought all the needed stationery supplies.

With Irving's back still causing terrible pain, it was here he began dictating letters to me. Up until that point, he managed his correspondence and virtually all drafts of poems on his own. Now unable to sit up for any length of time, he lay on the sofa with his legs bent at the knee, reading the mail and firing off his responses. Soon, I was also transcribing drafts of poems into my handwriting and then typing each consecutive correction. This grew into a methodology of sorts. Once Irving completed a poem, I prodded him to make triple sure of every word, only then typing it on premium cotton rag paper. The crowning touch: noting "Master Copy" on the reverse in pencil. Once *that* happened, he had to convince me to retype it for even the slightest change. Which he often did, turning the "Master Copy" into yet another draft.

Still in San Jose, Irving one morning watched as I slept while dawn broke through the silhouetted trees. I woke to the smell of coffee and before I was fully awake, he read his newest poem to me. "Lady Aurora."

As he had done countless times, he observed an ordinary scene — me not yet awake just as dawn was breaking. He sat by me, letting emotions course through him, and just as naturally harnessed emotion to intellect. In the last stanza, he waits until I open my eyes which, like the sun illuminating all that it touches, will make him "blaze more brightly than fern or bush."[2]

As he began reading the poem to me, I closed my eyes and listened closely to the way he read. His voice. His words. Though disconnected and solitary in his lines, he describes how the sound of my breathing binds him to me. Not only for the joy it gives him but more pointedly, for the courage to live forever. When his voice stopped after the last line, we remained motionless for a few moments, letting an almost holy stillness roll softly into the space between us. I opened my eyes again to the life we shared.

The bed linens were indeed white; sunlight pierced the dark through our bedroom window just above the bed. I vividly recall that morning, my tumult of dark hair splayed on the pillow and sleep-warm skin perhaps seeming to him like a gift. Youth, vitality, a kind heart, and unfettered love were all I could give him, along with a desire to make his life as complete and comfortable as possible. Knowing how he wrote poems, how they started with a flood of images and emotions that must be sheathed with rational thoughts and ideas, I did not at all object to the opening line. Knowing too how intimate we were, I did not then, nor do I now, think of "my woman" as a reduction or objectification of me. In the space we filled that morning, indeed during our entire time together, in our shared kisses and intermingled lives, I knew that "my woman" was inspired by me and no one else. Once the poem was complete, the woman can be whomever the reader wishes. When I read it then, when I read it now; the "she" is me, the "I" is exquisitely Irving.

Its title, Irving explained, came from the myth where a wish for eternal life is granted, but the person forgets to ask for eternal youth. Whether Irving deliberately conflated or contrasted the image of my head on a white pillow with that of his mother's head on "the cold pillow" in the poem "Keine Lazarovitch 1870–1959" is anyone's guess. In "Lady Aurora," sexuality suffused with love is what fuels the biblical burning bush. The poem moves from pagan sensuality to love — sexuality robed with respect for one another — and closes with the biblical reference. Unlike mindless sex, eros tempered with affection bound by moral tenets is divinely human love. "'Lady Aurora,'" he continued, "is a hymn to the élan vital, a profound tribute to woman and the way she represents the élan vital. The last stanza puts woman and the cosmic forces together. It is a joining of the Greek and Hebraic teachings. Both her eyes and the dawn are expressions of the élan vital. Precisely because he is filled with peace that he can go into battle and keep fighting for the élan vital."

The California trip included visiting Irving's brother Hyman in Petaluma. He had a comfortable stuccoed house where he lived with his wife, Ruth, and one of his two adopted sons. Ruth had first spoken to Irving about Boschka, then just plain Betty, the crazy cashier girl working at the Venus Grill on Montreal's Ste. Catherine Street. Ruth insisted they meet and, by all accounts, the attraction was instant and mutual.

Hyman retained his movie-star looks and witty repartee all his life. At one time, Irving told me, Hyman had rented a room and set himself up with a typewriter. It didn't last long. Imagining his older brother in a garret trying to break into the writing game broke Irving's heart. Hyman claimed to have once shared a room with Arthur Miller. His true gift would have been in theatre, stand-up comedy, or acting. Irving always grew serious whenever he spoke of his brothers. All favoured with good looks, wit, and lively minds. None of them, Irving noted sadly, lived up to their early promise, a tragedy he attributed to his mother's harshness and inability to instill confidence in her children.

Hyman and Ruth took to me straightaway and, like his sisters in Montreal, were relieved Irving seemed well looked after and was not alone at his age. Before we left, Hyman showed us his garage where Irving's early books were lying about helter-skelter. Privately, Irving remarked to me how a thin streak of envy was still worming through Hyman. "See, he's showing me he still has my books, but wants me to know they are in his *garage*, not on a shelf in the house."

Not realizing we would spend the night, I had not packed a change of clothes, not even a toothbrush. Ruth prepared the fold-out couch and left Irving and me to scramble under the sheets, stark naked. Hyman came in for a chat, sitting on the edge of the fold-out. I tucked the sheet up under my arms, Irving oblivious to the comical tension in the air. Later, I lay in the dark as Ruth, her sister, and Hyman had a late-night chat in the kitchen. "She's really sharp, natural, and *very* good!" Ruth proclaimed. I felt like a piece of cheddar cheese, that is, until she added I should be upstairs with their son rather than with Irving. I suppose we made an odd pair. It was the last time Irving saw his brother and I am sure they both knew it.

We arrived for the reading at Berkeley, hosted by Peter Dale Scott (the son of F.R. Scott) and, to my utter dismay, there were only about three students in attendance. I felt bad for Irving. Putting oneself out there could be a brutal game at times. All the work, effort, preparation — the mad desire to commune with strangers was an enormous rush when the stars lined up and everything went well. I looked at Irving and saw how determined he was to keep his dignity and spirits up. For a moment, filled with pity at the sight of him busily thumbing through his books and checking his reading list, I felt like bursting into tears. When it came time to give the reading, the audience still numbered three people. I asked if he was going to even bother. "Well, of *course!* Listen, these students took the trouble to come out after a whole day of classes and I respect them for that. I will not disappoint them."

Irving read as if he were before three hundred students. Afterward they came up, eagerly wanting to talk with him. Scott announced we were all to meet at a bar or club, indicating the large white porticoed building up in the distance. The students followed excitedly all the way to our parked cars. We got into Scott's car; they pulled up behind us. If it was the porticoed building, we should have turned left. Instead, Scott cut sharply to the right and zoomed away from the campus, bringing Irving and me to his home. We spent the night there, pleasantly enough, but too timid to ask why he shook the students like flies off our tail.

Irving's agenda shows Cody's Bookstore on March 7, a landmark that was later famously bombed after displaying Salman Rushdie's *Satanic Verses*. He gave readings at San Jose State and Stanford, though the dates are not marked in his agenda. On March 18, we returned to San Jose from Hyman's, two blank days, and then an 8:00 p.m. engagement at Toronto's New College, returning to Montreal at the end of March.

Being back in Montreal felt like being on spring break, if only for a few days.

20: On the Inside Looking Out

LENDING A MEASURE of urgency to everything was Irving's bad back and its intimation of mortality. He had many projects in the offing, not the least of which was writing his autobiography and seeing another edition of *A Wild Peculiar Joy* to completion, as well as several Italian editions. He was also being filmed for a National Film Board documentary that demanded significant time and energy, all the while adding steadily to the manuscript of *Final Reckoning: Poems 1982–1986* (Mosaic Press, 1987). McClelland & Stewart was planning a new selection of love poems called *Dance with Desire* (1986), which was followed by *Fortunate Exile* (1987), the best of his Jewish-themed poems. Both selections involved countless hours of going through his body of work, selecting poems, and fine-tuning the manuscript.

Irving plunged into all of the above. I helped with same, and saw to chores such as lawn mowing and weeding (manually, in lieu of chemical sprays), hedge trimming, snow removal, painting the basement stairs, hiring carpenters, electricians, etc., plus grocery shopping, laundry, cleaning, organizing tax receipts by category and date, filing letters, and whatever else needed attention. Together, we kept up with Irving's correspondence and tried keeping social obligations to a minimum.

One of the first errands after returning from California was going to the bank to put a stop on the monthly cheques going out to Boschka. There was a backlog of unanswered mail and more coming in daily. Somehow, we ploughed through it all. With a new second-hand desk and three low bookcases in my study, a wobbly antique dresser and a filing cabinet, I was set to plunge into what we came to call "Layton Enterprizes" — namely, his correspondence and literary work — while I still hoped to carve out my own writing schedule.

When faced with an abundance of requests, we'd start the week by listing all that needed doing under the heading "Layton Enterprizes." I enjoyed these moments intensely, despite the work involved. Pen in hand, blank pad before me, I loved the sense of authority those sessions lent. I was on top of the game and knew what was important, in step with Irving's penchant for disciplined order. The longer the list, all the more satisfying to see it turn blue as I marked off completed tasks.

Everything Irving did was performed with varying degrees of insistence. Letters *had* to be answered as soon as possible. No matter if it was a high school student from Renfrew, Ontario, a Ph.D. student from Rome, or his Swedish translator — *everyone* received a response. While I typed the morning's dictation on my manual typewriter, carefully making carbon copies of each letter and noting by hand on the copy any enclosures, Irving read or worked on drafts of his latest poems. Soon the routine included working on *Waiting for the Messiah* for some ten hours a day, a process that would go on for a year.

After lunch, as required, I spent the afternoon typing and retyping poems. On many drafts now in Concordia University's Layton Collection, there are cryptic sums added, subtracted, and divided. These were my calculations for centering poems on the page. First, I would count the spaces and characters in the longest line, subtract that from the total available spaces, and then divide by two to assure equal spaces on both margins. If it sounds tedious, it was; but it guaranteed perfectly centred poems.

Life seemed ready to point me toward furthering my own writing, at least in theory. I was reading snatches of prose and poetry between tasks. Before things became too chaotic, Irving instigated informal tutorial times when we'd read poems such as Matthew Arnold's "Dover Beach," Hardy's "Neutral Tones," and Frost's "After Apple-Picking." I read the poems to myself first, then often Irving would read them aloud, placing emphasis where it belonged. After I had done my best to interpret the poems, Irving would elaborate. In Frost's poem, for example, the two-pointed ladder represents paired constant opposites such as finite/infinite, particular/universal, and temporal/eternal. These opposites make poetry, which is also the two-pointed ladder because poetry reconciles these opposites. The ladder points toward heaven for its ability to reconcile.

Irving told me "'After Apple-Picking' is a marvellous combination of particular and universal. The sight is *strange* because poetry transforms, enhances, makes you see the thing anew, afresh. Magnified 'stem-end,' 'blossom-end' are the perfect poems you hope to write and that haunt you. Frost's sleep was troubled by thoughts of every poem he could have but did not write. Frost introduces a dumb woodchuck to deflate the tone, make it less ponderous. This is why I put a 'heh-heh' in my poem 'Opiums.' The woodchuck, unlike the poet, has no such nightmares, and here's the irony — 'just some *human* sleep.' It is really the woodchuck's sleep that is ordinary, mundane. Though *we* have nightmares, poets are superior creatures precisely because we are capable of being haunted — and of writing. The philosopher knows his art begins in wonder, but the *poet* also has an overwhelming sense of *gratitude*. The poet praises, but the philosopher dissects and analyses. The trouble with modern poets is that they are literary. They have distanced themselves from the real world of crime, pain, and above all, they lack those two all-important things that make a poet: gratitude and wonder."

"The journey of a good poet is from hedonism/paganism to Hebraism," he remarked when discussing British poet George Barker, the married man who fathered five children with Elizabeth Smart and which she raised on her own. "That journey George did not undertake, or he was incapable of." Another pair of opposites was passion and wisdom. "Keep your passion as you gain in wisdom," he counselled, warning how difficult it was to do. "It's the problem of reason versus energy."

Irving just as easily came up with less high-minded quotes, such as when he completed a particularly troublesome poem. "A genius! I'm a genius!" he proclaimed, "Un*erring* — I can inject electricity into a heap of wet manure!" It was all about *energy*. "Energy is the guiding line.

Then, you can take any conglomeration of words and shape it into a poem." On the same scrap of paper I scribbled these quotes, two other tiny snatches from that conversation: "Art and love-making both defy death" and "A fly is not an eagle or a hawk."

Nor is the nesting female free to wear the same plumage as her mate. More simply put: a home has only enough oxygen for one artist. With the tremendously stimulating atmosphere Irving created, and his unwavering desire to see me grow as a writer, I thought it would be possible to make good on my own creativity. In truth, I overestimated my ability to set aside time for my work and underestimated how all-consuming his last years would be.

Not long after settling in Montreal, my journal notes "another teary scene" after Irving reproached me for lapsing into a somewhat irritable mood, albeit not as black as the *dybbuk* episode. I again hastened to explain there was nothing amiss between us. My inability to draw a line between his time and mine was making me fume with self-reproach, frustration, and impatience. The anger stemmed from within, but one day came out as a querulous tone and what Irving called my relentless nitpicking, which increased after failing, again, to transcribe "caught scraps" into my journal.

Sitting at my desk was not enough to signal my need to be alone. Besides, his interruptions were always so entertaining. This teary episode began with getting letters done and mailed, bringing groceries in, and then going into my study to make a stab at journalling. No sooner was my *tuchus* on my desk chair I heard, "Anna! Do you want to hear a whimsical letter?" Naturally, I did, and so I perched myself on the corner of his desk. This time, it was his response to John Robert Colombo's questionnaire for his book on authors and places.[1] It was Irving's way of sharing his enjoyment at having dashed off a funny piece.

Back in my study, trying to make a start, he tasked me with looking something up for him. I didn't mind, but it took me away from my journal. A short while later, he came in wanting very eagerly to share a cigarette and talk. I could never resist, not just for the smoke, but the intensely stimulating confabulations. If I was addicted to anything, it was talking with Irving. Not only was I learning more than if enrolled in a perpetual graduate seminar, these talks allowed me to practise expressing myself passionately and to learn to think fast. Like any great teacher, he made learning into a game that we both relished. My writing time gone, I made lunch.

That same day, Joyce Rankin stopped by to pick up the rest of her things, and of course I chatted with her while Irving was already back at his desk, writing. The day slipped away and I began to simmer. Irving asked me to help catalogue packets of letters destined for Concordia's Layton Collection. Gladly, I sorted through letters from Boschka, Max, Naomi, and Aviva. Wanting me to have a clearer picture of his former life, he read one painful letter after another to me.

Those letters, along with ones from and about sixty other correspondents, had to be put in chronological order. I typed out the names while Irving cursed and called himself a fool for having entered into so much correspondence, asking why couldn't he be more like Leonard Cohen or Mordecai Richler. According to Irving, they could leave letters unopened, gathering dust in a drawer. The self-excoriation continued, Irving saying it was his day for being hard on himself. He bemoaned having sent all those cheques to Boschka, signing the property to Harriet, and answering letters from everyone, even the cracked ones. Then, looking at the neatly bundled letters destined for Concordia, he sighed and said, "Yes, but this, you see, is where my poems have come from." Irving felt less wretched, but with that, another day eluded me. I gave up, made supper, and hoped for better luck the next day.

By the following morning, however, I was fuming at having mismanaged my time, prompting Irving's remark that I had regressed during Joyce's stay with us. I was in too sour a mood to argue. When he again floated the notion that he may have made a mistake in getting involved with me, it set me off like a small anti-personnel device. It ended badly, me snivelling from self-reproach. Adding insult to injury, Venie had recently visited, nattering away for hours, making it impossible to relax or to write, so I griped some more over that.

Irving tried to calm me, gently urging me to stop crying. I was to try and let go of that chain I kept dragging, whereas he admitted to suffering from set patterns and preordained reactions to certain triggers. The most irritating of these was what I called "brick-walling." If he did not like my tone of voice — that is, if it was slaked with a querulous tone — he brick-walled by turning abruptly and walking away. My reaction? Ramping it up several notches before giving up in petulant dismay. This particular scene ended with his going for a walk, slamming the heavy oak door behind him.

By the time he returned, we had righted ourselves, both agreeing that jettisoning old emotional baggage was no simple thing. He wondered whether this waste of energy stemmed from my not being sufficiently challenged during my adolescence, which may have crippled my mind and emotions. I found no cause to disagree, not because I was malleable, but because it rang true. "All I want is a calm, cheerful wife," he said, to which I answered, "So, you want nothing short of a complete personality change?" We ended up laughing and hugging, Irving cheering me up with a jaunt downtown. Neither of us was perfect. Perfection would have been terribly boring.

Journal writing, after all, is an art like any other. Irving cautioned me that just mentioning him in no way guaranteed success — far from it. I was to work on my entries as though they were poems. I should include only relevant things, make them flow together, and liven them up with metaphors and crisp observations. He also encouraged me to colour it with my own biases and personality. I often fell short, hating myself for every flaccid sentence, each unfinished entry.

In letters to my friends, I wrote of life with Irving as being fabulous. It was that, and more. I think it fair to say we were spontaneous, fiery, and high spirited. Irving was exceedingly good-humoured and even-tempered with me as I was with him. We were both very complex, but not at all complicated. His experience coupled with my energy made us a formidable team.

I began writing short stories, and Irving was every bit as excited about them as I was. Wanting to encourage me, he threw a literary party in my honour, inviting Professor Wynne Francis and several other couples. In hindsight, perhaps he was being ironic when introducing my story, saying it put him in mind of Hemingway. What is important is not how true or false the comparison, but how it thrilled me to the core, providing a rush unlike any other. At Irving's insistence,

I squelched my nerves and read the story despite a terrible shyness. Irving was without doubt my strongest supporter, always encouraging me to do my utmost.

Over the next several months, taking letter after letter in dictation, I grew dismayed and then embarrassed at how often the well-intended phrase, "Anna is working on her second short story" came up. Months later, I was still on my second short story. Rather than degenerate into a parody, I asked him to stop mentioning it altogether. Indeed, over the coming months, all efforts to sustain my short story writing came to a slow, painful stop. Of my prodigious energies, all were poured into running our home and Layton Enterprizes.

It soon dawned on me that in order to succeed at life with Irving, I would have to fold up my creative impulse and put it away for the long road ahead. At some point in those early Montreal years, with great care, I gathered the innermost core of my self, put it in an imaginary box and placed it carefully at the back of my desk's bottom drawer. With luck, I said to myself and no one else, my creative self would survive in the warm dark. For however long it took until I could retrieve it, I had to believe it would still be viable — that one day, I would unfurl its delicate folds and breathe life back into what had been the very wellspring of my identity.

21: The Golden Boy

THURSDAY, JUNE 7, 1984. Easily legible in my handwriting, Irving's agenda notes: "Golden Boy: 10:30 a.m." For Irving, there was only one Golden Boy, and this was Leonard Cohen. Many journalists lapse into a bizarre fog when writing about Irving and Leonard, as if the combined aura of these two Montreal Jews blinds them to basic facts. One article I read declared them classmates. Irving was born in 1912, Leonard in 1934, making the Golden Boy twenty-two years Irving's junior. Irving grew up on and around Ste. Elizabeth and De Bullion Streets near St. Laurent Boulevard, also called "The Main," an area then teeming with immigrant Jews, Italians, Greeks, and Poles, with mostly French-Canadians just to the east. Leonard grew up in Westmount, Montreal's genteel, largely Anglo, upper-class neighbourhood. His family's fine home is still extant, not bulldozed like the tenement houses of Irving's youth. Neither chose their parents, both were born with an uncanny ability for sounding out the human soul. Recently, I read somewhere that Leonard was Irving's student at Herzliah High School, which is equally absurd.

The inaccuracy that annoyed Irving the most, and which has now acquired a life of its own, is that Irving was Leonard's mentor. Each time Irving heard or read this, he winced as if hearing fingernails scraping on a chalkboard. Unfailingly, he told me how false this was and that he recognized Leonard's unique genius at their first meeting. Leonard, then in his early twenties, braved one of Irving's famous Friday night gatherings. Anyone who was a poet, or thought they were, could drop by Layton's tiny house on Kildare any given Friday night. They could expect a hearty welcome and a fully engaged audience as they read their poems aloud. From what Irving gave me to understand, participants quickly learned to gird themselves against exacting criticism. Arguably, modern Canadian poetry was born in Irving's living room. The gatherings became so popular that the RCMP began spying on him, and presumably his guests, from the house across the street. Authorities feared Irving was using poetry as a cover and that his literary get-togethers were actually Montreal's best-attended Communist seeding ground.[1] In time, this too proved to be another nasty falsehood about Irving.

Leonard's verses left Irving almost speechless with admiration. "I knew he was a genius from the very beginning," Irving said many times, emphasizing that Leonard never needed his mentoring. What Irving did for the Golden Boy was to bring him along to Toronto and introduce him to key players in publishing and media. Other than that, Leonard Cohen was and is *sui generis.*

I no longer remember the occasion, but Irving, Leonard, and I were standing close together at a Montreal soirée. Irving made it a point to tell Leonard, clearly and most decisively, how he hated it when anyone called him Leonard's mentor. The Golden Boy seemed to know this, as though it needed no saying. Nevertheless, I recall his acknowledging the clarification with a smile and a slight nod.

That summer, *Quill & Quire* published an interview with Leonard. Irving asked me what I thought. I told him I could see why critics like Bruce Powe and Ekbert Faas tended to classify him as a fake. "These two, especially Powe, are heavy as lead, whereas Cohen is light as a feather — a feather with substance." Irving observed that Cohen's elusiveness is such because "he has no program. That he is a genius when it comes to words, I have no doubt, and he is a genius in the art of staying away from pigeonholes. He seems to have his fingers in many ideological pies, but his fingers never get dirty."

My nerves short-circuited with dread and wild excitement as I sweated out the minutes that sweltering June morning, awaiting Leonard's visit. I had taken two showers already, willing my heart to beat more slowly and more quietly. Irving milled about, happy as a clam. Their last meeting had been in Niagara-on-the-Lake when Leonard brought his friend, artist Morty Rosengarten, who sketched Irving for his *Lines of the Poet* lithograph series.

I asked Irving what I should say to avoid sounding like a Hollywood interviewer. He calmly advised me not to gush. "Just be yourself." To break the tension, I dashed to the convenience store for extra coffee and cookies, hoping there was time to fix myself up before our famous guest arrived.

Moving through the sticky morning air left me damp with dread. Now perspiring like a walking sprinkler, my one "meet Leonard" outfit was dotted with exclamation points of wetness all over my big white man-shirt and burnt-orange gaucho pants of terribly thin cotton. I went upstairs to ready myself. Too late, for before I could wipe down my face and neck, I heard footsteps mounting the porch steps, a knock, and then "*Irving!*" in that unique voice.

"*Leonard!* How nice to see you! Come in, come in!" Irving called out with delight. I heard the sound of open palms clapping against one another's backs. They were still embracing when I ventured downstairs.

With Leonard smiling up at me, I became Marcel Duchamp's *Nude Descending a Staircase,* slightly robotic, but hoping for graceful insouciance while trying to banish idiocy from my speech and manner. Just make him feel welcome, I said to myself, make our home into a little oasis, an obligation-free zone where no one could ambush or exploit him. I must have succeeded, for he visited quite a number of times. Still, it did not help my trying for Zen-like serenity when Irving put his hand on my shoulder and said, "Anna, let me introduce you to your hero."

I hung Leonard's black raincoat in the closet, noting how neat and spare he looked in a black T-shirt, dark grey jacket, black pants, and boots of buttery black leather. There was grey in his slicked-back hair, a few lines around his pale eyes, and more distinct ones bracketing his mouth. His voice was invitingly deep, full of rich, mellow tones.

We stepped into the living room where, like a stray chess piece, that engulfing burgundy velvet armchair now sat. Its springs no longer worked; using the chair required an extra pillow. To my horror, Leonard sat before I could warn him, plummeting virtually to the floor, elbows suddenly level with his earlobes. It was impossible not to guffaw as he extracted himself. I slid off the sofa onto the floor, still laughing. Leonard sat on the floor across from me at the low coffee table, Irving beside me on the sofa.

Leonard's effortless manner and elegance quickly put me at ease. He was funny, extremely gracious, humble, and spoke with such elegant phrases that I felt one could subsist on them in lieu of food. Anyone could see how Irving and Leonard enjoyed each other's company. They caught up on each other's lives, speaking fluidly and easily. Words were like gems between them, carefully chosen and set to delight and please each other. None of the encounters I witnessed ever had the slightest trace of competitiveness or envy. What I saw each time was a relaxed warmth and profound appreciation for one another.

Years later, when Leonard spoke at Irving's funeral, he said that what had passed between them was a private thing. I remembered that while looking through my notes, debating whether to share their contents. Irving often commented on Leonard's work, and watched me scrambling to keep pace, trying to write everything down. Many of his observations are so original and illuminating that I would feel remiss if they were not included here, and hope Leonard will forgive any perceived breach of confidence.

Some of Irving's comments may seem trenchant, harsh even. His more colourful turns of phrase stemmed from frustration. Watching the short musical film *I Am a Hotel,* for example, made Irving very uncomfortable, as if seeing Leonard in a stylized video embarrassed him on Leonard's behalf. The video's visual content detracted rather than added to Leonard's words. Irving's response was "I Am a Hotel," a wry poem published in *Final Reckoning,* to wit: here at last was one Canadian who had resolved his identity crisis.

Two months before Leonard's first visit, Irving and I lounged about on Easter Sunday. He was in high spirits. As often happened, Irving seemed to collect his thoughts like a baseball pitcher winding up to throw a strike. Whenever I sensed this shift in energy, I knew something of note was about to pour forth, which had me reaching for paper and pen. Here is an example, a word-for-word transcription of his thoughts on Leonard.

He is not comfortable, but not for the reasons he would have us believe. His tragedy is the tragedy of a narcissist who's incapable of loving himself. People are beginning to get wise to his pose of spiritual collapse — he's been collapsing for thirty years. If he ever cut his throat before the publication of his next book, it would be a runaway bestseller. There have been no suicides among Canadian poets. On the other hand, the U.S.A. and the U.S.S.R. have been more fortunate. We have no poets brave enough or desperate enough to make a decent end of their lines and lives. A Canadian Hart Crane or Yesenin would give more credibility to Canadian poetry and is the only thing lacking to make the world take it seriously.

After Leonard left that June day, I took down Irving's comments, titling my notes "On Leonard's latest book and newest songs." The book mentioned could easily have been an early draft copy of Cohen's *Book of Mercy*, published by McClelland & Stewart in March 1984.

He has taken the old timbers of Judaism to build airy castles in the air. The clash between Greeks and Jews was that the Jews upheld morality over beauty. What Leonard has done is to use moralistic, religious-sounding language to create beautiful things. This is almost blasphemous in a sense and comes from having dropped down to absolute zero. To use another analogy, more vivid and perhaps more to the point, it's like if a beautiful woman went into a synagogue and clasped her hands in prayer and was more concerned with the effect of her beauty on the congregation than in the fervour of her prayer.

In these poems, he's not asking you to admire his sincerity or authenticity, only to admire the beauty of his language. He's used a religious tone because these are highly evocative words that arose from deep well-springs of emotion. So, it's baroque in this sense for its sheer beauty. The real religious painters were interested only in expressing the religious emotions and faith; baroque painters brought beauty out just as Leonard has evoked beauty from religious language. My final opinion still is dissatisfaction because I don't like baroque art. I think it's a perversity, but his ballads I approve of wholeheartedly because they come from profound personal despair and that is truly religious art. What I said before still holds true: still perverse, still illegitimate. We have no right to wear a beautiful blouse and try to convince people that you are wearing a hair shirt.

He's not posturing about the abyss; but he really does know about the abyss. That's where people like Ekbert Faas can't distinguish between the posture and the stance.

He's lost credibility because he's cried wolf once too often, and people want to see blood, except they keep getting more words. But he really *has* been in hell. People, however, can't or don't give him credit for that. To sum it up, he sounds operatic. It's like in *La Bohème*, she's in despair but she sings so beautifully that people can't believe she's in despair and if he were here, I'm sure he'd underwrite everything I've just said. He said himself today that if people could read him properly, they'd know he has *no* message for them. Leonard's significance is that he is not deep, but that he has gone into profound depths and, without wanting to, he brings you a report. What makes Leonard despair is that the abyss yielded *nothing* but a reflection of his own emptiness writ large. [David] Solway has not yet arrived at that point.

Solway is the better poet; Cohen is the more significant. His empty mirror reflects the emptiness of the whole world. His genius is in the way he has universalized his emptiness. And the only way he makes us see the emptiness of these figures in the figures is by throwing garments made up of old words on them. That's why he and his work strikes people as being elusive. It's not Leonard that's elusive; it's his figures that are.

Seymour Mayne [referring to the Ottawa poet's book
Manimal as "Minimal" with a chuckle] doesn't have the
breadth. He accepted certitude too early in life and aban-
doned the home and hearth of uncertainty, which should
be the domain of every poet. He's already settled the big
issues; he didn't wait 'til he was seventy or eighty. [Ken]
Sherman is also a better poet than Cohen, but will never
match him. Cohen never studied the craft like Solway and
Sherman. He made the decision not to.

Contemplating Leonard continued as we lingered after dinner
talking about *Book of Mercy* and Leonard's songs. Now that I had met
him and heard more of his music, I pressed Irving for details. This is a
transcription of our conversation:

I: What gives authenticity to this book is the fervour with
which he is washing his hands. He started out with so
much goodwill and kindness and the evil around him, the
philistinism and rapacity, has stunned him.

A: Is he in pain?

I: No, it's like someone who's had his gums frozen and his
anxiety is thinking about when and if the anaesthetic will
wear off; how badly will it hurt?

A: If I were to spend a day and night alone with him on
Hydra, what could I do that would "please" him, what
would he want from me? A discourse on the cosmic reality
of an empty coffee cup?

I: He would want only that you go away. There would be no
meeting on any level whatsoever with you.

A: Is this then a sign of depth and complexity, or is he
somewhat off-balance?

I: No, no, he is highly complex and very, very subtle. He makes most Canadian writers look like farmers. Peter [Lindforss] is very disappointed in him.[2] You know that if it were reversed, if a book of his were coming out in Norway, for example, and I was well known there, well, you know how hard I work to write something for him. You see, that's the difference. This book of his is the first time I've seen an example of Jewish baroque. And you know what I mean by baroque, where the painters and sculptors concerned themselves primarily with the colour of the Virgin Mother's dress or the fall of her cloak. And he went back to the Old Testament, which is Judaic, and immersed himself in it. That's why to a Jew, it smells bad, phony. Because Judaism is a religion that concerns itself with ethics, conduct, action, behaviour, not on beliefs or faith. And he has used the Old Testament to come up with something spiritual.

A: What gives him pleasure? He says he hates the country, yet he goes to a bare rock like Hydra. Does he enjoy swimming in the Aegean, for example, and then he's in New York ... ?

I: Writing. Words. Making the right sentences to express this emptiness he sees and feels. Yes, his music gives him pleasure. He's a consummate actor. [Irving smiled broadly here]

A: If he is so "out of this world," spiritual or otherworldly, how can he go on?

I: Habit. And he gets involved in these projects because he has to (i.e., make a living). Read *Beautiful Losers* and *Energy of Slaves*. There you'll see the beginning of all this. He started out full of goodwill and promise. You know, I told you that I *never* heard him speak despairingly of anyone. Now, for the first time, he showed his displeasure at _____ for having made him do that *Hotel* thing, and against _____ who also wanted to use him. That's a sign of how disappointed, disillusioned he is with people. People just bore him now. He discovered that he has an audience willing to pay to watch him expend energy in washing his hands. You must understand he does not want to change, improve, or reform anything. Other people wash their hands because they are dirty. He has no dirt on his hands. He's one man who would be perfectly comfortable in a loony bin, if he could find loonies that were on his level. What concussion has done for some loonies, complexity has done for him. Got it?

In July 1986 Aviva came to stay with us for a brief visit. She wanted to see Leonard and gave him a call. No one could blame me for gritting my teeth overhearing her warble that she was inviting him to *our* place, pretending for a moment she and Irving were still together. It was only a joke and she quickly laughed it off, but I surmised her laugh held more regret than mirth. She had her chance, her kick at the can.

Leonard suggested we meet him on the Main for lunch. Aviva *insisted* I bring my camera. This was the last thing I wanted to do. I had never tried to have a picture taken with the Golden Boy, nor dreamt of asking for his autograph out of a single-minded desire to spare him that sort of star-treatment. I made protesting noises; Aviva *demanded* I bring my camera. Fine, I obeyed, slinging my Pentax over my shoulder with a little smile. There was no film in it.

We lunched at the Hebrew Deli, one of Montreal's classic greasy spoons, near Leonard's old three-storey greystone. The slanting afternoon light was rapidly turning from gold to orange as we ambled up the Main back toward Leonard's house on a tiny park occupied mostly by old Portuguese men. Aviva began prodding me to snap photos. "Uh, well, there's no film in it." I shrugged. She looked at me as if I were a cretin and either bought film herself or ordered me to get some. Maintaining my no-star-treatment policy was now impossible. Looking back, I am glad for Aviva's nagging insistence. She took one of Irving, myself, and Leonard next to a neon sign that says "Poète." I am standing between them, with bra alarmingly visible through my open-weave top. Though I shut my eyes against this perceived breach of Leonard's privacy and my hair hangs thick in a blunt cut around my face, I am thankful the photograph exists.

Leonard did not seem to mind the intrusive camera, so by the time we got to his place, I snapped a few more. In one shot, Irving is leaning close as Leonard demonstrates the word processor that McClelland & Stewart supplied, hoping it would help him assemble poems into a manuscript. He played with the doodle feature, sketching Irving and printing it out for me. All told, a perfect afternoon with the Golden Boy.

One morning perhaps several months or even a year later, Irving and I were at the dining room table lingering over breakfast. CBC radio was airing a feature on Leonard. "Bird on a Wire" began to play. Irving sat very still, his eyes closed, letting the words and melody seep into him. Suddenly, he exclaimed "Anna! *Quick!* Get me Leonard on the phone!" I did so without question, given the urgency and emotion in his voice.

"Hi, Leonard, Irving wants to talk to you," I said, handing the receiver to Irving.

"Leonard, you *bastard!* You've done it again. You've gone and made me cry!"

With the song coming to an end, Irving's candid praise filled the room as he thanked Leonard for writing such a perfect lyric, his voice catching and breaking with pure, unmitigated love for his unique friend.

22: How to Dominate Reality

ACCORDING TO IRVING love was one way, imagination another. I found writing feisty letters was yet another way. On my desk beside me is a manila envelope stuffed to bursting with drafts and copies of my letters. Some hand-written, many crisply typed. The earliest capture my first rapturous exclamations at having met Irving, later ones tell of my life with him. While it pleases me to say I can look back on the happy, exuberant chance-taker I used to be with tremendous affection, other letters leave me smiling through involuntary shudders.

Letters marked "Never Sent" across the top, mercifully, served as epistolary spittoons. That said, I have no guarantee that slightly different versions were also unsent. A letter from home compelled me to return its enclosed twenty-dollar bill. My mother had sent it as an Easter gift, along with choice comments about Irving. It is one thing for a parent to be concerned about their child's security; quite another to refuse to hear a word the adult child is saying. My mother's insults and digs were like a pastime for her. I responded by archly returning the money, assuring her I was settled in a lovely home, writing poems and short stories under Irving's guidance, and that I had always valued creativity and love more than money, carefully confining love to an abstraction rather than a personal thing between Irving and me.

By this time, Irving had sprung the news on me that Jesus was Jewish, a fact my mother found to be distasteful and untrue. Loftily, I quoted Jesus, asking what shall it profit a man if he gains the whole world and loses his soul, closing with my sincerest wish: "that my dear cousins have a future as assured of adventure, happiness, and security as my own." That letter does not have "Never Sent" across the top.

One thing I can be sure of is the many conversations Irving and I had about her attitude toward me, how she could only manage to refer to him as *ton vieux* — my *old* man. Surely it must have hurt him to feel that kind of old-fashioned Jew-hatred, for I think his being a Jew troubled her even more than the age difference. He spent countless hours comforting me after each barbed letter from home. It seemed to me she prayed I would fail and return to Belleville like a beaten dog.

By October of 1984, I ventured further afield with a letter to the editor of the *Globe and Mail*. For someone with no prior knowledge of Marxism, Suriname's government, nor Cuba's political machinations, I wrote a resoundingly political letter, blasting the *Globe* for interring the story of Cuba recalling her ambassador from Suriname on page eighteen. Barrelling right along, I lavish praise on Ronald Reagan for his astute anti-Communist policy. Clearly, the letter grew out of Irving's remonstrations against the spongy Left being soft on Communism. Of my own accord, I shape-shifted, melded my stance into something that looked like his, and started swinging my own little cudgel. I recall his bemusement, smiling as he edited my letter. He was pleased not because I had imitated him, but because of my capacity for absorbing ideas and becoming socially engaged. He was, moreover, confident that my own voice and ideas would form with time.

By November 11, 1984, I had spun my turret toward the unwitting editor at the Academic Press, firing my potshots at him for allowing Robert J. Ireland's *The Poet's Craft* to "Cuisinart poetry, spontaneity, ecstasy — in short, the spirit that moves the poet — and dole it out like sugary shortbread cookies to unsuspecting pupils.... " I bemoan how no one would ever know from reading "the pat, cheery notes that poets have been, for the most part, rebels, iconoclasts, madmen, and glorious shit-disturbers such as Jeremiah, Amos, Blake, Shelley, Ginsberg, Layton, Prévost, Mayakovsky to name but a few." It goes on in this vein, concluding that the publisher need not have a crisis of conscience at mice and vermin who will nibble at the unsold copies, the contents being too bland to upset their digestion.

Just as plainly as with the letter about Suriname expelling the Cuban ambassador, here too, Layton looms large. I do hereby apologize to Mr. Ireland and the Academic Press for my intemperate tone, but not for the passion infusing that letter. I had grafted some of Irving's personality onto my own and was beginning to thrive. His lifelong battle against anything that stifled creativity or threatened to turn poetry into bland verse was now a meaningful, vital battle of my very own.

From an impersonal political letter to the editor, to one championing Layton among other iconoclasts, I wrote another concerning Layton himself. This one, dated November 7, 1984, is to a Maureen of the *Sonoma County Stump*, the local paper where Boschka used to live. The October 29–November 5 edition ran an article about Boschka. Maureen sent it along and requested a copy of Irving's 1965 *Collected Poems* that she had seen at Boschka's place, the one with Irving's handsome face a gold background. That book being a collector's item, I sent her the newest edition of *The Gucci Bag* and a letter correcting the article's errors.

No one would confuse the *Sonoma County Stump* with the *New York Times*. Nevertheless, it contained whoppers that angered Irving. One can only guess at the source of these myth-making exaggerations. Irving would have none of it. He read the article, pausing to correct each error. I took note and wrote to disabuse her of the "grossly misleading notions" such as: Boschka had not come to Montreal to join "her brother [John Sutherland] on a publishing venture and they founded the *Northern Review* literary magazine." Irving and John Sutherland founded *Northern Review*, not John and his sister. Irving was not exactly a "young poet" when they met in 1942. He was already published and ten years her senior. Nor was Boschka "tracking down poems"; she was working as a cashier at the Venus Grill, had no interest in or knowledge of poetry, nor had she any to show Irving. Her interest, Irving recalled, was in painting and sketching. Irving was not surprised that she had "no interest in political poetry" because, according to Irving, who knew her, she had no interest in politics whatsoever. The article's claim that Boschka became his poetry editor was as preposterous as it was irksome.

The article also characterized their union as having been "tempestuous" for its entire sixteen-year span, something Irving flatly denied. I wrote down his words, to wit: "It became 'tempestuous' only in the last two years when Boschka became dissatisfied with the lack of recognition that her painting was receiving in Canada. About the same time, she developed yearnings to become independent and to write."

In my letter to Maureen, I allude to Boschka's letter to Irving, expressing her envy at his growing fame and success, adding, "Previous to that time, the union could be described as a harmonious and productive one." As to her finding it an impossibility for a single woman and daughter "to survive on the income she received as a charwoman in the Carmel Valley," Irving corrected that romantic image, as in truth, Boschka received "every single red cent from the sale of the house and studio (that Irving had practically gone into debt to obtain for her)." Furthermore, Irving held down five jobs "so that he could send her and her paramour a monthly cheque of $300.00." If she lived in India on pennies a day, Irving could only wonder what she had done with all the money he sent, and continued to send, every month (though a somewhat diminished amount) "until the day she died." The myth she or someone was trying to forge was far from the truth. In putting Irving's words into a letter to a newspaper, I was taking my first practice run at what became a two-and-a-half year battle against his pseudo-biographer and her supporters.

On December 22, 1984, I was in Belleville for Christmas. Desperately alone in a house suddenly full of enemies, I wrote to Irving. There was no one else who could begin to understand my discomfort and bitter disillusionment. The visit started badly just after I arrived; my coat was still on as we watched the 10:00 p.m. news. There was Dr. Henry Morgentaler, being let out of jail again or perhaps going to jail for his humanitarian pro-choice abortion rights activity. Nothing like visiting home for Christmas, and your mother making faces at the Jewish doctor, accusing him of trying to kill six million Christian babies as revenge for the Holocaust. It went downhill from there.

Dearest Irving;

I'm beginning to get an inkling of what you had to fight against all your life, but I never thought my own family, especially the father whom I used to idolize, would turn so violently against me.

Everything I say, he's got a quip or comment to parry it with, no matter how matter-of-fact or innocuous my comment had been! Like I told you on the phone today, he's become an antisemite. That f_____ priest has done a marvellous job. If I didn't think it were so hopeless, I'd go over to the glebe house tomorrow and ask him what the hell he thinks he's doing with these people? I'd love to call him an antisemite to his face...

I tried giving Ma & Pa a few revolutionary ideas ... i.e., how Christianity adopted so many Jewish ideas. His answer to that was that any religion or group can claim to have done all the 'glorious things', and just because it was in a book meant nothing. I told him about *The Anguish of the Jews* being written by a Jesuit, and he wouldn't hear of it, thought I was making it up. So then, he pipes up about the Acadians having been just as badly treated as the Jews. That's when I dropped my fork and walked out of the room. This happened during the course of our first supper together in 2 years.

I told him to read a couple of books. He firmly refused to do that, but to continue living his life as he has been because the world goes on, nothing will change it, nor will he.

Never before have I encountered such obstinacy, ignorance, and stupidity rolled into a big ball of fear and prejudice and envy. What on earth have I got to do with these people is beyond me. It is so supremely frustrating. However, I told Mom that while I'm in this house, I will **not** tolerate any more antisemitic slurs.

They have grown worse with age, and with the tender ministrations of that cursed priest. Anyway, it's helping me to forge my outlook, character, and convictions. And I have got a dilly of an idea for my next story. Give me Layton, Lawrence, Hemingway, Shakespeare, Byron, Blake, and all the other greats in whose shadow I am but beginning to walk. **NOTHING** else matters. And that, I've discovered, is a very "uplifting" or "releasing" concept. Having spent this time in this ugly grey village[1] with my irreparable parents, I feel somehow divorced from the mundane, the banal. It is to their opposites I am now wed. My family is cut off from me by a wall whose blocks are of ignorance, held firmly together by a mortar of fear. Should light and knowledge penetrate even the smallest chink, they rapidly set to work repairing their wall with new blocks, more gobs of fear. This wall is the self-same one against which one throws the proverbial peas.

You've taught me to hang on to my peas. I dislike phone conversations, and even this letter falls short of what I want to say. "Mere words" would truly debase all that I have in my heart for you at this present moment. Therefore, I shall divulge everything right into your ear and all down your face and neck in a torrent of clucking, cooing sounds and syllables of love when I see you. Your stink, as ever.

Scads and scads of love,

Anna — Poupala — Smell

By the end of 1984, the handful of friends I had fell away, some due to geography, others because our common ground eroded from under our feet. Now cleaved from my family, is it any wonder that I melded so fluidly into Irving?

Joyce was not the only guest I invited that January. Our mutual friend Dave Swick from Halifax was coming through by train from a trip out West. How fun, I thought, to have all of us under one roof, having met Dave the night of Irving's Halifax reading. I told Dave he could spend the night. Irving thought Joyce would have left by then, but had no objections to another new face for a day or so.

Then Irving's lawyer phoned. Irving was to attend yet another court hearing about the divorce and parental rights situation. Harriet's maneuvrings had nearly depleted his savings, and all avenues seemed exhausted. Whatever the reason for this latest court appearance, Irving became so distracted and upset that he asked me to un-invite Dave. With old wounds bleeding afresh, he could not bear seeing anyone or to feel guilty for disappearing while he prepared for the hearing. Joyce had not yet found a new place. She joined Dave and me at Ben's, a Montreal landmark that survived until the 2000s.[2]

Joyce, Dave, and I sat glumly in the hazy fluorescent light, greasy air injecting itself into our hair, clothes, and pores. Above us, famous patrons smiled down from dozens of autographed glossies, including photos of Irving and Leonard Cohen. Dave's anger and disappointment was growing with each bite of his fries. Coldly, but rightly, he told me he did not want an explanation, just an apology. I felt sick about the whole thing, but my loyalty was to Irving and to no one else. Dave, I rationalized, was an experienced traveller who would figure it out. Though the decent thing would have been to find him a room and pay for it. Unfortunately, either it did not occur to me or I felt uneasy spending that kind of money, having already fallen into the habit of being frugal. Dave survived. Our friendship did not. Soon afterwards, Joyce left for an au pair job on the East Coast.

From then on, my former life and friends from my past slipped further and further away. Beyond the odd letter or card, a brief afternoon visit or two, I had no peer group whatsoever. When I came out on the other side of this experience many years later I was able to again take up with Caroline, Helen, and Moire, for whom neither distance nor time mattered, as is the way with true friends. In 2014, via the Internet, I found that Dave was teaching Journalism at Halifax's King's College. We enjoyed catching up and, mercifully, he'd forgiven the snafu.

Life with Irving meant sharing his exuberance, vast experience, excitements, and talent. He was more than enough, and precluded any wish to seek friends my age. I wanted to spare myself the awkwardness of meeting a young would-be poet and discussing their love and breakup poems — not when I lived with a man whose best work stands among some of the finest poetry in the world.

More hurtful or irksome than a lack of friends were those occasions I found myself left out, such as that time in Rome when Adrienne

Clarkson happened along as Irving, myself, Gilbert Reid the cultural attaché, and his inamorata as we wended our way through Rome to an open-air trattoria. Adrienne, whether on holiday or business, was walking along on the sidewalk. Gilbert stopped the car and she readily agreed to join us. We parked and sauntered the last bit of distance, Adrienne linked arms with Irving, pulling him ahead of me on the narrow sidewalk. Gilbert led the way with his girl, deep in conversation. Throughout the meal, Gilbert and his inamorata talked to each other. Adrienne sat close to Irving, her torso ratcheted gracefully toward him all evening. I sat, enjoying my food, playing with my food, counting the gay overhead lights strung above our heads, musing as to why my country-bumpkin self seemed to have more natural manners than sophisticated worldly types. Irving tried, on many such occasions, to include me in the conversation, usually by drawing attention to my writing or photography skills. All too often, however, he let the guest set the tone. If they found me a bothersome inconvenience, so be it. Perhaps I should have interjected myself more, but that night in Rome was a wash.

Now more solitary than ever before, with my innermost creative core set aside until time became my own, much of my identity or life-purpose blended seamlessly with that of Irving's. His genius was never in question, accruing along with my reading and deepening appreciation of literature. Therefore, whenever dishonest articles or biased reviews appeared, I felt their sting as slaps across my own face. I responded with instinctive, visceral fury, attacking his detractors with a passion that surprised even Irving at times.

Mercifully, we were not always under siege. Late summer 1984 had brought another Italian reading tour — and an invitation to lunch with Federico Fellini.

23: Lunch with Ettore and Fellini

PLANNING THE NEXT TRIP to Italy was a welcome distraction. As with any reading tour, Irving packed his worn leather attaché case with books he might read — an anthology of poetry, perhaps a volume on philosophy or a novel. I made a detailed checklist of what to buy, do, and bring. If the schedule included radio or press interviews, Irving could wear the same clothes for each appearance, provided no photos were taken and the clothes were not soiled. I brought laundry soap, a small brush, a sewing kit, aspirin, tweezers, safety pins, band-aids, etc., in anticipation of every possible emergency. Irving had an infamously nervous stomach, which made some trips more like a series of near-catastrophic adventures than straight reading tours.

We left for Italy on Sunday, September 9, for a glorious nineteen days overseas. Irving revelled in this time of the year. For most of his adult life, he arranged his summers so that he could write, usually completing a new volume of poems by September before plunging into a new school year.

Energized and refreshed, we were eager to see our Italian friends again. Ettore found us a pleasant little hotel near the old part of Rome for the first few days. The Eternal City never failed to enthrall us with its sun-drenched ochre-orange façades as we walked through clouds of incredibly stale air leaking up from grated rectangular mouths, agape and level with the black cobblestone streets. We ambled carelessly, hoping to become lost, always finding our way back. Irving in a place like Rome on a late summer afternoon was at his most elemental.

Dark thoughts, if any, stemmed from his awareness of recent European history rather than personal troubles. He was completely relaxed and, at the same time, taut with excitement as poems formed in his head and on his tongue. Walking alongside him, I too felt my nerves rippling and sparking with pleasure at the sights and sounds all around us. Even the ubiquitous Vespas buzzing past could not faze me. I wanted not just to walk through Rome, but to twirl like a paper cone picking up the spun floss of steaming espresso, cigarette smoke, languid whispers seeping from potted oleanders and oh-so seductive perfumes wafting from the necks of sleek men and beautiful, beautiful women.

Ettore left us to our devices to acclimatize ourselves for a couple of days before coming by to announce a mysterious lunch invitation. Somehow, someone had told Federico Fellini that Irving Layton was in town. Ettore asked if we could meet Fellini at his offices in Cinecittà, then join him for lunch at his favourite restaurant on the outskirts of Rome. We were thrilled at the prospect and very grateful to whatever Fates arranged for this.

On Thursday morning, Ettore and his friend Janice picked us up in his old white Mercedes and drove us to Cinecittà. I practised my best nonchalant-but-deferential facial expressions. Irving remained his usual exuberant self. A studio representative led us to Fellini's suite of offices where we seated ourselves on sofas in a somewhat cluttered waiting room. Suddenly, the Maestro himself was standing in the open doorway, his body leaning slightly to the left like a cartoon character jamming on the brakes, his powder blue jacket and white shirt making a bright splash against the darkened hallway. Introductions were made, warm handshakes done. He asked through Ettore if we would like to visit the sound stage where they had just finished shooting *E La Nave Va*. I was beyond excited, as was Irving, who was probably pinching himself as hard as I was.

One of Fellini's producers accompanied us, as well as a young woman who was his interpreter. Ettore and Janice could enjoy themselves without the stress of having to translate for Irving. We made our way through the studio and stepped onto the cavernous sound stage. The massive ship's set seemed to fill the space, sitting like a used-up thing awaiting its destruction. Back outside in the hot midday sun, Fellini guided Irving and me toward his vermeil-coloured Mercedes, opened one of the back doors, gesturing for us to climb in. Fellini sat on my right, Irving on my left. The interpreter swivelled partway around in case they needed translations. If there was anything beyond light conversation, I heard very little. Speeding through Rome, all I heard was the voice in my head repeating, "Oh my God! I am sitting between Irving Layton and Federico Fellini in the back of his Mercedes!"

The restaurant was almost out in the country, outside the city. I did not notice the name of it, but recall a brightly two-wheeled Sicilian cart near the entrance. It was painted yellow and white, laden with geraniums. Fellini led us around to the back where, on a wide lawn thickly carpeted with vibrant green grass, tables covered with blinding white linen waited for us under an expanse of yellow and white striped canopy. Tall shade trees cooled by stray breezes. Fellini sat across from me, with his translator next to him, the producer at the head of the table, me to his left, Irving, Ettore, and Janice to my left.

As I permitted myself longer and longer glimpses at the director's face, Irving's observation proved quite true. Fellini, though two or three inches taller than Irving and sporting a slimmer build, looked enough like him to be cousins if not brothers. Watching Fellini as Irving and Ettore recounted how they met and Irving's fondness for Italy, I felt sure he knew quite a bit of English. He spoke a few words, turning to his translator for longer phrases.

The maître d' and several waiters, all in white jackets, appeared and disappeared, Fellini waving them off with a bring-us-your-best gesture. Soon a tiny army of waiters approached holding platters of food aloft, others with bottles of wine. We ate, and they came back with other specialties, done to perfection.

Irving considered filmmakers to be poets with cameras in their fists. Every Saturday night found us tuned in to Elwy Yost's *Saturday Night at the Movies*. Getting out to a cinema was a treat, except for everyone coming up to talk to Irving when all he wanted was to feast on the latest Woody Allen or Kurosawa film. Those who approached were fans offering kind words; none were turned away. Other times, however, would-be poets thrust manila envelopes in his hands and begged him to comment on their work. So, we loved staying home watching old movies. Irving relished firing questions at me to impart knowledge by asking cryptic questions. Fassbinder's *The Year with 13 Moons* had me stumped. My go-to answer when other guesses failed, "Um ... he's a Christ-figure?" did not quite cut it.

"God can't do evil," Irving explained, "so He created man to do it for him. To compensate man, He enabled people to derive pleasure from the knowledge that a neighbour has done evil. Evil is insubstantial and must be conquered so the Hitlers and their works *cannot* continue to exist. The proof is that the world still exists." He went on to praise Freud for his genius in showing that evil is inherent, causing man to try to destroy himself. Irving's own life, he said, illustrated Freud's insight in his having done things that his conscious mind neither liked nor wanted to do. "Copernicus showed man was not the centre of the universe and thus dethroned man. Darwin showed man's animality, further dethroning man. *Freud* proved man was not even in control of himself. All three aimed their blows directly at man's pride." Such was a typical Saturday evening at Casa Layton.

Over the years, Irving had many running fights with movie critics and reviewers — even the general public sent letters to the editor demanding to know how Layton presumed to know what the director had in mind. The chance to meet Fellini had Irving fairly levitating with giddy anticipation. That afternoon in Rome, Irving was less interested in the pasta than talking film with Fellini. Fellini films, to be precise. With the same delight as a master chef deconstructing one complex dish after another, Irving began interpreting Fellini films to their creator. *Amarcord* was one of Irving's favourite films. *La Strada, 8 1/2, La Dolce Vita* each brought out the best of Irving's interpretive skills. He praised touches such as having a loud motorcycle drowning out the humanist each time he tried to speak, about the exaggerated features of the women and their powerful sexuality, *Casanova*'s mechanical bird symbolizing the sad result of the Church's separation of spirit and body.

Fellini sat quietly throughout this enthusiastic delectation of his work. With chin in hand, head leaning this way and that as the interpreter kept pace, Fellini listened closely. Even if I had a paper and pen, I would not have recorded Irving's discourse. To do so would have broken the spell.

Waiters silently cleared away dishes, refilled our glasses, and brought an array of desserts as Irving saluted Fellini's genius, expressing his gratitude for the pleasure the director's work had given him. Fellini sat back in his chair, looking steadily at Irving with what one could call wonderment. Then, pausing briefly, Fellini pulled his jacket close around his torso, slid down into his chair said, "What can I say to a man who makes me feel completely naked?" It was the apogee of the entire trip.

No one wanted to leave the table. We lingered over espresso, *digestivi,* and more conversation. Irving spoke of Ettore's paintings; Ettore described his discovering Irving's work. They all called each other *Maestro,* and rightly so. All three artists were at the top of their game. Watching the body language and listening to the inflections in their speech, there was no doubt painter and filmmaker deferred to Irving, pronouncing *Maestro* with a touch more emphasis and nuanced tones. Painter and filmmaker saluted the poet as *"il miglior fabbro"* — the best smith. We said our goodbyes with handshakes and hearty embraces all around, thanked our host, and stopped at the Pantheon for yet more espresso with Ettore.

Still a bit dazed from lunch, I accompanied Irving down into the café's restroom area. A wizened *guardacessi* (washroom attendant) handed out toilet paper in exchange for a few coins. Only later did we realize Irving had lost his famous silver medallion. The *guardacessi* declared she never even saw it. Irving must have left it on the counter when splashing water on his face. And that was the end of the medallion, obtained in Morocco years before. The medallion and a broad silver bracelet, he explained when I asked if they had any meaning, were to ward off bad vibes. Depending on his mood, when others asked, he told people he won the medallion for deflowering fifteen virgins in thirty minutes. Other times, he upped the number of virgins and cut the time, all to test people's gullibility.

We headed to Fiano-Romano for a few restful days with Ettore. Irving was already working on his poem "Fellini." More lines came as we drove toward the Etruscan Tombs to see where Ettore had painted several landscapes. Irving and I were in the back seat. The lines kept coming and soon I was reaching for my notepad and pen, writing down the first draft of the poem.

Suddenly, I noticed a strange phenomenon happening to Irving. Let me emphasize here that no one in the car was smoking. There were no lit cigarettes, cigars, or pipes within miles of Ettore's fast-moving car. The ambient temperature was closer to body temperature if anything. One can joke about Irving being "on fire," or burning with creative abandon, but these would be metaphors. Yet, plain as day, not inches from my face, I could see bluish-white smoke curling out from Irving's nose. I had seen it happen before at least once, both of us lying in bed, my head on Irving's chest as we talked. It was very early in the morning. There too, the room was pleasantly warm. Against the incoming light, I noticed strange smoke curling languidly from his nose. Again, neither of us was anywhere near a cigarette. The room was too warm for breath to condense. Both times, the smoke had no odour, and left no trace. Nor was Irving aware of it until I pointed it out. I asked Janice and Ettore to have a look. They saw it too, and were equally mystified. It was so unsettling that I rarely, if ever, described the bizarre occurrence to anyone, nor has anyone explained what caused it.[1]

Irving, busy with writing "Fellini," took our word for it, but was obsessed with completing the poem. Four days later, we sat at a café in the Piazza di Spagna, where he distilled his love of Fellini's work, suffusing each line with the energy sparked by their meeting.[2]

On that same trip, Ettore brought us to an Etruscan burial site a short distance from Fiano. It was a wooded area, with a meadow below a tree-and-vine-covered escarpment. Here and there, like black orbits in a skull, foliage opened to burial chambers cut into the low cliffs. Ettore had made a painting of one such scene very close to where we stood. Irving ranged around the meadow and up into some caves while I did my own exploring. Along for the ride that day was Ettore's friend, Dante Gardini. Dante spoke very little, and knew no English whatsoever. He had approached Ettore one day while installing an open-air sculpture in a town near Modena. Dante, we learned, had survived time in a concentration camp and never fully recovered. To a stranger, he appeared a bit simple.

Dante followed behind as I picked my way through the overgrown meadow, and kept up a steady flow of mumbled words. His mutterings began to jangle my nerves. I would never have another chance to absorb these Etruscan ruins. If he piped down, I would hear only birdsong and wind-rustled leaves animating the ancient site. I bit my tongue and broke away, joining Irving in a burial chamber with carved stone benches on which corpses had once lain, and vented to Irving about Dante's disruptive mumblings.

Irving listened sympathetically, but there was little to do other than try to keep my distance. Suddenly, as we walked out into the meadow, he exclaimed, "I smell death! I smell death here!", his eyes widening as he scanned the earth beneath his feet and up toward the cave openings.

"No you *don't!*" I scoffed, my village upbringing and carcass smell expertise coming to the fore.

"Yes! Yes, I *do*. I smell death here. It's coming from the ground all around us."

Dante's presence or, more precisely, the terrible scenes he carried with him, seem to have conflated ancient Etruscan death with the stench of the Shoah's mega-death. Irving's capacity for empathy meant that, for a time, he became Dante Gardini, became of the six million dead. I paused, closed my eyes and tested the air. So I let Irving be as he drifted away from us in a semi-trance, already writing "Etruscan Tombs" in his head. Irving dedicated the poem to this simple, damaged man, the smell of death never having left Dante's nostrils.

By the time we arrived in Bologna, Irving's back began to give out. Thinking he could make it, we walked from the hotel to the university under Bologna's famous arcades. With pain radiating from his lower back, he began to go pale, clamping his jaw shut against the worst of it. Somehow, with short pauses here and there disguised as window-shopping, he made it and gave another inspiring, well-attended reading.

Amazingly, he gave readings in Victoria and Cranbrook, British Columbia, barely one week after returning from Italy. Days later, he read at McGill University and Dawson College, and was interviewed by Jane Lewis for the CBC over a three-day span. On the fourth day, his agenda is marked "Bed Rest." Irving was never one for bed rest. The back pain was a sharp reminder that time was becoming extremely precious. There were a few more poems to write, and a memoir to complete while he still could.

24: On the Writing of
Waiting for the Messiah

IRVING HAD BEGUN dictating his autobiography to me upon returning from California in March 1984. His disciplined approach made it easy to stick to a productive routine. When it came to prose, he was just as fanatical seeking *le mot juste*, but his methodology differed from what he used to write poetry. Poems took shape in Irving's mind and haunted his every waking moment until completion. During my time with him, I helped in transcribe hundreds of drafts, often acting as sounding board when he sought to confirm the chosen word or phrase. In challenging me to select and then explain my choice, he was teaching me about poetry. It was a game we relished.

Prose, however, needed only consistent working hours. With few exceptions, we spent approximately four-and-a-half hours per day on dictation, five, sometimes six days a week for a solid year. After our return from Italy, work resumed in earnest. A typical day began after an early breakfast; the *Gazette* and interesting mail read, I cleared the table. By 9:00 a.m., each with our second cup of coffee, an ashtray and cigarette fixings between us, we readied for a solid writing session. That is to say, Irving spoke, and I wrote down his every word as quickly as I could, keeping up as unobtrusively as possible. If he spoke quickly, I wrote quickly. If he lapsed into a lengthy silence while reliving boyhood scenes in his mind, I sat patiently, whiling away the time by putting tails on every *a*, or making sure each *b* was distinct from *h*, *k*, or *l*. The silence could last upwards of twenty minutes as he shaped his thoughts. I stayed put, waiting, watching as he sometimes enacted a scene to find the right words and the best rhythm. Describing his mother bargaining with French-Canadian farmers to stock her tiny grocery stand, Irving recalled how astute she was, despite not speaking a word of French or English. Though only a young boy, he waited for his mother by the Admiral Nelson statue near the Bonsecours Market, cart at the ready for when she finished her shopping. One day, an onion rolled off his cart and down into the gutter. It was a small catastrophe, for all purchases had to be sold. It was how Irving's mother supported the family while his father, aside from his cigarette and cheese-making endeavours, read the holy books.

Irving remained silent for a long time, recalling the scene's every detail. Cupping the air with his hands as if giving shape to the errant onion, then spinning his wrist and making small, slow motion circles with his outstretched arm, he mimicked the onion's movement down and away from him, bringing a six-decade-old memory to life.

From my side of the table, it was unthinkable to get up to do random chores. Out of respect for the process and for the man, I melted into the furniture while he collected his thoughts. Some sentences took twenty minutes to write. Other times, words flooded out, pages at a time. Keeping up with such bursts was a challenge. I had only a few shortcuts, such as the medical notation of a *w* with a bar on top for *with* or the same plus a *ch* for *which*. I wrote furiously. I never bothered to learn shorthand, fearing the panic of not being able to read or recall what I had scribbled. To prevent such a disaster, I wrote out virtually each word in its entirety.

In one such frenzied bout, my right hand began to tighten, then shake, until it cramped around my pen like a stricken claw. Irving was looking off into the distance, unaware of my distress. Beads of sweat began to trickle from my brow. Not wanting to interrupt his flow, I switched hands and continued writing as best I could with my left. Irving stopped several torrents later and exclaimed, "I didn't know you were ambidextrous!" Which begat a terse but proud, "I'm not." Many years later, Concordia marked Irving's birthday with an array of items from its collection, placing them in glass display cases in the Vanier Library. It gave me quite a start to see the notepad open to a page showing my handwriting suddenly turning into a crabbed scrawl.

As the text took shape on the page, it became increasingly subject to my observations. The process was simple but laborious. Irving began by quickly rereading transcripts of the interview sessions with himself and

David O'Rourke, a former York University student whose interviews with Irving for his thesis started Irving on the path to writing the memoir. From those unedited transcripts, Irving selected scenes, giving them depth and shape while dictating the text to me. I heard the text spoken aloud; wrote it longhand; then, after lunch, typed the morning's work, all of which familiarized me with the evolving text. Moreover, each afternoon I read the typed copy back to Irving for him to make verbal corrections, which I noted on the page. He made further revisions while rereading this corrected copy, which I typed and retyped. Though intensive, this method enabled me to signal Irving if he repeated an adjective, adverb, or turn of phrase, prompting him to word his thoughts differently. By the time we finished, I had typed each chapter as many as six times over.

For the better part of an entire year, we sat at the dining room table working on **Messiah**. The table was large enough to hold a miscellany of books, papers, poems, photographs, and such, while leaving plenty of elbow room. Oblong, with seating for six, it was almost too large for the room, so I placed it on the diagonal, creating two pleasant triangular spaces on either side. Behind Irving, a large, delicately lead-paned window illuminated my work area. Behind me, through open French doors, the living room's identical window let the morning light in, illuminating Irving's face for my benefit.

The well-crafted woodwork and soft light made our home a perfectly suited writer's cottage. The rooms were quiet; any sound we made fell into the living room's luxurious wool carpet. I never tired of how the sun tumbled over it, picking out the ethnic designs in brown, orange, saffron, and burnt reds. On the wall behind Irving's left shoulder, I hung Ettore's oil portrait of Irving. The blue eyes gazed defiantly toward an invisible horizon. From a distance, the complexion glowed with an abundance of robustness and health. Close up, the canvas held flecks of cadmium green, pinks, purples, and surprising dabs of orange. Ettore's colours were a fitting record of how alive and vibrant Irving had appeared to the painter. From my seat at the table, I had two Irvings before me: the portrait radiating a vitality that remained fixed and true, while the flesh and blood man before me gestured, spoke, laughed, descried, bemoaned, stormed, and sometimes broke down before my eyes, sobbing as the most heart-wrenching memories became too painful for words. These facets of the man glimmered before me, sometimes each in turn. Riveted to my chair, there was no other place I wanted to be except there, a few feet away from the most intriguing, funny, beguiling man I have ever met.

Jews and Israel were frequent topics of conversation. Not only was Irving mulling over his own cultural identity while writing his memoir, but almost daily news reports on Israel's invasion of southern Lebanon made for muscular discussions. Irving feared Israel would become the cemetery of Judaism, that it could end up being its "womb and tomb." He could not make up his mind whether invading Lebanon was a wise move.

"It's easy for me here, but if I were living in Israel ...," Irving began one day. "Nor am I sure that it was a good thing for America to allow itself to be defeated [in the Vietnam War].That's all I can say. I can see both sides very clearly, but I don't know the answers. With regard to the Vietnam War, I would still say what I said at the time: morally right, practically wrong, because it was a mistake to think they could win a war in so foreign a country. They were misled about the nature of the war they would have to fight."

As the memoir took shape, I noted Irving had yet to explain why he had always been so sound. Where, aside from his congenital foreskinlessness and apart from the tension absorbed from his mother's practicality and his father's spirituality, where did all that conviction, resolve, and confidence come from? Irving, having just read Eileen Simpson's *Poets in Their Youth*, paused a moment, and then said that he had never been plagued by questions such as *Am I a poet?* or *Am I any good?* I had first-hand knowledge of his impatience with whiners. If one looked past the rhetoric and saw him as I did, they would see a man who, despite dark thoughts about human nature, was fundamentally joyful and resilient. In countless conversations, particularly once the dust settled, what came through was Irving's preternaturally generous nature. For Harriet, he had an abiding sense of gratitude and even warmth. For Aviva, he had nothing but good wishes and respect — though he of spoke of her with exasperated frustration bordering on regret, those feelings always gave way to remembering how much she had going for her and how close she came to being his lifelong mate. Irving said it came down to her "maddening inability to understand a few simple facts about poets and poetry."

For critics and reviewers, he espoused abiding compassion. For those who had used his name for their own purposes, he had but a shrug and a quid pro quo attitude. I surmised that perhaps because he knew they were all doomed to insignificance — remembered only for the amber poems that captured their fly-selves, if at all — perhaps *that* was what fuelled his happy disposition. In truth, Irving was a man far more sinned against than sinning, blaming only himself for the deep pain of various relationships. He loathed not only whiners, but also those who rationalized their mistakes to avoid responsibility for their stupidities. As for his own stupidities, at least he made use of insights and wisdom gleaned from them.

These and many other such musings went into the making of *Waiting for the Messiah.* Irving's interpretation of the Messiah is somebody who comes to save the Jew — not by bringing certainties but to break old certainties; not to bring new dogma, but to reveal the drama of life. For Irving, the Jew at his best was a troublemaker, a shit-disturber.

His memoir is an account of his youth and the key events leading to the realization that he was a poet. Details about his marriages, teaching career, and all the rest held relatively little interest, as he already had covered that material in thousands of poems and letters. *Waiting for the Messiah* contains many of the same tropes as his poetry: sex, death, accident, unreflective nature, guilt — they can all be found in the opening chapter. These are the eternal elements of humankind. Only monsters, Irving pointed out, are ever free from guilt. In the face of these elements, Irving manifested a Nietzschean outlook long before the term became popular. For Irving, this meant being aware of the pain and terror of living while having the courage to go on. Nietzsche did not believe in Christianity's romantic evasion of these elements, which made him anti-Christian. Irving, like Nietzsche, held to a gospel of courage and endurance, or "stoicism with a smile," as Irving put it while I typed the last draft of *Waiting for the Messiah*'s first chapter. I pushed back from the keyboard to ask about Nietzsche.

His long-time friend, Concordia professor Dr. Wynne Francis, had written about Nietzsche's influence on Irving. One day, her essay came up for discussion, starting with Irving's dismay. "These pedants! I tell you, it's a *shamda na bischa!*" Which was Yiddish for "a damn shame." Irving went on, "I like the way Wynne comes out with these 'revelations,' Nietzsche's influence on Hemingway — these ideas that I put into her head years ago. I tell you that before she met me, she knew about as much about Nietzsche as this glass does." He lifted his brandy and soda and set it down with a thud. "Now she comes out with these revelations!"

When I asked about the propriety of naming names, whether in my journal or his memoir, his tone softened. "It's the truth. You have to use names, Sweetheart. Don't listen to what anybody tells you, just what I tell you. If I had hemorrhoids, which I don't, I can tell you in all honesty, one of my hemorrhoids would have more knowledge and sensitivity than all the Canadian literati put together. All the writer needs to know is what's alive and what's dead. My anger should stem from the fact that these people don't value poetry. They don't value the beauty of what we have."

In that opening chapter, various images provide clues to Layton's poetics. Seeing his father's fur hat knocked off by Jew-hating children hurling horse dung made a lasting impression. He likens the hat to a stunned animal, and describes how his father retrieves his hat, straightening, his dignity restored. Unlike animals, man has the potential to elevate himself above animal existence. He suffers, the pain made bearable by pride, that complex human quality that helps and hinders man.

Irving's recollection of everyone being in the street either giving or taking blows sums up everyone's life experience. Free will and independent thinking are rare qualities, particularly since human nature is so easily given over to mindless violence and unreason, and so subject to herd instinct. When someone spits to land a "dismantling blow to the devil" thought to be standing near the boy Irving, he is expressing how impossible it was for him to enter into a pious, orthodox religious life. The "devil" in him, namely creativity and a free imagination, was something people around him guarded against. If unleashed, an unfettered imagination could destroy their unreflective orthodox way of life. Indeed, his father's yellowing holy books are well thumbed but crumbling. His father reads constantly, but is not *creating* any new holy books. Only creativity can prevent death and oblivion. Epiphanies, Irving discovers, were possible. Such epiphanies prefigure the certain coming of the Messiah, and as such, give the first clear hint that for Irving, the Messiah is the triumvirate of poetry/creativity/imagination. With this realization, Irving declares his independence of mind and establishes the holy creed by which he lived his life. Reinforcing this stab at independence is the awareness that his father's prayers rise toward "the unanswering skies."[1]

From his earliest days, Irving was aware of antinomies, paired-opposites such as his parents. The black of his father's beard, the Shabbat tablecloth's whiteness; the hard and soft sounds horse dung made when

Catholic boys hurled it into the front door while his mother was serving a customer (hard in winter; soft in summer); his mother cursing, his father's silence. In the first chapter, he describes an encounter with a rusty sword, a symbol for the cruel, evil world. His mother curses, whereas his father turns to his holy books. Irving realizes that he will get his insights from the larger world and resists his father's last attempt at forcing him to adhere to an orthodox life. From that point on, he would continue to battle for his freedom and independence of mind.

Luck plays its hand in anyone's life, putting us at the mercy of forces beyond our control. Irving was equally aware that money or force equalled power. People respected power. Years later, Irving sprinkled rumours such as having made a fortune in Mexican jumping beans. He did so not to be self-aggrandizing, but to do an end-run around schadenfreude. Weakness, or the appearance thereof, could be fatal.

We savoured the afternoon light and quiet after I finished typing that first chapter. Irving looked through the pages and said, "On the one hand, I was alive — vociferously so; on the other hand, my dominant mood and one that I've battled all my life was the futility of action since it led inevitably to suffering and death. But the point is, my anti-nihilism is purely genetic, not intellectual. My chromosomes refuse to agree with my vision. My mind tells me one thing and my balls another. It makes me tear my hair to hear these smart alecks, who know from nothing, go on in such a superficial way about Orwell or films or books. What gets me is how incapable most people are of looking beneath the surface. Whenever I touch the subject of death, it comes from my heart. And yet, I'm not melancholy or given to brooding about death, certainly not a skull-and-bones death. Death for me is a metaphor for oblivion and the poet in me responds to that metaphor. That's why I keep going back to the subject of death."

Irving observed his own father starting out with ideals and the notion there was something better than this world but, for many reasons, he fell short. Irving thought constantly about abstractions such as God, death, art, and what the Messiah signified, turning them over like sides of an invisible Rubik's cube. "Man," he said, "has accepted the suffering of the crucifixion, but has gone on to create something greater: *Art.* God created Man in his image, that is, creative; *Man* created the Messiah. The Messiah is a much nobler creation than Man because Art is the result of the pain and angst that God rejected."

Another conversation led to my asking what made his work original, why he was confident it would last. "Because I've had the courage to walk through the gates of hell, shake Satan's hand, and come out praising God. I've never been fooled about Man's nature, and yet I've remained a Dionysian. This is what is original. [Essayists] Erwin Weins and Valerio Bruni see this. This is why [*Messiah*] and my body of work will be around for a long, long time."

At last, on April 23, 1985, to be exact, and with fingers sore from pounding the keys, I typed the final period on the last revision. *Waiting for the Messiah* done, a deep stillness filled the house. Irving reread the concluding chapter while I slipped downstairs to make *mamaliga*, a Romanian dish of corn meal, cottage cheese, butter, cracked pepper, and green onions. Fittingly, it was his favourite boyhood food. Spring sunlight filled the living room. Neither of us said very much as we ate. It had been an exhausting year, writing and rewriting nearly each day, maintaining correspondence, entertaining visitors; all had taken their toll.

I leapt up from the table, ran upstairs for my camera and the draft chapters, stacking these next to him. Fourteen chapters, with five or six drafts of each chapter, made an impressive tower of words. I wanted to document the moment, so, dovetailing the drafts on the sun-flooded living room floor, I bade him come sit on the sofa. My camera caught a look flickering across his face, a look I saw on that morning and at no other time: relief, joy, fatigue, all grimly mixed with a haunting, sorrowful ache. He was nearing the end of his life. The account of his boyhood through to becoming a poet, like one of his metaphoric butterflies, once free and mutable, was now pinned for display.

25: The Fire Is All That Matters

SPRING 1985 WAS an unrelenting onslaught of obligations, social niceties, and, of course, the last rush to hit the deadline for *Waiting for the Messiah*. On top of which, director Don Winkler had begun to shoot *Poet: Irving Layton Observed* for the National Film Board.

Links to the past were disappearing steadily into the ether. Poet F.R. Scott passed away in January. Naturally, we attended the memorial service, crowding in at the back of McGill University's ornate chapel. Midway through the service, Irving became increasingly impatient, irreverent even. To Irving's credit, his agitation stemmed from the memorialists' skipping over the more vital and pertinent elements of Scott's life. Impatience became stage whispers. Rather loud stage whispers. "Irving! It's a *memorial service*. Now *shhhh!*" He began writing "Two for the Road, Frank" virtually before the service ended.

On March 29, his sister Gertie died, adding a vivid *schmertz*, a painful nostalgic pang, to scenes he'd been reliving while working on *Messiah*. Seeing her imitation rococo furniture, the pile of old photographs seemingly discarded, dismayed and saddened him. The furniture was no loss, but the photos? Finishing *Messiah* had become all the more urgent.

Amid the frenzy to complete the memoir, and with Winkler's crew taking over the house to shoot interview segments, there were also last-minute preparations for a trip to Athens. With one week to go before the deadline and departure, we entertained Dino and Barbara Siotis.

Dino was the Greek cultural attaché who was to accompany us. The Winklers came for dinner, which meant cleaning the entire house, a grocery run, and being on top of whatever Don might need for the upcoming shoot. Somehow, we found time for Joy Bennett, Concordia's Layton Collection librarian, to come over and discuss accessions to the library's collection. According to jotted calendar notes, Aviva landed during this whirlwind. Oddly, I have no memory of her being with us, only the unremitting drive to finish *Messiah*.

On Saturday, May 4, I picked up the manuscript from the professional typist whose word processor made for a cleaner copy, packaged and shipped it to McClelland & Stewart, scurried about for shoes and clothes, got a haircut, rushed home, packed, got Irving spiffed up, and caught a night flight for Athens.

Three years earlier, I was a chambermaid at Hotel Alma, a two-star hotel off Omonia Square, for six dollars a day, living on yogurt, peanuts, Pavlidis chocolate, and the occasional souvlaki pita with retsina wine on good days. How very different for Irving, too. To my best recollection, it was his first time back since 1977.

That last visit had seen the end of Irving and Aviva's marriage. She had chosen Molivos, a tiny fishing village on the island of Lesbos where Irving had spent the previous eleven summers working on poetry, to end what she had termed their "open marriage." It was not a pretty end, as his poems attest. "Night Music," "Hills and Hills," among others, chronicle the end of their life as a couple, and his becoming Molivos's most famous, perhaps most pitied, cuckold. Poetry, his stalwart garburator, had long ago disposed of all that. In his hands now: a paperbound Greek-English edition of his poems and Irving, triumphantly marking his return.

But first: Athens! Mythic; timeless!

Suffocating. Crowded. Dino Siotis met us at the airport. In light of political unrest, bulletproof vests were thoughtfully provided. We declined, politely, as Irving found even seat belts challenging. Heavy for his frame, getting in and out of cars provoked colourful denouncing of small cars, bad designers, and imprecations against possible heart attacks. We took our chances in the back of the government sedan.

Irving's literary agent, Lucinda Vardey, joined us at the Chandris Hotel on Syngrou Avenue. Her no-nonsense professionalism and wry British humour was spot-on. Cool as the proverbial cucumber, elegant, graceful, we enjoyed the oasis she created just by entering a room. The itinerary she devised allowed for a day or so to acclimatize, then two brutal days of engagements with Don Winkler's camera crew following our every move, and then on to the island of Tinos for more shooting.

Covering the trip were Marilyn Powell for CBC Radio's *Anthology*, Brian Shein from *Toronto Life*, and print journalist Jeff Richardson. Richardson confirmed my own recollections of the trip while I researched this book. "Irving was *fun!*" he began. "He was just a lot of fun, gracious, humble, and he was having an incredible time." Richardson, then a young freelance writer, had never before met Layton. Like many Canadians, his image of Layton was skewed by chronic negative portrayals. In fact, he confessed to embarking on the junket with "negative expectations."

"There were a lot of strong personalities," he remembered, "Marilyn Powell, Lucinda Vardey ... but the moment we landed in Athens, I knew it was going to be an awesome time." The group was supposed to queue up in a long line for luggage inspection. Lucinda, however, deemed that an unnecessary waste of time. She sailed past the line, turned, and, raising an elegant arm, waved her hand imperiously. Her crisp British diction was like a beacon, trilling, "This way, everyone. Come along. Follow me," and we all sauntered blithely along, skipping past inspection.

Richardson also recalled how Lucinda was intent on promoting Irving for the Nobel Prize, as a top-notch agent should. What stands out twenty-eight years later, he said, is how Irving was having none of it. "I remember his humility, enjoyment, and how gracious he was throughout — and his sense of humour. He was just having a great time. No matter what was arranged for him, he went just went along with it."

One such event was the reading at the University of Athens, hosted by the chair of the English department, Byron Raizis. Jeff recalls feeling rather bad for Layton, supposing the students knew little about him. Even if they were familiar with his work, one can only guess at their command of English. In any case, presented with a classroom filled with eager faces, Irving delivered a lecture on Canadian poetry that would have enlightened even Canadian students. Don Winkler included part of it in his documentary, capturing the passion, eloquence, and fierce conviction with which Irving spoke — not of his own work — but of Canadian poetry's distinctive history, from pioneers to modernists.

"The one regret I have after the trip is the article that appeared in *Saturday Night*'s Back Page section," Jeff told me. "Here I'd been on this wonderful trip and wanted to have something to show Lucinda." His article covered the launch of *Where Burning Sappho Loved*, held at the Vorres Museum just outside Athens and hosted by Ian Vorres himself. There were well-heeled guests, Greek dignitaries, and Canadian expats, including Montreal poet and hellenophile David Solway and our cultural ambassador, the bespectacled, bow-tied Jean-Pierre Gamby. I wore a white linen skirt, mismatched with a cotton clearance-bin Geoffrey Beene jacket, and an azure silk blouse in tribute to our Greek hosts. Irving was not easy to dress, and he was rough on clothes, so we made do. I wish his shoes had been of better quality, his pants and jacket a bit fresher, but his personality was such that only philistines noticed the quality of his clothes, or lack thereof.

Vibrant blue skies turned violet at dusk as whitewashed walls exhaled the day's heat into the great open-air atrium. Under a waning moon and the film crew's spotlights, we took in the stunning gardens and museum with artwork covering four thousand years of Greek history, relished exquisite finger-foods, sipped wine, mingled, and simply basked in the beauty of it all. Our host, who could have stepped from a *GQ* magazine, stood up on a low wall and graced us with kind words about his guest and the book. Irving then clambered up and spoke briefly, with customary gusto.

In short, a splendid evening. Richardson's account, unfortunately, displeased *Saturday Night*'s editors. Their euphemism was "edgy." As in, it wasn't "edgy" enough. After numerous rewrites, and despite the author's intent, what came out was a send-up of our cultural ambassador. True, Gamby had been a bit bureaucratic, uptight, yes, but he did not deserve ridicule. The editors were happy, though, as *Saturday Night* once again avoided publishing a positive story about Irving Layton. Could chronic chicanery like this be at least partly responsible for his lambasting of "Canucky shmucks"? Lucinda looked for the positives: at least they hadn't mocked Irving outright, just ignored the salient points of his ever-growing success. "In hindsight, I wish I'd stood up to the editors," Richardson said, but being young and wanting to have his name on that Back Page column was important and very understandable. "Irving," he remembered, "was larger than life, but more of a contained presence, if that makes sense. I'd expected something else," he said, pausing as he cast about for the best adjective. "*Authentic!* That's it, he was authentic."

We had lunched with Irving's Greek literary agent, launched *Where Burning Sappho Loved* amidst Greek VIPs and media, spent two intense hours at the University of Athens, given a reading that same night at the British Consulate followed by a private dinner and small talk on poetry with the Canadian Hellenic Group, and were filmed by the ever-present NFB crew — all in the space of two days.

Mykonos, for lack of a better island, beckoned. Despite the tourist trappings, Irving revelled in just being there, Dionysian to his Hebraic fingertips. Books and writing materials were always within reach, as he never vacationed completely, never stilled his mind. My journal, dated Friday, May 17, describes how

it must have been around 6:00 or 6:30 a.m. Roosters were crowing. I had not slept very well. The horrible dankness, must, and urine smells kept gathering around my nostrils. When the dankness abated, I'd feel the damp mattress scratching against my bare skin. It was with relief that I heard Irving's familiar happy voice ask in the darkness, "Wanna have a cigarette?"

He seemed more than wide-awake as he poured himself a little Cutty Sark in a glass and reached for the lit cigarette. Nodding towards Tennessee Williams's memoirs, he said, "Do you know what the value of a memoir like that is?"

No.

"A memoir such as that is as valuable for the things he shows us about people who are greater, more brilliant and far more interesting than himself. As far as literary value, it

has none whatsoever. He just describes a few of his homo-
sexual experiences, but doesn't tell us why he's a homosex-
ual, for example. He shows no insight or depth."

The fragment ends there. I must add that Irving was not at all
homophobic. He was, however, disappointed with Tennessee Williams's
memoir, and it came out as irritation.

We set sail for Tinos. Aboard ship, Irving worked on a poem he had
begun in Athens, while Dino explained Greek political cartoons to me.
We toured the island and readied for a full day of filming. Irving, Dino,
and Irving's translator, Katerina Anghelaki-Rouk, lunched and chatted,
the cameras rolled. I bided my time, off-camera but never far. By night-
fall, we regrouped at a taverna where the crew had stowed their equipment. It was getting very late, our gang exchanged pleasantries with the
locals. I had been feeling splendid, if somewhat on the periphery. The
Greek females, including Irving's translator, seemed nonplussed that I
spoke some Greek and could even read it. Tension was building.

Someone put a coin in the jukebox and the entire taverna reverber-
ated with flamenco music. *Flamenco?* The great Antonio Gades himself
had once kissed me on the cheek. *You want flamenco?* I thought. *I'll
give you flamenco.* Kicking off my ill-fitting shoes, I began to dance,
slowly at first, undulating toward the centre of the dusty terrazzo floor.
The white linen skirt fit close around my hips, flaring out in countless
narrow pleats. Aside from a wan fluorescent tube over the counter, the
place was lit with only a few bulbs no stronger than candles. As I turned,
rolling my hips more daringly with each phrase, the men gathered in
one corner of the bar, scrambling over one another and the equipment
crates for a better view. Some crouched by the dance floor, dangerously near the hem of my twirling skirt. Their faces flashed in glimpses
caught through half-closed eyes as I swayed and turned. Their glowing
eyes followed my movements, their hands clapping, some now smash-
ing down on the table in rhythm with the music. I sensed a quickening
in the air, knew that I was creating it, and kept dancing.

Irving, however, had already picked himself and his red clipboard
up from our table and moved to the furthest corner, his back to me.

So I danced, determined to wrest his attention from whatever he was writing. With the men and even the women now emitting shouts and clapping furiously to my beat, I danced with redoubled passion, arms swanning out, down and up over my head and down again, breasts cocked like guns, torso, hips, thighs, gyrating, wrists snapping my skirt like a bull-whip; I danced, an Odalisque come to life. Irving stayed at the far table, never once glancing up.

Later that night, or perhaps the next day, he handed me the poem "Black Tourist in Tinos."[1] That the lady in the poem was dark-skinned, clumsy, with pocked thighs, puzzled me. Surely my movements had been a bit off, and cellulite was a fact of life. Still, it rankled that he never once looked, never received the gift I was trying to make. "I didn't have to. I could feel it."

A few years later, finalizing the manuscript for the expanded *A Wild Peculiar Joy,* I retyped the poem, still mystified that he had not watched me dance or described me more accurately. His explanation flowed into or from a discussion on where he parts company with Plato. "I want to make it clear that reality is flawed, so, she does not know the movements of the dance, has pocked thighs, *but,* 'the island gods are happy', so are 'the mortals in the *kafeneion*.'" It was *my* dancing, however, that burned away the chains and gyves of reality. "Read Shelley's 'Hymn to Intellectual Beauty,'" he urged, for "this is where I part company with Plato and Platonists. Your dance," he continued, "was *energy* incarnate. Platonists say *forms* are eternal. I say *energy* is eternal."

My role in dancing like that was to fill the poet with the epiphany, the inspiration that "... *makes of form itself a ruinous blaze* ... "

"What an exquisite philosophical paradox!" he exclaimed, warming to the subject. "God made the fire, and after the entire universe disappears, the 'fire' of creativity, passion, love, will remain. The 'awakened seed' is also a symbol of creativity. Keats's 'Ode to a Grecian Urn' deals with this theme, too. Plato believed that real things were a smudged copy of the *ideal* thing. I part company with that because the ideal thing is just an abstraction, a mental construction, which does not exist outside of Plato's mind. Shelley's intellectual beauty is a pure *form* or pure thought. This too is merely an abstract entity."

For Irving, the fire in "Black Tourist in Tinos" is a *real*, existing thing. My dancing exemplified the same fiery energy that fuels the universe. Therefore, he distances the reality of my dancing as much as possible, endowing the dancer with imperfections to show that the passion and fire within her "transcends all flaws and imperfections."

"Your dancing enabled me to have the epiphany," he explained. "The structure of the poem *insists* on certain facets being observed. Just as murder and lust, etc., in a play by Shakespeare is different from real life, murder in the street is different from murder on the stage; the poem's purpose necessitates I make her black, pocked, and clumsy. The 'faults' or deviations from the actual scene are there to heighten the contrast between reality and the *fire* which is real, constantly perfect, and eternal." The fire is all that matters.

Whenever I watch the documentary, it hurls me back in time to that night in the taverna. Winkler had hoped to recreate the previous evening's flamenco dance magic. Around noon the next day, he captured Irving and me dancing together in the same taverna, hands holding, eyes locked, me circling him until the music ends. Irving catches me in his arms, both of us laughing as if there was no one else there. In the film's closing scene, Layton, now in wintry Montreal and still working on the poem, voices its closing lines:

> When she leaves, taking her dark skin,
> the lit place loses radiance
> and we become patient mortals again.

26: Full Swing

ALMOST IMMEDIATELY upon returning from Greece, Irving boarded the train for Toronto. Ellen Seligman, Irving's editor at McClelland & Stewart, thought editing *Messiah* would be easier with Irving present. They worked well together, her New York smarts and editorial skills parrying Irving's effusiveness. She won out enough times to dilute the book's inherent spice, dismaying and frustrating Irving at times. Too much spice, she warned, and the Canadian public would shy away. Reluctantly, he conceded many points, generously praising Ellen's good sense and intuitiveness in the acknowledgements.

So, upon his return to Montreal, we attended a PEN Club dinner in his honour. Novelist Hugh MacLennan introduced Irving, maliciously calling him a former communist. If my own jaw clenched at that false, inflammatory label, I can only imagine Irving's disgust. Irving limited himself to thanking the organizers and giving a brief, gracious speech, mentioning he had just finished his memoir *Waiting for the Messiah*. Just then, a man came up alongside me, having arrived late. The man on the other side of me, oblivious as to my identity, turned to the latecomer and said, "Hey, you just missed the Messiah."

"Oh yeah? Where? Who's the Messiah?"

"Over there. Irving Layton. He just said he thinks he's the Messiah," the jerk asserted. No such words had left Irving's mouth. I found it difficult to stomach brazen misrepresentations like these, but somehow held my tongue. Insecure twits, I realized, will always project their failings onto someone like Irving.

Messiah came out that fall with a double crescendo: launch parties in Toronto and Montreal, with attendant media blitz. Interviewers such as CBC Radio's Peter Gzowski sensed Irving would perform better with me seated in the studio so that Irving could see me. As I will describe shortly, the battle against Elspeth Cameron, his erstwhile biographer, was already in full swing. Presumed friends, colleagues, and scores of writers whom he helped over the years fell away like psoriatic flakes. Fearful, perhaps, of offending grant-dispensers and literary powerbrokers, their tongues cleaved to the roofs of their mouths; their fingers, suddenly bereft of bone or muscle, were unable to write of their support for Irving. Now, it all came down to Irving and me. My presence at the interviews calmed him enough to perform well in the midst of all this.

Jack McClelland had us booked into the Windsor Arms Hotel for the Toronto event. Though terribly agitated from trying not to dwell on the battle with Cameron, the subject proved unavoidable. A consummate professional, each interview was a performance in the best sense of the word. He came prepared, was quick-witted as ever, using humour to syncopate forceful, lyrical, informative bursts. "Always be prepared, know what you want to say, and stay in control of the interview," he advised, as though predicting I, too, might one day be in the limelight. So I practised, discretely pretending the questions were aimed at me and getting used to the taste of adrenaline. By now, seasoned and able to anticipate almost every need, Irving relied on me even more. I had immersed myself in his work to such an extent that in time, when someone requested a poem for him to read, Irving glanced at me for the page number. Three years in, we had become a superb team.

At the Windsor Arms Hotel, we rested and dressed for the big night. In the reception room, we were quickly engulfed by fans, media, and publishing insiders. Even Irving's son David showed up. He looked wistfully towards his father, already hemmed in before the huge fireplace, besieged by reporters, cameramen, and photographers. With lights in his eyes and the people forming a barrier between them, David seemed shut out of his father's shining moment. I stood at his elbow, telling him how happy Irving was going to be to see him, but I don't think he stayed very long, perhaps even leaving before Leonard Cohen made a surprise appearance. Had David stayed, Irving would have been touched at the rare display of interest from his son.

Another David showed up, just as unexpectedly. David O'Rourke's name appears on the inside page of Irving's autobiography, as someone who wrote the book "with" Irving. His contribution had been the interviews, early on, that O'Rourke had conducted while seeking primary source material for his thesis on Montreal's early literary magazines. O'Rourke's visits began back in Niagara-on-the-Lake, and continued through to 1985. Many times, David confessed to feeling wretched over the inordinately long time it was taking to finish his thesis.

Their relationship had been rewarding, even stimulating for Irving at times. He likened David to an Irish rogue. We looked forward to O'Rourke's visits, for there was nothing of the dull academic about him. Over several years, he was a frequent houseguest. Typically, Irving helped defray some of O'Rourke's expenses; not realizing David's wife worked for Air Canada, Irving helped pay for his flights from Toronto to Montreal, as well as providing a room and abundant meals. Once apprised David flew for next to nothing, Irving still helped David with film and developing costs for all the photos David was taking. This was done out of empathy for anyone starting out with ambition, mortgage payments, and a love for literature.

O'Rourke's early interviews about Montreal's small presses and the key literary players of the era happened at the same time as Elspeth Cameron's, and their contrasting styles prompted Irving to think his initial assessment of Cameron's abilities was correct. Worse than her flat-footed obscure questions, Irving shuddered at her glassy-eyed demeanour. The most he hoped for from Cameron was a reasonably drawn chronology of his life. It was David's thoughtful probing that led to Irving's decision to conclude his memoir with his becoming a poet. Everything else, he said, was dross. The marriages, the disappointments, they all paled in comparison to the pivotal moment where he realized he was a poet, giving rise to *Waiting for the Messiah*.

Since O'Rourke was not involved in the writing, only the early interview process, Irving was not prepared for the phone call from his

editor Ellen Seligman wondering why a David O'Rourke was suddenly
calling in a frenzy, *insisting* his name appear on the cover as co-author.
This was mid-August 1985, and the memoir was well into production.
What made this incident exceptionally painful is that Irving thought of
O'Rourke, a former York University student of his, as one of his spiritual sons. Furious at McClelland & Stewart's balking at naming him as
co-author, O'Rourke called Irving, drunk, belligerent, and almost in-
coherent, insinuating that *he* had written the first draft of *Messiah*. As if
that was not appalling enough, he dug himself deeper into the cess, demanding ten thousand dollars for his name to be "bought off the page"
— his term. Still fuming at Irving, he vowed not to attend *Messiah*'s
launch party. Irving, shocked at first, grew more incensed with each
new absurdity. In an icy-firm tone, he let O'Rourke know how far off
base he was, suggesting he call back after he sobered up.

O'Rourke had told Irving repeatedly that he hoped the interviews
would bolster his academic career. Other times, David dropped remarks on how a close friend of his was getting good press over a short
story collection — his voice crimped with envy when mentioning the
writer-friend. Out of pity, Irving permitted O'Rourke's name to appear
on the inside page as if O'Rourke had written *Messiah* "with" him.
David's angry call was sad and brutally disappointing as it was unfore-
seen. Even more pitiful for O'Rourke, Irving had planned to mention
him at the launch party, publicly acknowledging O'Rourke's help and
how he helped Irving's most relevant memories to surface.

Contrary to his belligerent vow to stay clear of *Messiah*'s launch
party, O'Rourke turned up at the Windsor Arms Hotel. With a black
look in his eye and nary a word to Irving. O'Rourke stormed in and
thrust a binder of photos at me, a selection of candid shots he'd taken
during their interview sessions. Irving, surrounded by well-wishers,
never saw O'Rourke, who left as abruptly as he arrived. If Irving *had*
glimpsed the ersatz Irish rogue, there is no doubt in my mind that Irving
would have greeted him cordially, perhaps even warmly, and given an
abridged speech thanking David. Their relationship never recovered.
O'Rourke later sold all the photos he took to Concordia University. If
there was a thank-you, I do not recall one, nor did the token payment

promised to Irving materialize. Sad as Irving was over this colossal falling out with his spiritual son, it pales in comparison to what lay in store
with his biological sons.[1]

After the celebrations, Jack urged Ellen, Irving, myself, and Leonard
into the Arms' restaurant where we enjoyed a late-night dinner to mark
the hugely successful event.

Back in Montreal, the launch party went off without a hitch — at
least from Venie's point of view. She jumped at the chance to stage-
manage the whole thing, something I was too busy and too exhausted
to prevent. Aside from celebrating Irving and his book, the occasion
was rife with opportunities to upstage me. Would I have done the same?
Impossible to tell, since I lacked her, shall we say, directorial gifts.

Venie selected her friend Sharon to host the party, for Sharon had
a beautiful home in Westmount. Venie organized everything and even
prepared a speech to laud Irving. We mingled, imbibed, knoshed, and
I felt my cheeks grow warm with the wine. At least I had my ethnic
number dress on, and felt relatively comfortable as I made conversation
with some of the familiar faces, none of whom had any idea of how
much effort I had poured into helping produce *Messiah*. The spacious
living room had a fireplace, books, pale ivory-coloured walls, and high
ceilings typical of Montreal's old-money homes. In the corner: an imposing wing chair. Beside it, in front of the fireplace, sat a quaint little
antique milking stool.

As the shank of the evening approached, Venie herded everyone
into the living room. Before I could make my way next to the wing
chair, she gripped my arm, steering me toward the stool. I was to sit
there, she whispered. Why? Because I could see better from there, or
words to that effect. I looked toward the wing chair thinking I should
be next to Irving, given the work I did. Venie's face contorted in a panic
as she read my mind.

I was to sit on the tiny wooden stool. *That* was what her script indicated, and by damn, she was going to make sure I followed directions.
Her whispers grew sharper and more insistent. Then came soothing
implications that she had good reason for my having to sit on the
tiny, three-legged milking stool. "You'll see," she said, appealing to my

vanity. Maybe she was going to acknowledge my dedication and hard work. Maybe the moon is made of old car tires?

As usual, I gave in to her *farce majeure*, gingerly dropping down to the rickety stool. It did not take long to see what she had planned. With Irving ensconced in the wing chair, she sat on its arm, letting her haunch slide onto his lap. For support, she then had to snake her arm around his neck, her free leg dangling like a femme fatale's in a Bogart movie. Thus installed on the poet's throne, she extolled Irving and his memoir, while I sat like a random fan on the sidelines. Irving caved just as I had done. Hopefully everyone saw through her *mise-en-scène* and noted how I had kept hurt feelings or anger to myself.

Suffice to say that when we got home that night, Irving was made aware of how I felt at being stage-managed onto to a damn milkmaid stool during the launch party for a book still warm from my feverish efforts. We were too intelligent and in love with each other to waste much time bickering over Venie's spiteful tricks, especially perched as we were on the eve of a battle royal.

27: The Cameron Affair

IF ONLY IT WERE a B-movie or a beach romance, as inconsequential as newspaper blown by uncaring winds against a sewer grate. But no. "The Cameron Affair," wherein Elspeth Cameron wrote a pseudo-biography called *Irving Layton: A Portrait*, is far from inconsequential. Nor will it be so long as honesty has not gone the way of buttonhooks or the emu's capacity for flight.

Simply put, it constitutes Canada's literary Dreyfus Affair. In both cases, a Jew was maligned, his name and reputation smeared by characters not fit to polish their victim's shoes. At least Alfred Dreyfus had an Emile Zola to take up his cause and shame France before the world. Lofty comparison? Delusions of negative grandeur on my part? Perhaps, but not by much. Any lingering skepticism or ignorance of the facts is understandable, as this took place in the mid-1980s. More pointedly, only two people know the inside story: the target of the "portrait," now dead, and myself, who helped him battle night and day for some three years against Cameron's calumny. Cameron has had many opportunities to come clean as to her motivation and why she could not resist sloppy scholarship, an egregious cultural bias, and other whoppers. It is doubtful she will do so any time soon.

In a large plastic storage bin I keep, along with the silver wine goblets we first drank from and other Laytonia, a plastic bag straining to hold fourteen-and-a-half pounds of ephemera documenting the fight against Irving's purported biographer. When it came time to write this chapter, I dragged out the bin for the first time since it all happened. If only someone else, anyone else, could have sorted through this material to bind truth with supporting facts, and spare me the agony. Unfortunately, no one but me knows what we endured: not the violation, the outrage, the all-consuming campaign for truth if not justice, nor, years later, the sweetness of seeing public opinion begin to turn.

On two tabloid-sized sheets, buried deep in the ephemera, is a handwritten list that brings the time back. November 1985. With Irving away on the reading tour for *Messiah*, I took advantage of rare unfettered solitude to catalogue the unfolding events. For twelve straight hours, I sat on the living room floor, the sofa for a table, coffee table for a desk, listing articles, events, and the epistolary missiles launched to date. It was only the beginning. Upon Irving's return the battle became so heated, the engagement so fierce, that all I could do was to watch the stack of evidence grow — our disgust with Cameron and her ilk growing exponentially along with it.

Quite apart from my animus against Cameron's mumbo-jumbo mess of a book, I will never forgive what she stole from us. In 1985 Irving was — after decades of single-minded dedication to his craft, teaching, and everything else — still in splendid health. He had earned the right to enjoy life as only a poet can. Together, we had worked hard on *Messiah*, selections of his poems were in the works, his collected letters were being collated, there was pension money coming in, birds chirping in the honeysuckle-festooned garden, music, movies — the whole nine yards. By any standard, we were enviably happy, more so for the ever-percolating creativity that we thrived on. Nothing challenged our belief that conjugal life would continue resonating with joy such as only we could spark from the flint of any given day. Instead, his best remaining energies and all of my efforts disappeared down the Cameron Affair drain. Had those who knew Irving been less cowardly or more honourable, the battle — as much for Cameron's sake as ours — would have been mercifully quick. Had she written an honest but mediocre "portrait," it might have been acceptable, I suppose. But a compendium of odious lies? Why would *anyone*, famous or obscure, sit back and let filth pass for fact?

Cautiously, reluctantly, I leaf through these old articles and letters, recoiling as white-hot rage roars upward like a thousand angry birds. Twenty-eight years on, I am still agog at Canada's mealy-minded poltroonery. My disgust has not abated, not one iota, nor had Irving's up until his very end. The Cameron Affair never should have happened. We had better things to do with those topaz mornings, those silvery afternoons. Disgust notwithstanding, I am bound by, and committed to, the truth.

If honesty and ethical standards have any intrinsic value at all, then the Cameron Affair is an MRI-image of how a country failed its most renowned poet. Looked at forensically, Layton's lifelong iconoclastic stance, his attacks on gentility, philistinism, hypocrisy, etc., all made the Cameron Affair inevitable. Sure as darkness begets daylight, the loud uppity Jew was going to get it in the neck. Canadian society — or at least Toronto's ersatz intelligentsia — delighted in the caricature, its mocking debasement and ridicule of the poet. In so doing, Layton's success, including his Nobel Prize nominations, could be overlooked, his scathing critiques rendered pooh-poohable. La Cameron was WASP Canada's made-to-order ice princess-cum-literary assassin, straight out of central casting. Inevitability, however, does not lessen Canada's disgrace, not by a long chalk.

So how did her book come about? Though I was not yet part of Irving's life when he was the University of Toronto's writer in residence for the 1981–82 school year, what I can attest to is that his account of how they met never altered in tone or content. Whether speaking privately to me, to guests in our home, during interviews, or in published letters, his retelling never varied. To wit: Cameron approached him; she asked to sit with him; and she asked permission to write his biography. The genesis matters because Cameron's version is where she first strays from the truth. In falsely stating that Irving approached her, Cameron throws the first mud-ball, invoking the tired but saleable stereotype of Layton as predatory megalomaniac.

For evidence of who asked whom to write Layton's biography, compare Cameron's taped interview to Layton's account. In the fall of 1985, Toronto poet, editor, and journalist Judith Fitzgerald interviewed Cameron for *The Windsor Star*.[1] The article appeared on October 12,

1985. In the transcribed interview, as well as in the published article, Cameron reveals that she is forty-two years old, on her third marriage, teaching various courses in Canadian Literature and Women's Studies on a contract basis, and is not part of any University of Toronto department. On the topic of the decision to write a Layton biography, she states, in the taped interview:

> I don't know if I told Irving or not it would be a good idea to do the biography to help me get tenure. I certainly think that's true ... the MacLennan book was an attempt to prove to the U of T in that publish or perish syndrome that I could publish a good academic book that could increase my credentials and raise my profile, then they might offer me some kind of position with tenure.

A few sentences later, she wavers: "I don't think I told Irving it would help me get tenure." She did admit that she may have told novelist Hugh MacLennan something similar, though, as that is "how one gets up through the ranks." She describes approaching novelist Morley Callaghan for permission to write his biography. He declined, according to Cameron, because "he was working on his memoirs and he wanted to do it himself." Judith contacted Morley Callaghan on September 30, 1985, to verify Cameron's statement. His response:

> Elspeth Cameron wanted to do a biography of me, yeah. I didn't think she was the one to do a biography on me, put it that way. I had told her that it was too wide a field for her, I thought. She said Hugh MacLennan's the first Canadian novelist, but I was fifteen years ahead of Hugh, who's a friend of mine, and who knows the facts. She did as good a job as she could do in the realms of her imagination. She's an ambitious girl. I was astounded when she asked me. I told her she was silly. She had a rather weird view of the whole thing. Everyone knew it was silly.... It was too large a subject for Elspeth.[2]

Judith pressed her again as to how the Layton bio came about. Cameron said her "main connection" was Montreal. She'd not approached Gabrielle Roy, Dorothy Livesay, P.K. Page, or Phyllis Webb, as they weren't "part of the group 'til later," and were outside the time span she was looking at. The next sentence sticks out like a sore thumb: "Irving asked me to write his biography." If Morley Callaghan blew her off upon her approaching him, why in the world would Irving Layton suddenly jump up and ask her — of all potential biographers — to write about him? It defies logic.

As does her convoluted account of how they first met. According to Cameron, she "took him to lunch" upstairs (from the downstairs pub) in the posh Faculty Club. It seemed "the hospitable thing to do," as the University of Toronto had "no welcoming committee, no budget" with which to welcome their writers-in-residence. Oddly, if she was taking Irving to lunch as a semi-formal welcoming gesture, she neglected to make an appointment, and he was already eating lunch alone in the pub when she approached, according to Irving's account.

Cameron says they chatted about her MacLennan bio and biography in general when "he really rather suddenly said have you ever thought of writing a biography of me and I said no, and he said well, don't you think that would be a great idea or something like that and I said I'd like to think about it. It sounds like a great idea." Cameron also stated, "In the whole four years I interviewed him, I've not encountered any negativity. He's been 100 percent cooperative in every way."[3]

When Judith did this interview with Cameron, the battle had already begun. Oddly, Cameron claims to have expected what she calls Irving's "change of heart," infantilizing and patronizing him by pronouncing his anger as "a continuation of a pattern of behaviour that began very early. Temper tantrums. That's all. He gets very, very angry."[4] Newsflash: betrayal and scurrilous misrepresentation usually spawn anger. The "change of heart" is disingenuous, for Irving had cooperated, despite never being shown a word of what Cameron was writing. One of the first inklings that it would be other than so-so came when Judith obtained a set of page proofs, but more on that shortly.

One of the Cameron Affair's opening shots took place in March 1985. *Books in Canada* ran a cover story on Elspeth, written by John Goddard. Irving took strong exception to three misleading statements. His letter to Cameron is a model of restraint, considering he is addressing what he deems to be lies. Forceful, written through clenched teeth, he nevertheless kept the irony to a minimum, the tone impeccably civil. To set the record straight, here is his letter:

Dear Elspeth,

Yesterday, David O'Rourke gave me the March issue of *Books in Canada*. I was delighted to find you on its cover, looking your determined, attractive self. I eagerly turned to the article by John Goddard. He had called me several weeks ago to tell me he was writing the piece for *Books in Canada* and wanted to have some of my observations. By now, you probably know I do not have a very flattering opinion of journalists, since readability rather than veracity is their first consideration.

However, there are several misleading statements that I'd like to clear up, lest they cast a shadow over the nice working relationship, and I hope something more, that has developed between us since you began on my bio.

To take them in order. I simply do not recall asking you to write my biography. I was having my lunch [in the pub below the Faculty Club], the place was crowded and noisy, my hearing is not as acute as it once was, so there's the possibility of error on either your part or mine. Three things, nevertheless, persuade me that my version is the right one. One, it was you who joined me and not the other way around. Two, I just can't see myself, for all my much touted megalomania, asking anyone to write my biography. Three, assuming such a notion would occur to me, I don't think I would have asked you to be my biographer for at the time I was quite ignorant of the exceptional qualities of mind and heart you possess and which were only revealed to me on closer acquaintance. I thought your MacLennan bio was well done, but that it called for a pretty straight-forward telling about the main facts of Hugh's life. If I'm not mistaken, I believe I pointed out to you at the time that there's a great difference between a poet and a novelist, and that my life was not that of a sedentary writer. Apart from the episodes that life has thrust on me, I have deliberately sought out experiences that no sensible man would wish to have. My motto, one that I've served stubbornly right up until the present has been that a price must be paid for the poem that hopes to withstand the ravages of time.

"I go about making trouble for myself.
The sparks fly.
I gather each one
and start a poem."

"Now Layton has reservations about the project." An absolute total fabrication. I never expressed any reserva-tions either to him or to anyone else. As you know, I have given you my fullest cooperation, withholding nothing and trying my best to be as candid and honest about my life — warts, carbuncles, cysts and all — as is humanly possible. What I remember saying to Goddard and what I have said to others is what I have said to you: because I'm Jewish, have been a rebel and maverick at odds with my environment, because I hold with Plato that poets are mad, because my models are Dostoevsky and Kafka and no Anglo-Saxon has ever been able to come up with any-thing too illuminating to say about either of these writers, etc., my career and writing would pose a tremendous chal-lenge to anyone with your background and sensibility. But, dear Elspeth, you know all this as well as I do, so there's nothing more that I need add.

"As if anticipating a shortfall in Cameron's work, Layton, while continuing to cooperate with her, also begun writing his memoirs." Why do journalists invent such lies? I didn't undertake writing *Waiting for the Messiah* because I anticipate a "shortfall". As I have explained to you several times, I am writing my memoir because I want to give a picture from the inside of the inevitable and, yes, often tragic conflict between poet and society. The book deals only with the first 30 years of my life and has for its main focus the development of the poet's mind and sensibility. You may call it my PRELUDE, for what I tried to do is what Wordsworth did in his great autobiographical poem. In no way do I see it as competing with your own work, or in any way making it irrelevant or unnecessary. My memoir is now more than three-quarters done and I hope to have it finished by the middle of next month. If you can make it to Montreal before you leave, I should be happy to read you several chapters. I'm sure I don't need to tell you how eagerly I am looking forward to holding your volume in my hands. It won't surprise me the least bit should it turn out to be the lively, insightful, and meticulous book we both want it to be. With a warm embrace,

Avanti,
Irving Layton[5]

Howsoever flattering it may have been, Irving did not need an Elspeth Cameron to write about him. When she sought his permission, looking for her next subject in the hope of getting tenure, Layton was in post-Harriet hell. In this context, against this painful background, he let her go ahead. No one could guess just how specious her "portrait" would be.

As late as the summer of 1985, Irving was still reserving judgment on Cameron's book. Then Howard Aster sent a copy of Stoddart's promotional booklet featuring a scowling, bare-chested Irving fixing the public in a sulphurous death-stare. Startlingly, it was an Arnaud Maggs photo taken in Oakville two years earlier. Had they sent Arnaud with a mission to catch Irving unaware? It felt like a betrayal, more so when a reviewer spit on Irving's photo by intimating Maggs should get a prize for the unflattering pose. It may seem trivial now, but the Cameron Battle began with many such questions, all unanswered, snowballing with alarming speed. The booklet's excerpts showed Irving in an unsavoury triptych: a suspected public enemy, a herky-jerky idiot big on coitus interruptus, and a man plagued by loose bowels. We looked at each other not knowing whether to laugh or cringe after reading it. If the biography was anything like its promotional booklet, Irving had better brace for a negative caricature, a literary kick to the groin. There remained only to see how hard the kick, how wide the gap between scholarship and schlock. Even more vexing, Cameron had his full co-operation and go-ahead to write a "warts, carbuncles, cysts and all" book.[6]

When Cameron's book was taken on by Stoddart, Judith Fitzgerald told us she sat in on an editorial meeting where Cameron was told to forget about facts and just "sex it up." Shocked and angered by the conspiratorial slap at her former teacher, Fitzgerald later smuggled out a galley proof copy and sent it to Irving. I sat in Irving's study reading it through the night. At dawn, turning off the light, my bleary eyes fell on Nadezhda Mandelstam's *Hope Against Hope* on Irving's bookshelf. In Russia, they put a bullet in your head. In Canada, they set an Elspeth Cameron on you. I resolved to do everything in my power to help Irving counter her malevolent book.[7]

Over the coming days, Irving and I passed the galley copy back and forth, instinctively beginning to classify her missteps as bloopers, whoppers, factual errors, anti-Semitic barbs, and sick-making libellous filth. When, for example, Irving read that, according to Cameron, he grew engorged with money lust at his mother's death (a Jewish trait, apparently), practically rubbing his hands together anticipating the of couple thousand dollars he was to inherit, Irving's disgust with Cameron became boundless.

Almost immediately after reading that slur, he hit upon the passage where Cameron says his alleged sex obsession petered out with the advent of the 1960s. Now irrelevant, she asserts he looked for something else to shock the public with, another hot-button topic to mine. Not only does that betray a stunning lack of awareness about the man, his work, and his poetic process, but she then makes the most obscene, vilest, anti-Semitic characterization imaginable. I say "imaginable," because until that moment, it was beyond Irving's imagination that anyone could even think such a filthy thing about him let alone publish it: that Irving consciously decided to begin writing about the Holocaust because doing so "posed almost endless market possibilities."

That she would claim that he, Irving Layton, had sought to up his fame and to make money from the corpses of his murdered kin rendered him speechless and physically unable to move at first. Then, slowly, there rose in him anger so intense that no word exists to describe it. From that moment until the day he died, he never spoke her name unless broadcasting standards forced him to do so. Irving's name for Elspeth Cameron from that day forward was *The Whore*. She brought it on herself with her fabrications and overtly malicious stereotyping. Lying through her teeth, she invented scenes, such as Irving in a fetal position with Aviva, me, and Boschka cooing over him. On page 460, her sexual hang-ups concocted this lie: me and our guests exchanging our wildest erotic fantasies and sex dreams when, *in fact*, we were laughing over our funniest crank call stories, and then — *gasp* — exchanging ghost stories. In a later interview with Joel Yanofsky, published in the *Canadian Jewish News* (December 19, 1985), she lies through her teeth, saying that Irving sent her "hate mail almost every day for three weeks" and spent three hundred dollars on postage. Irving refuted that in a letter to the editor (January 23, 1986) with these facts: from January 1, 1985, to the day of his writing this letter, he wrote 290 letters to 156 correspondents, at a total cost in the neighbourhood of one hundred dollars. My record-keeping made it easy to refute her slanderous lies. Anyone can see the proof at Concordia's Layton Collection.

If her book was so bad, why not sue for defamation and libel? That was one of the first things Irving sought to do after going through every line of the published book, highlighting the slurs, errors, and prejudice. I sent my copy of her book, blue highlights marring almost every page, to Norman May, one of Irving's former Herzliah students who had become a Toronto lawyer. Unfortunately, May informed Irving that, being a public figure, a lawsuit was futile. Even if he could afford a protracted court case and the many trips to Toronto that would entail, and even if he was lucky enough to get an impartial judge, the best Irving could hope for might be a nominal dollar bill as restitution many years later. Worse still, a judge would likely slap a gag order on Irving, forcing us to live with the stench of her book in our nostrils without being able to ventilate or elaborate. Curiously, Mr. May's office never returned my copy, despite my asking by phone and in writing.

That being the case, Irving decided if she could denigrate and slur his standing as a poet, he could challenge her claim to being an academic scholar. For amusement's sake, the blooper lists we sent to everyone whom Irving felt ought to know what her book, and her scholarship, consisted of, are reproduced in Appendix 2.

Cameron's obsession with Irving's alleged sex life set our teeth on edge. An honest biographer, spending as much time as Elspeth did in Irving's company and studying his work, would have known he was actually quite prudish as well as gallant. Irving's ex-wife Aviva confirmed as much to Elspeth. The Irving-as-sex-machine image, though amusing, was untrue. The facts about Irving would have startled readers far more than hoary stereotypes. Instead, Cameron chose to wrap the same old smelly fish in new paper. Yet, to his shame, Robert Fulford, then-editor of *Saturday Night* and arbiter of Canadian culture, penned the booklet's main blurb, trumpeting Cameron's book as "setting a new standard in Canadian cultural biography." Irving would later make Fulford eat that blurb with heaping sides of irony and scorn.

It became clear the media was far from impartial, with publications such as *Quill & Quire* routinely censoring the most salient parts of Irving's letters to the editor. In his response to Beverley Slopen's article "An Outrageous Life" (*Quill & Quire*, July 1985), Irving called Cameron out for never asking him about his personal life, rhetorically asking if this was part of her methodology for writing what she deemed an "experimental" bio. *Quill & Quire* censored his question. Likewise, it censored the entire passage where he related how Joy Bennett, curator of Concordia's Layton Collection, exposed Cameron for never looking at over 150 drafts of his poems. Had Cameron eschewed reflection and analysis in favour of her intuition? Fair question, but he was not allowed to pose it. He concluded the letter with an open-ended question about Cameron's motivation. Perhaps her project was all about mining a saleable book for lucrative excerpt deals with *Chatelaine* and similar women's magazines. If so, "no bloodhound could sniff a favourable breeze with more acuity."[8] This too was censored.

For years, Canada's intelligentsia had characterized Irving as a megalomaniac who was so full of himself that he needed someone to write his biography. Had that been true, Elspeth Cameron would be the last person he would have approached. Sadly, for Canada's sake if not his own, Irving's vigorous, archly sincere protests were either mocked or ignored. By November 2, 1985, the *Toronto Sun*'s Yvonne Crittenden had reviewed the biography and autobiography. "Competing Portraits of the Poet" opens with the regurgitated lie that Irving asked Cameron to write his biography.

For reasons known only to his detractors, Irving's word carried little weight. The media had built a stereotype of a loudmouth Jew, infamously tub-thumping his way into the public eye. Now, they turned the volume down, censoring and/or ignoring his questions, his objections, and his growing outrage. Did Toronto's literary cognoscenti get together and plot against Irving? No, I do not think so — certainly not overtly — but who knows what the cocktail party chatter consisted of? Surely, it is fair to ask why fact sheets and devastating exposés with which we blanketed the literary world went unanswered. The only notice William French took was to claim in a December 28, 1985, column that Irving was "scurrilously attempting to damage [Elspeth Cameron's] reputation."[9] Peter Worthington went further, likening Irving to Jim Keegstra, a contemptible anti-Semitic Holocaust denier, accusing Irving of hating on the delicate Ms. Cameron.

Some of the letters or collated items (such as a clipping cut and pasted to a sheet with a letter typed out, meant to be photocopied) were given names for our amusement as well as ease of execution. For in this, Irving was like a brigadier general, planning strategy with me to help deploy tactics. A blistering letter to, say, the president of the University of Toronto mentioning Elspeth falsely calling herself a full professor (among other things) was sent with "The Stunner," "More Cameronian Bloopers," and "The Vanderhoof" as enclosures. It can now be told that amidst the outrage and muscular campaign to expose her shoddy work, we also had moments of tremendous complicit glee.

As mentioned earlier, we had no word processor let alone a photocopy machine, so for those three perfervid years, Irving would set off toward Concordia University's Loyola Campus with a folder tucked under his arm, in a plastic bag if it was raining or snowing, on a photocopying mission. At the Vanier Library, Irving welcomed much-needed help from librarian Marvin Orbach, who restocked the paper tray and always made change for Irving. Even years later, we recalled Marvin's singular kindness, sometimes getting *verklempt* thinking how rare such souls are. By the time Irving came back, I had readied envelopes and would then carefully trim the photocopies to letter size, for they only seemed to have legal size copy paper. I hated wasting paper, so those strips were cut in half and the halves stapled together into crude little booklets used for notes. I still have a few of these, souvenir jetsam somehow too precious to throw out. They represent sleepless nights; our outraged minds; and our bursting hearts.

No one but a handful had the balls join the fight. Not his sons; not his nephew Bill; not his dear friend Musia Schwartz, who marched him to the notary on Somerled where, at her insistence, he perjured himself in an affidavit saying they had never been lovers. She was fine when it never went beyond nods and winks over the years, but now, in a purported biography, the lady did not want the word to get out. Ever the gallant, Irving lied to save her bourgeois reputation. I stood there, agog, while she, agitated and imperious, waited while he pulled the five-dollar bill from his wallet, paying for the lie she asked him to tell.

Despite all the evidence we circulated, Montreal's Jewish Public Library still saw fit to invite Cameron to speak at an event, on the eve of Hanukkah, no less. Their local poet, despite having his memoir out concurrently with the biography, was denied the opportunity to speak. So much for equal time or fair play. In a letter to Montreal's Jewish Public Library's director, Zipporah Shnay, dated December 13, 1985, Irving expressed his disgust for the library having invited Cameron to speak when the whole country had been apprised of her book's fatal flaws. He tells Shnay of listening to CBC Radio's *Arts Report*,[10] and hearing the catcalls, jeers, and insults hurled at me. The predominantly Jewish audience shouted at me to "shut up," "sit down," and "take it to a lawyer," among other things, when I held up evidence of Cameron's bias and incompetence.[11] The audio clip ends with my declaring her book a hatchet job, and that Cameron was not fit to polish Irving's boots.

Irving had not trusted himself to stay civil, so I had gone to the event alone, but armed with enough "Cameronian Blooper" lists to place one on almost every seat. As Cameron made her way onstage, I glanced around to see the lists fluttering throughout the room like white, rectangular aspen leaves. My attempt at questioning Cameron after her talk provoked an ugliness I had never thought possible (and which was only partially captured on the CBC report). Irving became incensed when told of what they did to me. After Cameron's talk, the emcee, Carole Burke, invited questions from the audience. I was already at the microphone. When I pointed out the shame of having the author of such anti-Semitic dreck here on the eve of Hanukkah, the audience shouted me down, particularly the VIPs in the front row. After my third attempt to ask Cameron why she had lied about interviewing me and why she published a private letter without my consent or permission, I was ordered away from the microphone. To Burke's hectoring and the audience's jeers, I walked with slow deliberate grace back to my seat. Standing in the middle of the aisle, I proceeded to do a very slow reverse strip tease, picking up my long navy blue coat and swinging it like a cape in a broad swoop over my shoulders. One sleeve; the other sleeve; then my scarf, then, arms extended and raised to about eye level, I donned one glove, then the other, pulling each finger down snugly, before walking slowly down the aisle toward the stage and a quaking Cameron. Left face; measured steps. I reached the lobby and nearly collapsed into an unknown lady's embrace. She literally took me in her arms and, if memory serves, was a psychologist who empathized as to the ugliness of what had just taken place. I do not recall her name, only her ineffable kindness.

In his letter to Shnay, Irving refers to me for perhaps the first time as his fiancée. He also promises to continue expressing his grievances and dissatisfactions until he saw convincing evidence of reform and change. In closing, he declares he can no longer consider himself part of Montreal's great Jewish community, vowing never again to set foot in the Jewish Public Library until they apologize to him and to "*Anna Pottier, my bride-to-be.*"[12] To the best of my knowledge, no apology ever came, nor did he break his vow.

That is but one of hundreds of battle scenes. To give a tiny glimpse at what it was like, here, on the following pages, is an example of my attempt at cataloguing the Cameron Affair. It covers only the period from March to November of 1985. After that, I had no time to breathe let alone keep track of who said what. What stands out vividly is how little impact our efforts had for the first two years. It was as if we sent envelopes stuffed with blank paper to Canada's intellectual elite for all the notice they took of the facts documented on the following pages.

As unnerving and angry-making this entire episode was, we managed to keep fighting. Nor did we lose our sense of humour, despite what anyone might think upon reading Irving's letters meant to set the record straight. Poems such as "Monsters" for Elspeth and "Herbert Vunce" for Robert Fulford, as well as more generalized ones, came from this fertile muck.

Happily, nothing stays the same. All wars eventually come to an end. It pleases me still to note how by the fall of 1989, close to four years after the Cameron Affair began, Irving lived to see the tide begin to turn, his reputation restored, and his critics dealt their comeuppance.

Ken Adachi, the *Toronto Star*'s chief book editor to whom Irving sent a blistering letter (September 27, 1985) pointing out how this was far more complex than a mere "literary feud," and another letter (October 7, 1988) excoriating him for, among other things, saying Irving was mad because Cameron hadn't praised him enough, was caught in a second plagiarism scandal and entered into a suicide pact with his wife on February 9, 1989. She lived; he did not.[13] Robert Fulford said he retired; others hinted he was pushed from his plum position as editor of *Saturday Night*. William French, when not ignoring the jaw-dropping evidence that shredded Cameron's claims of scholarship and academic rigour, did nothing more than ridicule Irving. Later, the Cameron Affair over, French found the journalistic courage to go off on on an author for having — gasp — misspelled the word "Ottowa". It left Irving and me shaking our heads in amazement."

TABLE OF CONTENTS

...page 2

45. Oct. 7/'85   Received copy of David O'Rourke's (Sept26) letter to CHATELAINE
46. Oct. 7/'85   Note to E. Cameron
47. Oct.10/'85   Letter to E. Cameron (...piss from a whore's diseased vagina...)
48. Oct.12/'85   Article in THE CITIZEN (Ottawa) by Judith Fitzgerald re: E. Cameron
49. Oct.12/'85   Article in WINDSOR STAR by Judith Fitzgerald re: E. Cameron/bio
50. Oct. '85   issue of QUILL & QUIRE with review by Robin Skelton of both books
51. Oct.12/'85   Excerpt of WFTM in MONTREAL GAZETTE
52. Oct.19/'85   Review in MONTREAL GAZETTE by JOel Yanofsky of both books
53. Oct. 19/'85   Review in TORONTO STAR by Ken Adachi of both books
54. Oct. 19/'85   Review in GLOBE & MAIL by William French of both books
55. Oct.22/'85   Letter to Editor of TORONTO STAR re: Item # 53
56. Oct. 24/'85   Mention in THE THURSDAY REPORT (Concordia U.) re: Irving and Elspeth
57. Oct. 25/'85   Review in MACLEAN'S (Oct. 28 issue) by Brian Johnson of both books
58. Oct. 25/'85   Letter to Editor of MACLEAN'S re: Item # 57
59. Oct. 26/'85   Review in WINNIPEG FREE PRESS by Allen Mills of both books
60. Oct. 26/'85   Review in THE CITIZEN (Ottawa) by Phyllis Grosskurth of both books
61. Oct. 29/'85   Letter to Phyllis Grosskurth re: Item # 60
62. Oct. 30/'85   Addendum to Item # 61
63. Oct. ?/'85   Letter to Editor of GLOBE & MAIL by Karen Pietkiewicz re: bloopers in bio
64. Oct. 30/'85   Letter to Editor of MONTREAL GAZETTE by Anna Pottier re: bloopers in bio
65. Nov. 2/'85   Review in THE VANCOUVER SUN by Jim Christy of both books
66. Nov. 3/'85   Letter to Doug Beardsley re: meaning of Layton/Cameron fight
67. Nov. 3/'85   Mention in TORONTO STAR by Beverly Slopen re: launching parties
68. Nov. 3/'85   Review in TORONTO SUN by Patricia Job of both books
69. Nov. 3/'85   Article in TORONTO SUN by Jean Sonmor re: battle
70. Nov. 5/'85   Notice of reading at Harbourfront in GLOBE & MAIL
71. Nov. 5/'85   Letter to Editor of TORONTO STAR re: Item #53 as it appeared
72. Nov. 5/'85   Letter to Editor of MACLEAN'S (Nov. 11 issue) re: Item #57 as it appeared
73. Nov. 7/'85   Article in CANADIAN JEWISH NEWS by Elaine Kahn re: bloopers in bio
74. Nov. ?/'85   Composite with Items # 73 and 58 sent to many people
75. Nov. 8/'85   Review in GLEBE REPORT (Ottawa) by Sharon Drache of WFTM
76. Nov. ?/'85   Composite with Items # 63 and 64, quote by R. Ormrod, bloopers & blurb
78. Nov. 9/'85   Letter to Editor in THE VANCOUVER SUN by F. Mansbridge re: Item #65
79. Nov. 9/'85   Letter to Elspeth Cameron
80. Nov. '85   issue of BOOKS IN CANADA with review by Bruce Powe
81. Nov. '85   Review in CANADIAN FORUM by Pat Keeney-Smith of both books
82. Nov. 11/'85   Letter to Pat Keeney-Smith re: Item # 81
83. Nov. 15/'85   Letter to William Taylor re: Cameron's book
84. Nov. 16/'85   Review in THE HAMILTON SPECTATOR by Howard Aster of both books
85. Nov. 16/'85   Notices in MONTREAL GAZETTE and GLOBE & MAIL re: WFTM
86. Nov. 22/'85   Mention in MONTREAL GAZETTE by Thomas Shnumacher re: Elspeth's reading

There was a sea change. New blood appeared on the scene; other critics found courage enough to say they reread Irving's work and had to adjust their opinions accordingly. The cherry on this rancid sundae would have to be the sublimely gratifying cover of *Toronto*, the *Globe and Mail's* glossy magazine insert of March 1988. The cover featured a staid white, middle-class couple like wax figures in a museum diorama of same. Before them, a large bronze plaque identifying them as the now extinct species: WASP Torontonensis c. 1800–1988. The cover had me and Irving guffawing, if not high-fiving. It was as if the *Globe* published it as a birthday gift for their erstwhile nemesis.

Like the tender green shoots of grass that always fascinated Irving, poking up through thick black asphalt, hope, too, sprang eternal. One of the happiest moments of our entire life together was the Saturday morning when we, holding hands, went "up Somerled" to pick up the papers. On August 19, 1989, we hoped but were unsure whether the *Toronto Star* would run a feature interview and review of *Wild Gooseberries*, Irving's selected letters. We hurried into The Paper Nook, our favourite newsstand. There it was. No two happier people ever picked up a newspaper. On the book section insert's cover, a full-page colour photo of Irving. He looked as impish, roguish, and rampant as I had ever seen him.

It was over.

We won. We had engaged Cameron and Canada's literary establishment as if Irving's life depended on it. In a way, it did. Had Irving chosen to "rise above it" as some advised, the enduring image of him would be that of a sex-obsessed, lecherous Jew; a risible skirt-chasing megalomaniac. Instead, we bested Cameron and her ilk hands-down, yes, but at tremendous cost.

Looking back, as I do now, fighting nothing but the tears in my eyes remembering how Irving thanked me for helping him win the battle, it pleases me to think how no one can ever take that moment away from him, nor erode my own splendid memory of that summer morning when, like two generals, save for the way we held hands, going up Somerled and all the way back home.

Irving resting his back, reading Graham Greene in our rented cottage, San Jose, California, February 1984.

I call this one "Me, More or Less" in the midst of doing "Layton Enterprizes," 1989. The desk was not always so messy, but I knew where everything was.
(Photo by Irving Layton, from the author's personal collection)

Irving, me, and Leonard Cohen, strolling on Montreal's famous Main after lunch at the Hebrew Deli.
(Photo by Aviva Whiteson, from the author's personal collection)

May 1985, moments after completing *Waiting for the Messiah*, the draft chapters splayed out to see the entire year's work. There was little time to enjoy the moment or recover from the strain, as we left for Athens shortly thereafter.

At the University of Athens where Irving was about to give a lecture on Canadian poetry.
(Photo reproduced with kind permission of Lucinda Vardey)

Crashing the Montreal International Film Festival closing gala,
September 1, 1986. When Giulietta Masina invites you in, you go in!
(Photo by Lois Siegel)

Taken September 17, 1988, this truly captures the time after the battle and a little before the downslide, savouring all that we had, all that we were.

(Photo by Irving's dear friend, the late Sam Tata)

May 25, 1992. On the balcony of the Olive Press Hotel in Molivos, Irving watched swallows building a nest. "Nest Building" became his last complete published poem.

Possibly taken on March 1, 1995, the day I moved out. Shaken by the ineffable sadness of it, I blocked the image from my mind. The negative, unseen for nineteen years, was discovered as I completed this book.

March 1, 2001. People left us alone that day at Concordia's reception marking the final acquisition of Irving's papers. These were the last moments of the last time we saw each other.
(Photo by Andrew Dobrowolskyj, © Concordia University)

28: Wedding Over the Atlantic

BY EARLY 1986, despite our fraught lives, we hadn't lost the knack for finding pleasure — or letting it find us. One day, it arrived in the form of Irving's *decree nisi*. A mere formality really, but we could marry if we felt like it. Fighting against the culture mavens' anti-Layton slant was an exhaustive test, forging us into much more than a couple. Nothing could possibly tear us asunder. Marriage was in the air.

There was nothing quite like watching Fellini's *La Dolce Vita*, huddled and cuddled in front of the fire, to ignite romantic notions. Sylvia and Marcello in the Fontana di Trevi; me and Irving strolling towards the same fountain on our next visit. I always made it a point to lob big Italian coins into the Trevi Fountain, ensuring a return trip to Rome.

Ipso presto, Alfredo Rizzardi invited Irving on a reading tour slated for early March of 1986. Why not get married at Rome's City Hall? It was as if we both envisioned the same imaginary newsreel footage, me daintily coming down City Hall's marble steps, perhaps with a small hat and half-veil shielding my bridal glow from lusty well-wishers.

We made an appointment with the Italian consul-general to ask if it were even possible. Yes, it certainly was, he told us, his face beaming his blessings, honoured we had chosen Rome for our nuptials. All we needed was to have our *documenti* translated into Italian. The flight was already booked, leaving no time to scramble for birth certificates, translations, and such like. We thanked the consul and trudged out, feeling a bit shrivelled with disappointment.

Another day, another plan: why not get married at *Montreal*'s City Hall, and turn the reading tour into our honeymoon trip? It sounded feasible, that is, until I went to City Hall and learned we had to fill out an application. I still have it amongst my papers, our names and address typed in, the rest of the form untouched. Irving was repulsed at the thought of some clerk, who would probably refuse to speak English, checking the application, perhaps grilling us on what we thought marriage was. Love subjugated by bureaucracy was offensive and absurd.

We needed no one's permission to be husband and wife. Love, trust, and a slender wedding band for me would suffice. I wanted to show the world my bond to Irving; he, as far as I was concerned, needed no such symbol. To put it another way, let's face it: I was his fifth and final wife, so for Irving to don such a conventional symbol bordered on the farcical. Besides, there was not a lot of surplus cash in the kitty.

In 1986 I was already sporting a tiny diamond solitaire. My mother sent it, presumably hoping people would think my *vieux* had given me an engagement ring, thereby mitigating the shame of my being "shacked up." *Shacked up, doormat,* and *indecent* were some of her favourite weapon-words.

That March, Irving and I took bus and metro down to Birks, Montreal's answer to Tiffany's. Bent over the long glass counter like a pair of apostrophies, we inched along and found a perfect gold band: slim, but enough to set me apart as a married woman. It was only seventy-five dollars, and they could resize it in a few days.

On a miserably cold morning, I set off alone to pick up my ring. Grey skies mirrored the sad, pensive mood taking hold. Irving had tried to come with me that morning, but it was too bleak, too icy. I did not want him falling or catching a cold just before flying to Italy. My red wool coat's sassy one-button closing at the neck and swingy verve bolstered my spirits as I attempted feeling coltish and giddy the way a fiancée was supposed to feel. Instead, a grim awareness took hold. Irving was becoming fragile, too old to accompany me safely on such a blustery day. Saddened, feeling a new kind of aloneness, I rearranged my thoughts as one would furniture in a room, determined to make the best of whatever lay ahead. My PincuVing was snug at home reading a book, no doubt blasting an aria on the radio, probably singing away. What was there not to be grateful for?

I tucked the ring in my purse so that Irving could place it on my finger later, and hurried to the stationery place, my second errand of the day. Now laden with typewriter ribbon, whiteout fluid, carbons, onion-skin paper, and premium stationery watermarked "Linen Record," I set out for home. As I stepped onto the sidewalk, a man with a fedora and horn-rimmed glasses ran into me almost hard enough to knock the parcels out of my arms. No harm done, I assured the odd, intense man. He seemed down on his luck. The once-elegant dark blue cashmere greatcoat and silk scarf were dander-flecked and frayed; his brogues salt-stained and worn. We talked a bit, the man asking about my paper and typewriter ribbon. Unable to contain my excitement, conversation turned to writing and that I was about to leave for Rome with my soon-to-be husband, a writer. Curious, the man politely asked who my beau was, nearly jumping out of his brogues when I told him.

"Well, I'll *be!* I've just met Irving Layton's Queen Bee!" he exclaimed with an amazed whistle and whoop. His face and entire demeanour broke into in a sudden joyful uplift. I noticed his eyes pooling a bit, probably from the cold wind, I thought. Then he confided his terrible secret. "I was going to go home and kill myself this afternoon," he said, intimating his despairing descent from privileged beginnings. Having met Irving Layton's Queen Bee, grateful that I had stopped to talk rather than push past him, he now felt hopeful enough to stay his plans. Whenever I think of the time Irving and I began calling ourselves husband and wife, I always remember that man, Mr. Clark — or was it Cox — his Boston accent, and the silvery stubble on his wind-red face as he smiled and waved me onwards.

There was no wedding per se. Jack McClelland sent a bottle of champagne, hand-delivered by the McClelland & Stewart sales rep. Word got out to the press. The night before leaving for Italy, I called home as I always did before travelling any great distance. After the awkward, forced cheeriness and intense confirmations about the weather that characterized our phone calls, I was determined to announce that Irving and I were getting married — and to ask their blessing.

At least we no longer had to maintain the housekeeper pretense, not after *Chatelaine* ran that full-colour spread promoting Cameron's book, outing me to the world as mate number five. Hopefully, they had digested most of their bile and embarrassment. Perhaps promotion to wife status would appeal to them, if only to soften the "shacked-up" shame. I could not have misread the situation more. Steadying my voice, I tried going for an authoritative, mature register. When I asked my mother for her blessing, there was only silence — a hollow buzz coming through the receiver. Feeling as though backhanded hard across the face, my voice cracking, I asked her to put Dad on the phone. Like a masochist pulling cuticles off in long bloody strips, I repeated my plans and gave my father a chance to offer his blessings. The only sound was me choking back sobs in a rising red-hot wave of hurt and anger. I can never forget the silence with which they answered my simple, impossible request. Nor the way Irving comforted me after I hung up, trying to soothe me so that I would not hate my parents, and perhaps even forgive them — they could not condone what they could not understand. Still, the rift widened, never to be bridged.

We told Montreal friends we were to marry in Italy. We told our Italian friends we had married in Montreal. So, somewhere over the mid-Atlantic on a night-flight to Rome, we toasted each other as Irving placed the slender band on my finger. From then on, we were husband and wife.

The Italian honeymoon was rife with sensory and intellectual delights, as though seen through a magnifying lens. Ettore arranged two nights for us at Hotel Sole, a three-hundred-year-old hotel looking out over the Pantheon. We then moved to the more economical Hotel Smeraldo where I was mistaken for Irving's granddaughter. Deeming the clerk's intent as innocent, I proudly showed him my left hand and, smiling like Gelsomina in Fellini's *La Strada*, set him straight with an "O nooon, Signore. Io sonno La Moglie!" (Oh nooo, Sir. I am the Wife!) He smiled at Irving, me, and back to Irving after only a momentary splutter. The Smeraldo became home base for a week of walking all over Rome, dodging Vespas, thrilled at every sight, taste, and sound.

Irving marked his seventy-fourth birthday with a reading at Rome's La Sapienza University and an interview with Vatican radio. There was even a jaunt with me to Naples where I showed him my old haunts. Ettore threw a grand dinner party at his place. Elegance. Ease. Talk. Exquisite food. Ettore kindly brought us to the local police station to help Irving report his stolen wallet. Always fond of tempting fate, he had done one of his "cheat destiny" stunts boarding a Rome subway car. Holding his wallet aloft, he shouted over the din, "See Anna, they won't be able to steal my purse, because I'm putting it right here in my *front* pocket!" He never felt a thing.

Ettore painted my portrait that evening, tired as he was, my red silk scarf vibrantly adorning my ponytail on the canvas. I looked Spanish, formidable, wise, and womanly. We never discussed purchasing the painting, nor did we ever see it after that night. I coveted it, wanted to hang it next to Irving's portrait. Alas, we never did ask how much Ettore wanted for it.

In Fiano, Irving and I smoked cigarettes with our shots of espresso, then strolled through surrounding fields toward the village, bringing back a few groceries. Local farmers peered at us from passing cars. Sometimes, their faces hardened, making me feel like Irene Pappas in *Zorba the Greek,* the victim of cutting stares if not knives. Ettore returned from his dawn to noon painting excursions with warm bread, salamis, figs, asparagus, pears, or whatever was freshest, and made a gourmet meal served with a cheeky Lambrusco or Villa Antinori red. The highlight of the day for us: going into the studio's anteroom after dinner to view Ettore's work. Irving voiced his admiration with articulate, heartfelt interpretations. Affection and respect floated in the air between painter and poet like music. Out of this communion came the poem "For Ettore, With Love and Admiration."

Next, a reading at the University of Bologna, then on to Milan for dinner at the painter Aligi Sassu's home, then other lunches, other dinners. In Milan, we stayed at a small pensione on Via Senato, making time to visit the Verdi home for retired opera singers. Aged performers shuffled about, still marvellously theatrical and self-centred as children, their voices all but gone. They moved Irving deeply. If he thought of himself as an aging artist who might one day need to be in a special home, he hid it well. Praising Verdi's generosity, we continued our ramble humming *Va Pensiero*, absorbing every pleasure we could.

Honeymoon over and home again, I soon took enormous pleasure sending letters to the editor, signing myself Mrs. Irving Layton. On one occasion, a CBC *National News* piece about the Intifada struck me as unfairly slanted against Israel, prompting calls to CBC's nerve centre in Toronto. Acting a part, but not acting, I'd bark into the phone, "Hello. Get me the news director!"

"Who's calling, please?"

"Tell him it's Mrs. Irving Layton."

To my surprise, it worked — at least insofar as being able to vent my grievance to the top brass. On my next two passport applications, I listed my name as Anna Pottier-Layton, not even providing proof of a name-change. Fact is, there was no such proof.

My name remained Annette Marie Pottier only on letters addressed to me by my mother. I expressly told her not to call me that. Anna Pottier-Layton was fine, as was Mrs. Irving Layton. She refused, angrily sending me a photocopy of her marriage certificate. Until I could send her a copy of *my* marriage certificate, she refused to honour my request. It was hopeless to think anything I did or said would ever meet with her approval.

Some time after returning from Italy, Irving was invited to Ottawa to give a reading. We took the train this time. It was now mid-winter. Irving sat at a window seat and began coughing loudly. I tapped him on the back as the fit continued. My hand still resting on his shoulder, I bent closer to see if he was choking and thought of running to get him some water, but the coughing subsided. About two rows behind me, on the other side of the aisle, a clear young voice called out anxiously, "Hey! Ma'am. Is your husband okay?" I turned to answer, happy that someone unhesitatingly called Irving my husband, and saw a small round face tilted to one side, waiting for assurance that everything was okay. "Yes, thank you," I said, "my husband is okay." The young boy, though with certain challenges, was not blind to love's distinctive shape. He was the first to see the invisible threads binding us together as a married couple. That clear, high voice rang with more authority than any judge or rabbi could ever command. With that, we considered our union witnessed and blessed as if by God himself.

PART FOUR:

RESOLUTION

29: Downdrafts

WE RETURNED FROM Ottawa to the usual stack of letters and requests; cold, icy streets; and the fight against his biographer. There were, however, some things to look forward to. Irving finally agreed to play Socrates for two performances in a fundraiser for Montreal's Centaur Theatre. Director Maurice Podbrey had gently pressured Irving for several months, coaxing him to sign on.

Irving's reluctance stemmed not only from lack of time, but the fear of not being able to remember his lines. Shooting the Tom Longboat movie three years earlier had not been easy. Back then, my reassurances eased Irving's anxiousness — of *course* it was hard to memorize someone else's lines, given how stressed he was from the divorce, and how packed his schedule. In 1983 he was tired, but still in full command of his faculties. Each passing year, his very real Alzheimer's anxiety grew in worrisome increments. In his poem "Senile, My Sister Sings," his sister Esther famously defies death and dementia by singing along with Irving, who prompted her with a song she had loved as a young woman. Irving told me how she one day tried returning home from shopping, only to become paralyzed with fear on a street corner, not knowing where she was nor how to get home. The disease incapacitated her for the last fifteen years of her life. Esther's fate haunted him.

Worse still, he would be live, on-stage with other actors depending on him to stay in character and with no way to edit mistakes. Irving's professionalism had initially driven him to refuse — flubbing lines and looking like a fool held no appeal. I could see how frightened he was, how he dreaded confirming that his memory was starting to go. However, both performances packed the theatre and were a triumph. Perhaps the most taxing part of the shows was staying in character for the live Q&A that followed. People asked about Cameron; Irving responded as Socrates, the experience resulting in his poem "Socrates at the Centaur."

As if dark premonitions about his brain's condition were not enough, Irving could always count on his family to provide even more anxiety. My wedding ring did not change relations with Irving's children. They continued to accept me as a fact of their father's life — nothing more, nothing less. Naomi stayed with us for a couple of weeks, being alternately sweet and trying in her unique way. She taught me how to make biryani and shared memories of her California girlhood. Some were upsetting, such as the time she was seated inappropriately on a man's lap in his truck while he drove down the highway. Her guitar playing, so determined, so close to divine, was heartbreaking as ever. Max also came to visit that summer.

In all honesty, neither Irving nor I quite looked forward to Max's visits. Tension filled the house the moment he arrived. We braced for his riptide recriminations, often tacit, sometimes thrown on the table like a virtual accusatory dead fish. I made sure there was wine and cognac, served nice meals, and let the philosophy debates rage. Well, Max raged, Irving mostly listened, countering enough to keep up the façade of a debate rather than a "son venting at his father" scenario.

The most harrowing visit took place a few years later in 1990. It started when Irving and I vacationed in the Dominican Republic in January 1989, contracting dysentery so severe as to require medical attention. I never wanted to set foot on that island again. David, meanwhile, went there to work on a novel and Max insisted we have a family holiday the following year. In a tragedy of errors, we ended up going, arriving just after Max left. Max claimed to have spent two thousand dollars on our travel package, oddly not telling us which hotel or flight we were supposed to have taken, and was enraged that we had "stood him up." Max probably felt we had missed him on purpose in favour of being with David (who was gone anyway, having headed home with

an eye infection). Beyond livid, Max phoned later to scream vulgar-
ities at his father. Irving listened, bemused, and handed me the receiver.
"Here! You explain it to him again."

Max went apoplectic, ordering me to put his father back on the
phone. "You're nothing to me, Anna, you mean less to me than a pot of
clay. Now put my father back on the phone."

"You've insulted your father quite enough," I said, banging the receiver down.

It was ugly. Angry letters were exchanged. After some time, Max
came to our home in Montreal and exploded in a display of menacing
wrath and malice the likes of which I have never seen before or since.
He was shaking with rage and decades of built-up resentment. Sitting
across from Irving at the dining room table, with me seated at the head,
Max began threatening Irving with a "curse" if he did not get Irving's
"blessing." Irving sat back in his chair, folded his arms, and braced for
the onslaught. Max's voice rose higher and louder with each grievance.
There was a "plot," he said, a plot to cast him as Esau to David's Jacob. The
biblical references were lost on me, but not on Irving, who sat there un-
flinching while Max, his purple-faced son, raised his arm high, holding
what he said was the jaw-bone of an ass. Veins popping, flecks of spittle
marring the corners of his mouth, Max shook his fist and threatened to
come back and "smite his father" if he dared treat his second-born son
better than his first-born son. He pounded the table so hard, his face so
disfigured with fury that I was ready to call the police at any moment.
Veering away from biblical characterizations, he then demanded to
know what was in the will for him, how much, and why could he not
get his share right now. At which point Irving reminded Max that he
already had in his possession a set of Irving's entire works, having given
Max his own collection some time ago, and reminded Max of the ten
thousand dollars he loaned him in order to help buy a house, but which
Max invested in a business instead. Max denied receiving the loan, until
I pointed out I had the cheque upstairs, it had been cashed and returned
for Irving's records. His memory improved suddenly, admitting he had
paid back half.

Irving said little else throughout these awful minutes, listening to

Max's threats and accusations until they all crashed down around him. Spent, and with something of a hang-dog expression, Max in turn bore the brunt of his father's response. Irving's voice, icy with disdain, reminded Max that he was still very much alive, and that he could do whatever he damn well pleased with his money and his estate. Only years later did it come to light that Max believed his father was wealthy. Nothing could have been further from the truth, if wealth were measured only in dollars.

There are other such stories of the family's disregard for Irving's feelings, such as Aviva actually calling Irving to ask if he knew of a good used-book dealer to whom she could sell her copies of Irving's books. The phone in the downstairs hallway had volume control on the receiver, which Irving turned up to maximum, making it easy for me to hear entire conversations from the dining room or kitchen. I was appalled that she would ask Irving where to unload books no doubt inscribed to her. Betraying nothing of the hurt her question caused, Irving suggested she try David Mason Books in Toronto and left it at that. After he hung up, it was plain to see her question had cut like the proverbial, poison-dipped knife.

As for my family relations, I was faring even worse than Irving. I had always thought of my parents as truly good people. That all changed when they realized that my allegiance, indeed my identity, became Jewish. My "conversion" happened while watching Anatoly (Natan) Scharansky, the famous Russian refusnik, being released to freedom. Watching on live television on February 11, 1986, as he crossed the Glienicke Bridge, I realized I was feeling exactly the same as all Jews watching around the world. That became my secular Bat Mitzvah. Catholicism had never taken root with me, at least nothing beyond the warm-fuzzies at Christmas that settled briefly over our non-demonstrative family. I was a natural-born skeptic. My mother could live with that, but *not* with my becoming Jewish, and my father had no choice but to follow her lead. On one visit home, I found a *National Geographic* that had a feature on the death camps, with photos of a mountain of eyeglasses and a vast pile of shoes. Hoping my father could relate to these personal objects and would, like myself, feel horror at the injustice done to Jews, I held the magazine up to him, my voice trembling, begging him to look, to understand. It had no effect. My mother's term for my interest in Judaism and my desire to take on the identity was "Jew jazz." As in, "enough of that *Jew jazz,*" which she wrote to me after I returned to Montreal.

In another letter she sent not long after our return from the honeymoon, she let her guillotine blade come flying down on what was left of our mother-daughter relationship. There was something I should know, she writes. Namely, my own mother informed me that should I be killed in a plane crash or if I died from a heart attack, she wanted nothing to do with my remains. Furthermore, my corpse was not welcome in the parish cemetery. There was no family plot as such, but for at least five generations, local Pottiers all ended up in the Ste.-Anne-du-Ruisseau cemetery.

It took some four months for the full import of her words to sink in. What crime had I committed? Was I a murderer? A prostitute? A drug addict, perhaps? No. But I had chosen to live happily as a free-spirited, independent woman. Also, I converted in my own way to secular Judaism and married a secular Jew — a life path apparently worse than all the standard shame inducers. A news story from those days about a missing sex-worker in Vancouver showed the mother holding her daughter's photo, tearfully pleading for the public's help as she searched for her prostitute daughter. If *that* mother could love her child, why couldn't mine love me?

My mother actually approached the Bishop to ask what happens to a Catholic's soul if they become Jewish. She was in a quandary, unable to bury me according to Catholic rituals, nor could she risk arranging a Jewish funeral, as that would compromise her ability to get to Heaven. I wrote back saying it was a pity my death interested her more than my life. While she rocked in her rocking chair and feared for her soul, I screamed to Irving through many tearful days and nights, "Even a mother cat does not do that to one of her kittens!"

Dad died in 1999. His will made no mention of me, presumably because he was unable to act independently of my mother's disdain. I didn't exist? Fine. I later perfected my non-existence by changing my name legally to Anna Pottier, effectively killing off Annette Marie Pottier. Visiting Nova Scotia after his death, I confronted my mother about pressuring him to disown me, and she could not deny it. She did, however, deny writing the letter about not wanting my remains. For what it's worth, I still have the letter. My mother, despite the appearance of a normalized relationship, tried to disown me as well. Only my brother's intervention prevented it at the last moment. At her death in 2011, I disposed of her things, staying alone in the house for an entire month. She had saved items such as leftover gauze bandages from the time my brother accidentally blew his finger off in 1972, newspapers headlining Pierre Trudeau election victories, and other such ephemera. My letters to her dating from 1975 to 2011, save two or three sent within months of her death, were never found and, I suspect, were burnt by her.

The one letter I wrote to my father was to tell him about the rejection of my remains. The letter and eight-by-ten black-and-white photo I sent, a self-portrait of my stunned, brooding face, went unanswered. After my mother died, I found the opened letter in its original envelope buried in the linen cupboard. She probably never gave it to Dad, and forgot to burn it along with my letters sent over a thirty-nine-year span.

On their one visit to Montreal during my years with Irving, they phoned a mile from the house, insisting I take a taxi to have dinner with them. They categorically refused to come to the house. I had hoped they would, wanting desperately to do the ask-Dad-about-renovations thing. Instead, I did my best with what I knew, updating the bathroom. The hired handyman did as much damage as improvements. Dad would never have allowed such bad tile work and scratched floors. The tiles stayed that way, for Irving's literary harvest work now began in earnest.

Despite the quickening pace and breathlessness of having several volumes of selected poems in the works, we relished it all while leaning on one another. These last poems and last books spurred Irving to get everything done while he still could. Yet he continued making time for me, letting my mother-anguish play out for weeks, listening patiently, watching me parse her hateful "remains" letter until there was nothing left to analyze. In retrospect, perhaps Max's anger at me stemmed in part from envy. I seemed to receive his father's best attentions, though a mate is not an offspring. Speculation, alas, serves no purpose after all the *sturm und drang*.

As to my mother's resentment: my crimes included following my heart's desire; daring to slough off the trappings of a conventional life; and, most unforgivably, being happy. Irving's tireless empathy allowed me to scrape my hull clean of her barnacle resentments and sail ahead all the more swiftly. Nor did Irving ever speak harshly against my parents. "Your mother has just done you a huge favour," he explained gently, "you can't bring her with you where you are going. Best to leave her behind. She's still your mother, you still need to call on her birthday or Mother's Day, but you can not bring her with you into your world."

He was absolutely right.

30: Of Triumphs and a Dedication

FOR IRVING, FINDING the energy to write poems rather than blistering *samizdats* was not a problem, as poems from this period grew from the same steamy swamp, becoming part of *Final Reckoning: Poems 1982–1986*. What changed was the level of urgency that began to take hold, slowly at first, then becoming fever-pitched by the early 1990s. Titles such as *Final Reckoning* and *Tutto Sommato* (1989) hint at Irving's desire to sum up, to distill the last essences of his poetic vision before the flame died.

Final Reckoning, Irving explained, was a summing up, a meditation on death. Death enhances our feeling for living; there is nothing depressing in *Final Reckoning*, because of its affirmation of Life. One night, after watching a PBS documentary on the Holocaust, Irving remarked how "we stand in awe, are terrified of the unknown pornography of death. [It] takes a very violent turn because we are extremely terrified of death. So, we familiarize ourselves with it in violent movies, in the Holocaust. In the same way we have an urge to throw a snowball at a man wearing a top hat, we want to degrade sex and death, because we are in awe."

In early January 1986, Irving worked non-stop for two days, writing many drafts of "Norbert Vunce." What began as a personal attack on Robert Fulford, editor of *Saturday Night* magazine, evolved into an indictment of Toronto's clannish gang of hacks, yuppies, and lazy journalists. I typed the final draft and saw Irving off to Concordia's Vanier Library to make photocopies. No sooner had I settled at my desk than Irving burst up the steps, coming straight into my study and asking me to make "one small change."

"I was just about to put the dime into the machine and run it off," he said excitedly, "when it struck me that the word *daring* was too grey, too dull to match *leaf green*. The word has to be *dazzling*. Oh! That's *it*! It has to be a colourful, alive word there, and *dazzling*'s the one!"

There was no denying such exhilaration. My eye rolls and laboured sighs were no match for his tsunami onslaughts. Besides, he knew my protests were pro forma, part of the games we played to amuse ourselves. My reward for transcribing and then typing draft after draft of practically all the poems of the last decade of his career was twofold: learning the art of poetry from a master craftsman; and being entrusted with the meanings of both older and his newest poems.

"Nazi Airman," written after watching a movie about the Second World War, proved challenging. Irving explained it is a parody of the Christian myth that God assumed man's form so that He might know man's suffering — another reason why God is angry. Irving wanted the antithesis between God and Nazi, so he has God looking directly through the crazed eyes of a Nazi airman. God is *angry*, Irving said, "He's angry with the world, men, Himself. He is a confused God." The silence is *leaden*, whereas stars are usually silver. There is no comfort, no illumination. The Crone's contra-God comment is there because Crones (important literary and mythological creatures with powers of divination, as the Crones in *Macbeth*), have intimate connections with supernatural powers. The Crone's presence signals this to be a supernatural poem.

Irving relished distilling observations into short, punchy poems such as "Anti-Abortionist," which he deemed one of his bitterest poems. It, along with "Leopardi in Montreal," tied in with "Maimonidean Perplexity," wherein Maimonides, the rabbi-philosopher-physician, author of *A Guide for the Perplexed*, ponders the ironic way man kills by the millions, yet keeps procreating. Miracle, or God's loving concern?

"Soft-Porn," another very short ironical poem, posits Death as being Life's pornographic twin. Irving said of the poem that "the originality here, the whole thing about poetry, is to be able to see things in a new light. I'm the only one to say that Death is a pornographer. Pornography is the debasement of the sexual relationship. How neat this poem is. Notice how 'a sudden heat-wave brought the mottling

spots of decay.' The title is perfect, because the spots of decay themselves are soft. Art is the great falsifier; it transcends philosophers. Plato
warned against Art's blandishments, of forgetting the reality underneath the aesthetic. Death is a pornographer who loves the wrinkles on
a woman's face. You have Love and its pornographic twin Death who,
like a vindictive twin, will debase Love to get back at it. 'Soft-Porn' can
be linked with Baudelaire's 'Carrion.' A perfect little poem, all because it
has an original connection. I would be heartbroken if someone pointed
out to me that another poet had written Death was 'love's pornographic
twin.' Heartbroken. That's how much I put into that line."

"See, nothing like poetry to freshen up life," Irving quipped after
we had talked about these poems for about an hour. "Without poetry,
life goes stale."

His poem "Overman" also holds important clues for decoding
Layton. He said of it, "The 'Overman' is surviving massacres, etc., and
has every reason to rejoice and love because *he* is surviving, but the
inhumanity also survives. Overman holds on to his humanity; for
example, intelligence and love. Accompanying that is the ongoing
inhumanity. Christianity is optimistic and romantic. I don't have this
outlook. All I anticipate is that people will be less stupid and cruel
— but [they will be] the more neurotic through having to repress his
basest instincts. Society will realize that it has to stop killing itself —
and the price will be a terrible repression and resulting neuroticism.
Look what forty years of peace have done. The well-constituted man's
job is to hang on to his individual humanity in the face of all this
inhumanity. I do not give in to despair or allow myself to be castrated
by Society. This is a kind of heroism that the ancients knew nothing
about. For Christians, heroes like Achilles, adventurers like Ulysses. I
repudiate the Christian martyrs. There is also the hero who sacrifices
his life for a cause or for the welfare of a nation or even mankind. To
the Overman, these attitudes are a surrendering of his individuality
and freedom. Nietzsche confirmed my own intuitions and gave me
the courage to live by them. For Nietzsche, the highest type of man is
the artist (but not the neurotic or romantic artist). Nietzsche's ideal
was Goethe because he accepted life. [Though for Irving, Goethe was

a ponderous German.] This is an *extremely* important key to under-standing all of my work. My body of work is one of the most com-pletely integrated bodies of work of any poet ever."

The back of his pay stub dated two days prior his performance as Socrates is crammed with notes summing up *The Symposium.* Qualifying it as a series of speeches on the nature of love, Irving deems it equal to or greater than *The Republic,* containing Plato's innermost conviction that it is the things not seen that are eternal and eternally important. Irving cites John the Baptist's words, "if we love one an-other, God dwelleth in us." Toward the bottom, he wrote: "love is the longing for immortality." As against procreant biological love, there is spiritual love, and "every one of us is a poet when in love."

His poem "Socrates at the Centaur" is a distillation of these thoughts. "Through Diotima, Socrates speaks of the daemonic or the Dionysian," Irving began one day after writing the poem. "This demon-ism has to be there if you want to write a poem. This is what is in *The Symposium.* Greeks were aware of the demon. This poem is a profound statement on what has happened to the demonic in our modern, com-fortable, technological civilization. One of the most obscene symbols of this for me is people getting monitored by psycho-physiologists while having intercourse. It's the ultimate obscenity.

"In the poem, you have to know Plato's *Symposium.* I am an *ordinary guy*, that is to say, not a philosopher, not Socrates, but an ironic Jew who can see the gap and gulf between the Ideal and the Real. But for all that, I come down on the side of Socrates who is demon-possessed. This is done in two ways. First, via tribute to Diotima where 'even Aristophanes was silenced'; and secondly, where I point out that Socrates is left 'dialoguing with two poets.' If you can't figure this out, if you can't understand the demonic, then don't even pretend that you're anything different from the herd. If you aren't daemon-possessed, then just take up basket-weaving.

"Rationalists have to be reminded of the demon in the human soul. If we ignore, or try to repress that, we get holocausts, riots, wars. People don't seem to make this connection and are always astonished at the carnage. The poet in the poem (and Irving Layton) says fuck you — you should be aware of the demonic and you should make it possible for people to be creative rather than destructive. If you don't get a Beethoven, you'll get a Hitler. There is nothing shocking about this, as least not for the poet."

Undated lecture notes from this time, possibly for a talk at Montreal's MIND high school, show the terse wit that made him such an engaging teacher. For example, one note states that it was "not possible for a Jew to believe in the divinity of another; and the poet helps preserve the beauty and elasticity of language [and] moderates the hate social conflict generates." This is how he spoke. This is who he was.

In the midst of preparing these poems for *Final Reckoning*, Don Winkler completed his documentary. There was an early screening preview for the crew, and by end of October 1986, *Poet: Irving Layton Observed* was ready to be premiered at Montreal's Saidye Bronfman.

October 28 was a night unlike any other. Before the premiere, Irving and I attended a fundraiser for the Writer's Development Trust at the Ritz-Carlton. Irving wore his usual, but still-splendid, white dinner jacket and black silk bow-tie, with a pale blue dress shirt, and fine dark blue pants I bought on sale at the *nec plus ultra* of men's clothing stores, Brisson-Brisson. Irving's energy level was so high that it might have tripped a voltmeter. We taxied to the Ritz and made our way up to the reception area. The crowd seemed to be in awe. After months of national press coverage regarding the Cameron Affair, publication of his memoir, and readings and interviews all across the country, everyone wanted to greet him. Adrienne Clarkson was there, rather like a gossamer of silk organza seeming to drape herself elegantly over Leonard Cohen's shoulders.

Everyone turned at once to take in the huge commotion coming up the main stairway: Pierre Trudeau, tailed by a scrum of voracious paparazzi. Irving and I were near the top of the stairs as the small mob ascended. Jack McClelland squeezed past me, urged if not pushed by an excited woman exhorting him to "get in there" — meaning, make damn sure to edge into photos with Pierre. *So, that's how it's done*, I thought to myself — not that I needed lessons in PR.

At our table, Premier Richard Hatfield of New Brunswick, fresh off his landslide defeat, eagerly told me of his law school days with Honourable Justice V. Pottier as his professor. With scant time to finish dinner, we left the Ritz for an interview with CBC television, though it may have been radio — the night blurs into one explosion of lights, flashbulbs, crowds pressing close, encircling us tightly.

Interview over, we then took a cab straight to the Bronfman Centre for the 8:00 p.m. world premiere screening of *Poet: Irving Layton Observed*. Even before we could see the Saidye's lights, we could tell it was an over-flow crowd from the cars jamming the streets and the people hurrying along. We stopped the cab, wanting to walk the last little way to collect ourselves and get a bit of fresh air. This was a rare moment of unadulter-ated triumph. The megawatt energy spent on giving Winkler whatever he asked for was now on film. Together, we had published *Waiting for the Messiah* and completed *Final Reckoning*. We were hard at work compiling *Dance with Desire*, along with other projects already underway. I had per-fected the art of getting Irving safely to readings overseas and in countless Canadian cities and towns. We had become man and wife and weath-ered my mother's unspeakable rejection of my very remains, all the while fighting a lone, furious battle against an entire country's prejudicial bias.

Now, arm in arm, we strode toward the packed theatre. With some fifty feet or so left to go along the sidewalk — up a few steps, across the dark rain-splashed terrace and into the glare of lights and a grateful, ex-pectant public — I felt exultant, ready to burst with love as much as pride. Just as we began the final walk toward the waiting crowd, I noticed a short, heavy-set woman coming out onto the terrace as if to meet us. "Venie! What are you doing out here?" Irving asked, surprised to see her out on the chilly terrace rather than inside enjoying a glass of wine with everyone else.

"Oh, I'm just waiting for a friend," she said vaguely. We broke stride for a moment to say hello, and that's all it took. Venie grasped Irving by the arm and quick-stepped him away from me, toward the teeming lobby. Ushers swept the central glass doors open for them as they en-tered together, arms linked. Not wanting to trail anonymously behind them like an afterthought as the doors closed against me, I was left with no choice but to veer off to the right and enter alone through a smaller auxiliary door, biting back tears.

You do not ever get a second chance to make such an entry. Venie the stage director knew this better than anyone, and had no right to steal it from me. Irving knew it was wrong, horribly wrong, but she had his arm in such a grip that the only way to extricate himself would have been via an ungallant jerking away and shoving movement. She banked on his gallantry, and mine as well, for neither was I free to stiff-arm her or degrade myself with a well-placed kick. It was wrong, all wrong. Irving bore some of the shame, but mostly, the shame was on her. Once again, I drew comfort from being the better man.

During the screening, Irving and I sat together holding hands as we watched the dance scene of us in that Greek taverna. Don placed it nearly at the very centre of the film. No one can ever steal that from us. And besides, there were other meaningful events in the days ahead, some much more intimate.

One such night was December 31, 1986. My calendar notes it as a day of working on *Final Reckoning*, and "Champagne, oysters, lox, roaring fire in fireplace." I always donned my red satin robe for our New Year's eves. A few days later, "Schmooze leads Irving to get more into Preface and Acknowledgements of FR." Irving had dedicated the book to me.

31: Weight of the World

WHILE WRITING THIS BOOK, I can barely bring myself to look over the agenda pages for 1987 to 1993, as the memories hit too hard. Those years, packed with non-stop engagements, saw me running on never-ending errands. No one but Irving knows how hard we worked, or how sweet the hard-won triumphs that thrilled us. In those same years, alas, came changes and signs marking the beginning of Irving's decline. Walking beside him, pausing as he leaned on parked cars to admire how that tree looked like an old Prophet, I saw he was not only being metaphysical, he was masking his need to rest. In those years, I never ran so fast, nor walked more slowly.

Fortunate Exile, his selected Jewish poems, appeared in 1987. Choosing the poems was particularly difficult, as it meant contemplating the Holocaust anew, recalling its horror. Irving's reaction to archival film footage of the Holocaust was always visceral. One evening, we watched grainy footage of bulldozers pushing naked Jewesses into a mass grave. Irving became so stricken that his response almost alarmed me. "That's my sister!" he cried, "every time I see scenes like that, it is my own mother, my sisters being shoved into the pit!" His capacity for empathy plunged him into depths of agony and outrage so profound as to be soul-shattering. He was, in that moment, as vulnerable and agonized as if he'd been skinned alive. How else is a moral person to respond to such archival proof of human depravity? This time, however, his anguish was so pronounced I wondered briefly whether something else was happening. Were his normally Dionysian/Nietzsche-like ramparts beginning to weaken? He knew of the Holocaust's atrocities since learning of them first-hand from survivors immediately after the war, but something had changed. Along with the revulsion, had I detected fear in his eyes? I willed myself to dismiss it and the intimation of further, possibly disastrous, changes ahead.

The one change that absolutely needed to happen involved my physical self. Perhaps it was the stranger who bought me a bag of chips that day of the car accident — five-year-old me wrapped in a woollen blanket on his wife's knee before the Mountie scooped me into his arms. From then on, stress pointed me to potato chips. In 1985, year one of the battle against Irving's so-called biographer and subsequent falling-out with my mother, I gained thirty pounds. It kept up through the late eighties so that by 1990 on a trip to Italy, I wore a size twenty-two sundress. Photos of our little foray over the border to Nova Goritza in what is now Slovenia show me huge with bloat and looking two decades older than my twenty-nine-year-old self. No wonder Italian men had stopped smiling and making throaty little noises when I walked through the Piazza Navona with Irving, feeling like a queen but looking like a schlump. Gilbert Reid, Canada's cultural attaché, confessed later, as did my doctor, that they thought I "let myself go" to look older on purpose, as though to lessen the age gap between Irving and myself. No, that was not the case. I had long before learned to adjust the cinch strap and carry that item rather gracefully. There would soon be a choice to make: keep ballooning and die young, or go on a diet.

Irving surely noticed my expanding diameter, linking it with the unrelenting demands made on us. He felt guilty at the amount of work I did, wretchedly so for not being able to provide much relief or reward as befits a treasured wife. After the Cameron fight, we had no real respite. Not only was he hugely popular again through the late eighties and early nineties, but he was better appreciated after waging and winning the battle. People wanted forewords, blurbs, critiques, opinions, along with the usual letters of reference and autographed books. They wanted pieces of Irving. Over time, those pieces began to be pulled from me.

As with most obese persons, the heavier you are, the more invisible you are. It is a way to pad one's self from social interaction too painful or tiresome to deal with. I could interact with Irving on a hundred different levels at once, less so with "civilians." My growing girth pushed them further away. Irving more than made up for all that stunted social interaction. Increasingly, he exhorted me to keep certain hangers-on and exploiters at bay. I did exactly as asked and, predictably, was accused by certain people of keeping "close friends" away.

My burgeoning expertise in all things Layton and my ever-sharpening writing style enabled me to take on much of the correspondence, often composing the bulk of his letters. Irving then had only to add a few flourishes and it was ready to go. An example of this is a letter to an Ontario poet. One of the verses he sent seemed to champion Hitler. In it, trainloads of Jews stop to eat chicken along the way and, being dirty meat-eating slobs, litter the tracks with chicken bones, suggesting the Holocaust was just deserts. Irving read the poems quickly, trying to find something kind to say while I kept coming back to the chicken carcass poem. In Irving's letter to the misguided would-be poet, my vitriolic words are virtually unchanged in the final draft. The letter was later included by Francis Mansbridge in Irving's selected letters. Mail answered entirely by myself was marked with an *A* encircled in green. For the record, I never wrote a letter using Irving's name. Ethics and common sense made that unthinkable.

In 1988 Concordia University established the Irving Layton Awards in Creative Writing. He selected the winners and presented the cheques, five hundred dollars for the best poem and the same amount for the best prose piece. Concordia also invited him to teach poetry as an Adjunct Professor in 1988–89. He still enjoyed teaching, though it left him utterly drained by end of term. In earlier years, teaching energized him for summers filled with writing. It was his last teaching job, and this saddened him.

The next major project involved recording poems from *A Wild Peculiar Joy* on audiocassette for McClelland & Stewart (1990). Julian Scher was the sound engineer, patiently guiding Irving through the nine hours of recording done over a three-day span. As soon as we began, it became apparent that something was off. It would have been too tiring to stand, so we had decided to sit at a small table, but the sitting affected Irving's breathing pattern, effectively changing his delivery's pitch and

key. Despite glancing up at me after every few lines, I could not provide
the same energy as a live audience. During breaks, I critiqued his delivery just as we did after readings. Having heard the poems read in perfect pitch hundreds of times, I urged him to key his tone up or down,
and modulate tempo and rhythms where needed. Irving agreed and
struggled through takes, but to no avail. It is as though someone placed
a capo on the wrong part of a guitar neck. His timing was off, and he
was in the wrong key. Still, better to have something than nothing.

During and immediately after putting *Tutto Sommato: Poesie 1945–
1989* together, he worked with McGill University's Brian Trehearne, who
wrote a splendid introduction to *Fornalutx: Selected Poems 1928–1992*.
These books came about in a fury that grew like an approaching hurri-
cane. By the late eighties, after his 1988–89 stint as Adjunct Professor
at Concordia, exhaustion was setting in, most noticeably that day after
handing out the 1989 Layton Prize. Waiting for a cab afterwards, his
knees suddenly buckled. I clasped my arm around his waist to keep him
from collapsing, guiding his body as it virtually fell into the cab, keeping
his distress hidden as best I could. Musia waved goodbye and surely
noticed his face turning grey as his overcoat, but she made no comment.
I do not think she wanted to acknowledge signs of encroaching age.
Neither did his audiences, kindly indulging him if he seemed a bit hard
of hearing or slightly distracted. There was no doubt time, or simply life,
was taking its toll. In the rush to get all these books completed, he confided feeling suddenly closer to death, his eyes large with something between horror and fear. Unable to shake the sensation when his energies
dipped like that, he kept a madman's hours. I was on stand-by, whatever
time of day or night, ready to type, number, list, collate, photocopy, and
repeat until each manuscript was safely in his publisher's hands.

There were still good days. We sometimes "played hooky" and took
long walks, usually to bookstores. At the Bibliophile on Queen Mary
Road, we bought Yoram Kaniuk's *Confessions of a Good Arab,* Dan V.
Segre's *Memoirs of a Fortunate Jew,* and a biography of Mayakovsky.
Many people stared, all smiled, some asked to shake hands. Between
writing a foreword for *Rawprint,* a poetry anthology, reading "Elegy for
Marilyn Monroe" at the Centaur Theatre's anniversary gala, we went to

the movies, including Pasolini's *120 Days and Nights of Sodom* as well as *The Naked Gun*. I was also busy with External Affairs, the consul-general in Chicago, and Rizzardi, arranging itineraries for upcoming readings in Chicago, Göteborg, and Italy (in 1990).

Countless hours were spent cataloguing boxes of papers destined for Concordia's Layton Collection. Irving read constantly, gathering his thoughts for upcoming readings or appearances. His 1956 book, *The Improved Binoculars*, was to be reissued by Porcupine's Quill in October 1989, involving pleasant enough discussions John Metcalf and a final photo shoot with legendary photographer Sam Tata for the cover.

There were other notable moments, such as the private dinner party in Westmount, where Irving and I sat at each end of a table set for about ten people, arranged so that Pierre Trudeau could meet Irving to ask him about himself and the state of Canadian arts and letters.

The Göteborg Book Fair in Sweden was another highlight. However, in Stockholm, Irving's mounting anxiety about his declining powers of perception tethered us to our hotel room. By now, he had already con-fided how death held no fear for him, but becoming incapacitated, being a burden, filled him with dread. On that trip, he was unable to bear my being out of his sight. I did everything in my power to distract, make light, and reassure him. As calm and soothing as I was on the exterior, my concerns kept growing. What was wrong with him? Why could he not settle down? Was this to become his normal state? He became ob-sessed with needing milk of magnesia and fruit; I set out to the sound of his plea, "Get me some fruit! I need fruit!" Unfamiliar with Stockholm's layout, perhaps taking advantage of the chance to explore, I walked for what felt like miles, increasingly upset at not being free to explore at my leisure. Finding no fruit, I returned to the hotel. Maybe walking would help Irving. We ventured out. It was only my imagination, but Irving seemed ill at ease, as if exploring was no longer as exciting. At last, a tiny convenience store had two crates of delectable Bartlett pears set out, shining softly yellow against sooty bricks in the thin orange light of late afternoon. "*What? A dollar seventy-five for a pear? RiiiDiculous!*" We kept walking, and stumbled upon the August Strindberg Museum. The photos I have of this foray are all blurry. One, taken by a passerby, shows me standing behind Irving, clutching his shoulders and smiling, in front of Strindberg's former home. We fluttered like two votive candles over the displays — his desk, bed, dining room table, and his water closet — and hurried back before darkness fell.

Mavis Gallant was part of the Canadian presence in Göteborg, and we joined her for breakfast. I was fascinated by her nervous movements, how her eyes kept darting about as if something bothered her, but she herself did not know what it was. Whenever the handsome waiter glided up to our table, Mavis would gaze up as if looking at Michelangelo's *David*, though this was but a lanky boy. She seemed to be making little simpering sounds, beseeching him with her eyes, her mouth, albeit asking only for more coffee. I made a mental note to never appear so wanting if I managed to reach her age, but gave her full marks for being alive to the world, still sensual. The taxi ride to the convention hall was one long show of Mavis's quirks; she seemed to be telegraphing *look how incredibly nervous and tense I am*. I tried not to glance at Irving, staving off a terrible giggle-fit. That said, she wrote like an angel and lived life on her own terms. I would gladly share a cab-ride with her again, if ever I could.

Despite the excitement of international travel and my knack for "collecting ambassadors," as Irving called it, I grew heavier and heavier. Three main forces conspired against me, any one of them enough to cut one's Achilles heel: want of my mother's love; bearing a huge responsibility while bereft of any real power; and the inability to pursue my own writing.

Incredibly, I still hungered for my mother's approval. We stopped communicating for a few years after the corpse-rejection letter, but the desire for her approval, perhaps even her love, continued. It became a sado-masochistic exercise, me telling her later, for example, of being in Arthur Miller's hotel room in Toronto where Irving presented him with a signed copy of the New Directions edition of his *Selected Poems*, the one with "Elegy for Marilyn Monroe." I waited for her sneering put-downs by return post.

Struggling to keep on top of both the demanding schedule, and Irving's increasing trouble keeping track of things, I gamely taped legal-sized sheets filled with to-do's on the edge of Irving's bookcase, hoping he might make a habit of glancing at it rather than ask me repeatedly was coming up. With the same reasoning, I bought a memo board and jotted down which calls needed returning or which visitor was dropping by. I tried to make it seem as if this was to help me keep things straight rather than for his use, but he still preferred asking me what was on the agenda. With his hearing deteriorating due as much to swimmer's ear from the pool at the YMCA as to age, I often had to unplug the iron in the basement, and go up two flights of stairs upon hearing, "Anna! Annaaaa, where are you?" Knowing he'd not hear me from the basement, I'd find him upstairs and ask, "What?" His "Oh, nothing! Just wanted to know where you were," was said with such impish innocence that I could never be upset with him. Exasperated, yes, but not upset. I could try to ignore, but no longer deny, the signs and portents. Irving had begun that inevitable decline.

No one helped; it was mostly all on me. After one time too many of someone like Musia dropping in straight from her Charles of Westmount hair appointment — and me not having showered in two days, exhausted, overwhelmed, and ticked at visitors who neither called ahead nor took the hint — I turned to Irving and said, "Can't I just *be* for a minute, must I be a function of what I *do?*" He understood my distress, but was powerless to stop the onslaught. This was the harvesting time and I had volunteered to help until it was all in. We commiserated during midnight talks, vowed to try keeping obligations to a minimum, and soldiered on.

Perhaps the best example of an inconsiderate guest was the lady who came all the way from another province in the hopes that Irving would look over her writing. Her husband distracted me with small talk while she made Irving read her entire manuscript of poems, correct each one, and then, hours later, she told me she liked her own versions better. She came again, offering to pay Irving for his time (which she did) and brought wonderful gifts, but it bordered on the absurd. She tried to set up a third appointment that it was clear would be yet another full day of manuscript editing. Irving begged me to keep her away as his doctor had ordered bed rest after his near-collapse in the street. I let her know he was under doctor's orders to rest. Suspecting she would ignore my plea and show up regardless, I settled Irving in bed, put a note in the door reminding her of the doctor-ordered bed rest (with apologies), then went up Somerled for groceries. Rounding the corner back onto Monkland, I saw a long dark sedan in front of our house. On our front lawn: the lady, her husband, and teenage daughter, all gazing up to the bedroom window. To my utter disbelief, they had sent their driver to the back of the house where handymen doing renovations had left their ladder. The driver, a Mexican with pure Aztec features, his skin so reddish brown as to be almost burgundy, sporting a full set of gold teeth, was now on the ladder, level with our bedroom window, tap tap tapping against the pane to wake Irving.

Before I could tell them to clear out and show a little mercy for a sick man who had, by the way, helped her enough already, Irving's white hair showed through the window in the front door, and, by habit if nothing else, ushered her in. I was never more aghast, rarely more livid, or so powerless. Rightly or wrongly, it felt as though everyone else could exercise their will or get what they wanted, while I could barely finish a thought or sit without interruption for more than a few minutes.

Doubtless, that was another reason for my ballooning weight: powerlessness. "Irving, I've got the responsibilities of a brigadier general, but the power of a buck private," I griped on more than one occasion. He agreed, but could truly do no more than tell me how much he loved me and appreciated everything I did for him. Easing his conscience, he kept assuring me that at least he was leaving me the house and its contents. If I wanted to live on at 6879 Monkland and perhaps take in a boarder, he suggested, I would not have to work. The house was fully paid for, all I would need would be a little for taxes and living expenses. It soothed both our tired minds to picture me ensconced in our little house one day. "This world is not made for people like me and you," he said. "I want you to have this house so that you will always have a roof over your head."

I assumed what he told me was true and made no concrete plans for my future. Nor was there time for me to obtain a degree, anyway. Some people have asked if perhaps Irving was afraid my becoming a student might mean meeting people — men — who might interest me too much. Having no interest in other men, my fidelity was unimpeachable. If anything troubled him, it was having recognized my penchant for single-minded obsession. I, too, could lose myself whole days when trying to write, even if confined to journalling rather than creative work. As much as he encouraged me, I suspect a part of him was relieved that I was too busy to write, for *that* would have pulled me away. He needed me. I think we both knew the cruelty and sacrificial aspects at play, but I was still young and, we hoped, I would get to my own work after his demise. No school could teach me more than Irving, but employers rarely take such learning into account. Perhaps I would make our house into a Layton Museum, he half-joked one day. Why not? And, assuming my wanderlust would resurface, maybe I would prefer to travel the world and serve as its curator. Both scenarios would prove as elusive as gold at the end of a rainbow.

I tried to make Irving feel less wretched; it was the situation, not him, that was wearing me down. Not being able to write, read, or have a moment's respite was taking a toll. Eating became the only thing I had any control over. I now could, and often did, devour half of a one-hundred-gram chocolate bar on the way home from Somerled, hide the half-eaten bar, and go back to purchase a second one, only to devour the half-eaten one the moment I returned home. Becoming obese and unattractive also fulfilled my mother's subliminal wish. I was her archrival, ergo, the more ungainly I was, the better. After twenty-nine years of hearing that message, it took root. I was doing what Mom wanted, like a good daughter.

Shocked at my appearance when I looked over photos from a trip to Italy during that time, and feeling even more bloated, with the odd chest pains and other complaints, I finally sought medical attention. Dr. Bronet sounded the alarm. Weight Watchers had a new program, she said, handing me their pamphlet.

It was 1990. I had no desire to turn thirty looking and feeling as badly as I did. Joining Weight Watchers was the first independent thing I had done since 1982. Well, other than the short-lived drawing lessons at the Saidye Bronfman Centre Irving suggested I take. My drawings delighted him and he urged me to study the craft. I quit after a few classes, unable to bear seeing the artist, Rita Briansky, trying to teach non-artistic housewives how to draw.

For a year and a half I wrote down every morsel I ate and logged every glass of water I drank. Once a week, I walked to the weigh-in. It worked. Seventy pounds lighter, I did not recognize myself in the mirror, or remember ever feeling so alive. I had gone from pillowy Rubenesque to an almost angular, highly kinetic abstract expression of youth and energy. This vibrancy beamed out like radio signals to men who suddenly began looking at me longingly. I had only a vague notion of what they were seeing. Still thinking of myself as invisible, I was unaware of the sensual power I had but could neither feel nor command.

My weight loss affected Irving in a big way, albeit the opposite of what anyone might have expected. Every movie, pulp novel, and cartoon ever published portrays the older man/younger woman pairing as every man's dream; instead, Irving became saddened and fearful that my change would take me away from him. I was now a size ten, having shed half my bulk, but these changes placed a burden on Irving. It would only occur to me later that he began to withdraw deliberately. It was his way of acknowledging I would soon need to learn how to negotiate life without him. Meanwhile, I can only imagine the bittersweet delight he took in helping kit me out in a new wardrobe. It took four hours of the salesladies' help and Irving's appreciative eye to convince me how good I looked in Lagerfeld suits.

In 1991 we embarked on an epic European tour with stops in Prague, Athens, Molivos (on the island of Lesbos), Rome, Sardinia, Naples, Glyfada (a suburb of Athens we stayed in for one week after missing the flight back to Prague). It was in Molivos that, for the first time, I shed my winter clothes and took to the beach, awkward, unsure at first, then revelling in my new body. Without Irving's support, I doubt if I could have tasted this kind of success.

The highlight of that trip was Irving's reading at the University of Cagliari. Despite jet lag, fatigue, and the hot Sardinian sun, Irving gave one of the most powerful performances I ever witnessed. Upon arrival, Irving and Professor Rizzardi were ushered into an antechamber. I continued into a huge white-walled, wooden-beamed baronial hall, joined by professors from Sardinia and the mainland, their spouses, and other university officials. We'd been told to expect a relatively small audience, as most students had left to study for finals. Instead, the hall was jammed, the students literally climbing over one another for better seats. When the massive door opened and Irving emerged, the place burst into screaming, whooping, shouting, whistling, and thunderous applause. I held my breath. Irving had been exhausted, with virtually no time to prepare. Alfredo's presence beside him on the dais reassured me somewhat. It would be a bilingual reading, Alfredo reading the translations. To my astonishment, Irving delivered one of the most galvanizing talks he gave in all the years I knew him. He was spellbinding, magisterial, funny, challenging, powerful and in complete control. That he had the energy to speak so compellingly was baffling, until I turned and saw the students' rapt faces. He was siphoning their energy, and giving it back tenfold.

This was a rare occasion where Irving had not made a reading list, so his closing with "I Take My Anna Everywhere" came as a surprise. An even bigger surprise was that Alfredo had only just finished the translation. As Alfredo concluded with this poem, Irving rose to stand beside him and the audience erupted, sending its appreciation crashing over the stage like breaking waves. Leaning slightly forward, I looked at the faces of those sitting alongside me. Even in the fading afternoon light, there was no mistaking that everyone, men and women alike, had tears streaming down their faces as they stood to give their applause. I realized I was weeping too.

We had shared a moment that would never happen again. Irving would not be returning to their university or to their island. There would never be another poet quite like him anywhere ever again.

Students began surging forward. Alfredo quickly helped Irving down from the stage and escorted him over to our group. My face still wet with emotion, I clasped hands with Alfredo, thanking him for his beautiful translation. Then, almost in unison, everyone pressed very, very close around us. Some actually reached out, wanting to touch Irving and me as if for good luck. Someone asked what it was like to be a living poem. I do not think I had a proper response, though my eyes likely answered more eloquently than words.

Having lost so much weight I now blended nicely in places like Capri, for example, sitting between Irving and Czesław Miłosz at his award ceremony for the Premio Capri. He told us how awful it had been to be declared a non-person. The two of them got on well, almost too well. When the ceremonies went on a bit too long, Miłosz leaned across my lap, whispering to Irving and me, "We suffer together." I braced for an exchange of stage whispers, relieved the two of them behaved themselves.

The summer of 1991 was our last good summer. Irving and I relaxed as never before, letters went unanswered, and phone calls sat on the machine sometimes for days. Years of basking in Irving's unconditional love opened the slimmest possibility of our having a baby. I no longer felt terrified of being emotionally or physically abusive to a child. At last, I could pass a toddler and not be singed with envy seeing it enjoy the kind of mother-love I craved but had never received. One Sunday, A *60 Minutes* episode on Yves Montand prompted the conversation about having a child. Montand had become a first-time father at age sixty-seven, and was ecstatic. He had the means to bring a child into the world; we did not. Ultimately, Irving asked if I felt deprived of the motherhood experience. No, I assured him, I was not suffering for want of a child. It was enough to know I would be a loving mother. Had Irving been younger, then perhaps yes, but it seemed terribly wrong to have a baby whose father would die within a few years. Still, if it we had a boy, we would name him Noah. We never got around to imagining a girl or picking out her name.

One night, Irving was already in bed as I stepped into the shower. It was that time of the month and I felt a rush of warmth exiting my body — some kind of clot. Curiosity piqued, I bent to pick it up. Nestled in the dark cushioning mass, there was a small whitish shape, no bigger than a small pea. I turned to get more light and gasped at what I was holding in my hand. One end was slightly enlarged, with two dark blue circles on either side. Down along one edge, there were tiny little white segments, all narrowing to an undistinguished point. We had made a baby after all. I can't begin to quantify the overwhelming desire I had to restore it inside me, safely housed and able to resume its life. But it was too late. A baby was not in the cards. So I cupped it in my hand very close to my face, shielded from the rushing water, and talked softly as if it could hear. The hot water ran cold. I finally decided to tell Irving. I sat on the edge of the bed and we communed with the little one enough to keep the moment sacred but not degenerating into a maudlin gush. That was that. I had completed the circle of life, experienced that volcanic surge of primal maternal energy, and continued with the even tremor of our days.

Irving's age and the soon-to-be-diagnosed condition became more marked, his irreversible downward turn more apparent. His public did not know any of this, and continued to make demands. I grew angrier and angrier at having time stolen from us by people who, in some instances, would send postcards just to milk him for letters so they could sell them to Concordia's Layton Collection. He was still in demand, though "handling" him in public was becoming more worrisome. For the most part, I am sure his audiences noticed some changes, such as his asking them to repeat questions. I could tell that often he heard well enough, but needed extra time to come up with a Layton-like response. Such intimations of encroaching age, like the occasional pee stain everyone saw but agreed to pretend was not there, were impossible to ignore.

In the meantime, despite such realities, I was enjoying my new body. Doing housework, I often put the radio to rock and roll oldies, bopping away while Irving read the paper. One day, a waltz came on, and I begged him to dance with me. He sat at the table, reluctant to set the paper down. I did coax him to dance a little, but there was such sadness emanating from his eyes, and even his body, that I scarcely dared ask him to dance again. Another day, deliriously happy with a new pair of jeans, I burst into the bedroom to show him how nicely they fit. Oddly, he held the *Gazette* open wider, raising it high like a curtain. Confused, hurt, I asked why. His answer matched what I had already begun to suspect. My size-ten figure and off-the-wall enthusiasm for life was beginning to make him feel as if he could not possibly husband me without turning the pair of us into something farcical.

It took all I had to convince him — and myself — that nothing whatsoever had changed between us. Looking back, I think he sensed the coming changes, and wanted to push me away, thereby forcing me to think about my future and life without him.

On February 26, 1992, his doctor drew a little sketch and put names on the miscellany of aging. According to the CT scan, the central reservoir of fluid in Irving's brain was getting larger. "Water on the brain." We could expect problems with memory and thinking, urinary troubles, and the tell-tale "magnetic gait." Parkinson's, but not quite Alzheimer's. Not yet. Dr. Kirk suggested Irving should "make plans" if his symptoms became more pronounced. I had a special journal that I called "The Changing Book," begun in 1981 and meant to record events that left me a different person.

Essentially, nothing really changed, other than having names put to the aging process, the "inescapable lousiness of growing old."[1] My entry in "The Changing Book" from March 2, 1992, recording the doctor's appointment says:

> I certainly don't intend for this to become a minutiae of Irving's health à la Simone de Beauvoir. He's a man, he's my husband, not a lab specimen.... I must add that as we sat watching TV (*Murder She Wrote* was about to begin), Irving turned to me and said with wonderful feeling in his voice that these past few days and weeks had been among — if not *the* — happiest of his entire life. We've been busy and there was some strain and pressure, but on the whole he said he's never felt so relaxed, so completely himself. He said again how very much he loved me and how I was the one who helped make his days such happy ones. And my heart didn't know whether to melt or jump up and down for joy. It did me such good to hear these things. How does that quote go? *We live in the dark. We do what we can. The rest is the madness of Art.* You see, he's made me. I want him to enjoy me as I am now. And he will, he will.... Now, he has his books, his music, gourmet meals, and of course, me, a nice little house, a garden and the knowledge that he's made it. What more could any man want?

As warm and loving as we were, Irving continued to withdraw physically. Later, I would wait until he was asleep to slip quietly onto my side of the bed, avoiding contact so as not to arouse or upset him. Eventually, my pent-up energy threatened to send me over the edge, such as on the night I found myself stark naked in my study at 2:30 a.m., dancing maniacally before the full-length mirror, without music, projecting a full range of sultry grimaces like I was in the spotlight at Studio 54. Something was going to have to give.

32: Israel: There's a Crack in Everything

"THE CHANGING BOOK" entries from 1992 and 1993 make my insides plummet as if I am crossing a gorge on an old rope bridge. Without detailing each instance here, I can only read a bit before having to put the journal down, recalling the downward pull, time's degradation carving away at him. As against his downslide, it is equally painful to remember my determination to grow in strength, confidence, and ability. It was rotten timing. How I would love to have met him in the 1940s or so, but Fate had other plans. There. February 26, 1992: an elaboration on a cryptic, cringe-worthy sentence written seven months earlier about Israel being where I shall "never die" and Greece being the place where I "began to live."

"Not dying in Israel" was an awkward attempt at expressing the degree to which I identified myself with the Jews, how timeless and infinite I felt amongst them. No wonder being so much younger than Irving did not matter. What's forty-eight years between two five-thousand-year-old souls? Some of my fondest memories are of "making" Friday nights. I taught myself the Hebrew prayer to bless the candles from a book of recipes and Jewish traditions. Irving was pleased his family's menorah had come to life again. The imposing antique, slightly battered brass candelabra had likely bumped along country lanes in a horse-drawn cart leaving Tirgu Neamtz when the family fled Romania, arriving in Montreal on Irving's first birthday in 1913.

One such Friday night, the house clean and filled with the smells of chicken soup made from his sister Dora's recipe, my grandmother's silk scarf around my head (a nod to my Acadian origins), I readied to light the candles and say the *bracha*. Irving put aside the book he was reading. "Anna, I've never been able to be fully myself with anyone else," he said softly, his words clouded more with wonder than regret.

Other times, as I put bright orange tiger lilies and purple clematis in a water glass next to the gleaming menorah, he'd tell me how so very happy he was with me. I miss those Friday nights, their sublime peacefulness, and of course, the place I had in his life. My sense of belonging with the Jewish people remains to this day. It never left, not after being disinherited by my father, not after my mother's disavowal of my remains, nor during the marriage to my second husband, a young Tunisian Muslim.

As good as life could be, we were under chronic stress. His sister Dora, slipping rapidly into the twilight zone, called repeatedly. Forgetting she had spoken to us and her devoted daughter, son, and daughter-in-law, she called again and again to say how lonely she was, how she had no one. On one visit, my hair newly cropped like a boy's, she mistook me for Irving's son — mine and Irving's son. She told me how lucky I was my father was a teacher and he could help with my schoolwork, and next time to bring my mother Anna. I stayed in character, same as one would so as not to wake a sleepwalker. Her voice, still accented with old-world Yiddish, had a catch in it like a terrified child. It was crushing. No matter how often we visited and tried to reassure her, nothing eased her paralyzing despair. Dora's calls hit Irving like hatchet blows. She was the sister who nursed him back to life when he set himself on fire as a small boy.

On Sunday, March 1, 1992, we readied for the Ottawa birthday bash/launch party for *Dance with Desire,* a collection of love poems spanning Irving's career, arranged by John Metcalf. After lunch (cauliflower soup, hot rolls of dark bread, salad, with cheddar cheese, pears and dates for dessert) as I tried on clothes to see what to pack, Irving stopped me to describe the fabulous faces he "sees." They were fantastically detailed three-dimensional faces of strangers, more often men than women, which appeared unbidden and "floated" in mid-air. Irving described them with bemusement. I put it down to his vivid imagination, hoping to allay fears of his deterioration. "If this is softening of the brain," he ventured light-heartedly, "then good! Let there be more of it."

He had seen such apparitions before, but something had shifted. This would be my burden, one more devastating than I could have imagined. Against the dark thoughts I confided to my journal, each good day was cause for rejoicing. The Ottawa launch party was so successful that police had to help control the overflow crowds. Irving could still put in stellar performances, but no one could guess what was happening behind the scenes.

Two months later, I nailed down the itinerary for a return trip to Greece and Italy, including arrangements for his son David to join us in Molivos where he'd spent eleven childhood summers. It would be Irving's last trip to Italy and Greece, his last dusty bus ride from Mytilini to Molivos, last glimpse of the Plaka, as well as the first and last time he would be together with his grown son in that magical village.

This fresh realization hit hard. I was about to witness the last of everything. In fact, he would write the very last complete poem of his career on that 1992 trip to Molivos. Smoking a cigar on the balcony, he put down the book on modern European poetry to watch barn swallows building a nest under the eaves. Within minutes, he began to write, tapping out the syllables, counting the beats with his blunt fingertips on the sun-bleached table. A small, awful feeling in the pit of my stomach prompted me to reach for my camera. I photographed him writing "Nest Building." Women my age were seeing their babies' first steps, hearing first words. I felt, among other emotions, privileged to witness the last milestones in a poet's life. In those last hours in the Plaka, with not enough light to photograph our table at Platano's or his last stroll through familiar streets, Irving's demeanor remained stoic. He accepted his fate, though his melancholy was palpable as a shroud.

Back in Montreal, the nervous agitation persisted. Not only was he compulsively trying over-the-counter Relaxol pills, he insisted I find his pipe and tobacco after we had mutually agreed to keep them hidden over a year earlier.

Convinced his time was almost up, he wanted to see his daughter Samantha, having not seen her in nearly a decade after reluctantly, and under extreme duress, being forced by Harriet to relinquish all visitation rights. He tried to maintain a link to Samantha via the name Layton, but that too failed. Harriet moved to change Samantha's name to Bernstein without his consent. Irving challenged her in court and lost, his ill-prepared lawyer bungling the case before an unsympathetic judge. Doubtful Harriet would take his call, I phoned her at work posing as an old college pal. It worked. Her assistant warbled about Harriet having "moved a million times" and gave me her home number. On March 5, 1992, I phoned, explained who I was, my reason for calling, and handed the phone to Irving. After some neutral chitchat, he asked if he could see Samantha. Harriet said she would let Samantha decide, adding that she'd not expressed negative things to her about Irving.

Three days later, Harriet called back and put their eleven-year-old daughter on the phone. The green steel cashbox sat open on his desk — it was where he kept his family mementoes: photos of Aviva as a girl, which unfailingly stabbed at his heart seeing her plucky-but-lost-little-girl expression; a baby bracelet that said "Lazarovitch," which Naomi had made decades earlier; and a precious few photos of Samantha. He had these photos out, a big-bellied toddler in little red pants and top. I stood in the doorway of his study, saw his entire body collapse inward as Samantha announced her decision. "No," she did not want to see him. She "still needed to think about it." Calmly, he pointed out that he'd very much love to see her, that he's thought of her very often all these years, and now that he is getting on with perhaps not much time left, it would mean a great deal to him if he could see her. The conversation ended. He hung up the phone, unable to contain his grief.

Samantha had at least promised to send a photo. Weeks passed. No photo ever came. Several months later, Véhicule Press published Henry Beissel's brainchild, a festschrift titled *Raging Like a Fire: A Celebration of Irving Layton*. Irving inscribed a copy to Samantha, enclosing a lovely letter. Harriet, in a brazen show of how unbiased she was, literally set fire to the book and returned its charred remains to Irving. It was too disgusting, too funny not to laugh. Drop-jawed, mouths open, fingertips blackened from passing the burnt book back and forth, we cursed and laughed, agog at the concept of a Jew burning a book — about a Jewish poet no less. This gesture, along with having handed his love letters to her lawyer, confirmed everything written about her in *The Gucci Bag* to be irrevocably true. Whatever regret he may have had, Harriet sent it up in smoke.

Black humour notwithstanding, old wounds reopened, old habits returned. He began waking at 3:00 a.m., agitated, drenched in cold sweat. He overate and was sometimes bearish. His doctor experimented with pills as though Irving was a prime lab rat: Xanax, Halcyon, Prozac, Zoloft, Sinemet, singly or two or three kinds together. They interfered with his memory and, I am quite certain, began altering his personality. Mostly though, he was still "my" PincuVing. We forged ahead, me still thinking I was capable of meeting the future head-on.

Not unlike an iron bar subject to repeated bending, I began to weaken. I too had a breaking point. Despite the vastly entertaining conversations we still had, my heart plummeted each time I heard him mutter, "What's the *matter* with me?", his voice tight with frustration.

I dropped everything to help find the lost glasses or wallet, soothing him with, "See? You're misplacing your wallet on purpose because you're addicted that rush of relief when you *do* find it!" And "Well, of course you're feeling groggy, you took this pill with that pill, that's why!" Some days it worked, other times not.

Housework or Layton Enterprizes would come to a dead stop at his jovial "Face time! Where are you? I must have face time!" By January 1993, Irving agreed we needed to concentrate more on our own lives and that too many people wanted too many things. "I've left a large enough body of work," he said, shooting down his desire to try his hand at short stories or a play because it meant dictating to me. I told him I would gladly do it, *if* we could put the kibosh on extraneous social obligations. Better yet, he continued, perhaps the best course of action would be for him to devote himself to my career. As revolutionary and flattering a concept, I knew life would not permit it. We concluded this long talk on a calm, happy, positive note. Both of us looked forward to 1993, thinking it was to be the year to truly enjoy each other fully, without distraction. Time was accelerating, he was slowing down, and I could barely keep up.

In March 1993, we boarded an El Al flight for Israel to attend the International Poetry Festival. The festival was sponsored by and located in the Jerusalem Foundation's Mishkenot Sha'ananim, a starkly beautiful residential building built in 1860. From our terrace, we drank in thrilling views of the Tower of David and the walls of the Old City above. Irving was the only Canadian participant.

The festival's theme was peace, coexistence, and language as a possible mediator or means to find common ground. Its organizers went from nervousness to dismay to alarm at seeing "Israelis" and "For My Sons Max and David" on Layton's reading list. Could he not select other poems? He resisted, albeit politely. This went back and forth until the organizers *told* him not to read these poems. He bristled, but acquiesced. When invited to a country surrounded by hostile neighbours, where peace is more fragile than a spider web, resistance for its own sake would have been perverse.

As a convert in Israel, one would think I would be beyond excited, reverberating with reverential kinship. In fact, I was and was not. Travelling with Irving had become even more exacting. In terms of adventurousness, we still shared the same desire to get fabulously lost when in a new place. The new reality, however, meant Irving was virtually confined to the room unless I was at his side. Unfamiliar surroundings triggered anxiety. If I left him in the room, happy with books, writing material, the *Jerusalem Post*, and handy to ensuite facilities, I could not be away for long. Standing on our patio after breakfast, like Moses, I gazed and yearned, unable to venture any closer to the Holy City.

My only solo foray was a quick walk to the Montefiore Windmill, hurrying past a group of day-care children guarded by men with Uzis. Returning to the Mishkenot, there was Irving up in the lobby area, holding forth with three young English poets, Simon, Peter, and Mark, whose last names I cannot recall. It was the old Irving in splendid form, asking about their lives, their work, enjoying a coffee. It was how he stayed current, soaking up all he could from younger poets, their likes, dislikes, and opinions. I could also tell he was unsure how to get back to our room. "Well, of *course* it's confusing! See, all the doors look alike," I said, hoping to tamp down his rising frustration along with mine. We linked arms and sauntered back to our room down the long, silent corridor of Jerusalem stone.

Another participant was the thirty-something sabra, Israeli-born Amir Or, founder of the Helicon Poetry Society. Our hosts herded the group, some twenty-five poets from all over the world, onto a tour bus with two guards with Uzis, allegedly, in their duffle bags. Amir revelled in the morning papers' full-page reviews of his latest book, *Limb-Loosening Desire (An Anthology of Erotic Greek Poetry)*.

We motored up to Kfar Blum, a kibbutz on the Jordan River high in the Upper Galilee. Amir told me how his father's generation of Sephardim had, regrettably, turned their back on European Jewry to focus on building their new country. Irving's white hair stood out vividly, as did his *anglit* (English) voice, making him a de facto representative of Diaspora Jews from that era. Amir observed Irving, watched how he held court, laughed. His energy and warm approachability won everyone over, even pragmatic sabras. We all toured the kibbutz, saw the bomb craters, and later enjoyed a patchouli kind of night, with cigarette smoke, guitar music, and wine-bottle candleholders amidst kumbaya songs and poetry.

The next morning we headed for the Golan Heights. To my surprise, the "Heights" actually have a flat-topped berm that tapers along its length from about six feet high near the parking lot, to about two feet at its far southern end. The group disembarked and all but the Swedish poet, an older man with a cane and bad limp, scrambled up the embankment. Our guide began explaining the Golan's history, and that we were a mere four minutes' flight-time from enemy strikes.

Eager to hear the guide, I was atop the berm in seconds. Irving, however, remained at the base looking up, assessing how best to attack it. Amir stood close by, watching. I glanced at our small group already gathered around the guide then looked down at Irving, whose determination broke my heart. His desire to clamber up was cancelled by frustration as he started up and half-slid, half-stumbled down. I wanted — with every piece of my breaking heart — to help him. Doing so, however, risked causing him to pitchpole all the way down. There would be red dirt all over his clothes, perhaps a twisted ankle or sprained wrist, and a big dent in his dignity. If I helped him up, I would miss the guide's talk.

These thoughts raced through my mind, each one cutting me to the quick. My muscles locked. I could neither speak nor move. Amir saw my hesitation. His poet's intuition made him privy to my unspoken thoughts. In one step, he was at my side. I looked straight ahead, down the length of the Golan Heights.

In what felt like slow motion, Amir's abundance of coal-black curls danced on the hot, playful breeze. His green eyes lit up, smiling, as he began to speak. Hot sun. Burning air. The only coolness seemed to come from his white linen shirt. Howsoever much the scene might drip with bad Harlequin romance imagery, there was nothing romantic about it. This was no mundane "innocents abroad" moment. It was the beginning of the end. Worse still, I was instantly aware of it. Details sank into me. Like expertly thrown javelins.

So I recall Amir's handsome, deeply tanned face, neck; his chest in the broad V of his half-buttoned white linen shirt. I sensed more than saw his mercurial body loosely enclosed in luxurious linen. Pristine. White. Linen. Silently, Amir filled the breach my hesitancy and fatigue had created. Ready. Set. His arm rose up before me. Slow motion. Authoritative as a train barrier. His fingers, surprisingly long, splayed open like a cock's comb. Delicate, vital, as he extended his hand to Irving. Then, I heard him say very gently, "Here, Mr. Layton. Let me help you. Why don't you come down further? It will be much easier to climb."

Momentarily free of my charge, my duty, my love, I could not move. Instead of going to hear what remained of the guide's talk, I stared straight down along the Golan Heights. Eyes stinging. Mouth parched. I watched Irving and Amir grow smaller and smaller in the distance until Irving's silhouette bent to the earth and clambered up, one hand on the soil, the other steadied by Amir's kindness.

In less time than it took for a heart to beat, I saw objectively what I'd been doing for Irving for some eleven years. Amir's simple gesture lay bare what I had not wanted to see. Up until that day the enormous amounts of energy that had been expended so effortlessly and with infinite love previously became grindingly difficult, almost impossible to muster. Without doubt, I felt the first hairline crack trace its way along the very foundation of our marriage.

The Festival's grand finale was a night of poetry and music at Jerusalem's Khan Theater. Irving had his usual white silk dinner jacket and black bow tie; I donned my Anne Klein dress, a fine wool crêpe, with a fire engine red back panel, the front a bright fuchsia. We stood out in whichever crowd we were in, everyone seeming to recognize Irving.

I made certain he went to bathroom before we sat down. Did he want to sit in the first row? No, the second. Okay. Near the aisle? No, in the middle. Okay. We edged in and took our seats. When the lights came back up, Jerusalem's mayor, Teddy Kollek, and his wife were sitting directly in front of us. In the interest of harmony, the evening's presentations were in Hebrew, English, and Arabic. To Irving, never the world's most patient man, it drew things out to excessive lengths. Soon, the unmistakable rumbling fidgets were starting. He needed to use the bathroom again.

I tried to distract him, saying it was almost intermission. The row on either side of us was packed. His discomfort grew noticeably worse. To my dismay, there were empty seats in front of us. The scenario was inevitable. Either he'd try and climb over the seats or he'd trample everyone in our row on his way out and then get terribly lost, as the men's room was on the mezzanine. Even if he made it in time, even if he found his way back sans telltale watermarks on his pants, and even if the ushers let him return to his seat, it would be mortifying. I had held my head high for years in such situations, daring anyone to judge a man his age having to answer nature's call.

But that night, after what happened on the Golan Heights, I could not continue as before. All eyes were on me. Four hundred pairs of eyes watched the young wife of the famous poet stay glued to her seat as her eighty-one-year-old husband opted for the trample-exit, struggling to keep his balance and dignity. *Please God. Please. I can't any more. Please let someone else help him now*, I pleaded in silent despair.

Irving's puckish face, grinning mischievously, soon appeared through the little window in the theatre door, an usher keeping him out in deference to the performers. At intermission, he was swarmed by well-wishers, former students, fans. It did my heart good to see him looking so hale, still bright with that familiar charisma. I asked him again if he was *sure* he didn't need the bathroom before the performance resumed. "No. No. No. I'm fine," he confirmed, grinning exuberantly. We took our seats. The same seats.

When the lights came up this time, Kollek was gone from the seats in front of us, replaced by prime minister Shimon Peres and Mrs. Peres, flanked by two bodyguards. Was there ever a prime minister with a finer haircut, a more elegant suit? I think not. Irving and I exchanged oh-my-gawd looks, suppressing involuntary giggles.

Soon, the dreaded fidgets began, replete with verbal and non-verbal sounds of discomfort and mounting anxiety. I cautioned him to shush, driving a discreet elbow into his side, "Peres knows what putz means, now cut it out!" This time I *knew*, by his eyeing the empty seat next to Peres's bodyguard, that he would try for the step-over exit. The seat would flip up. His foot would go through. He'd ride the seat-back, momentarily centre-hung, straddling it, trying to leverage himself off by rocking side to side while smiling benevolently at the audience as if they'd paid to see this. And the prime minister's bodyguard would react like a lion. There would be a violent wrestling scene, soiled pants, news clips, embarrassing photos … I went numb. Again, four hundred pairs of eyes burned holes through us. Silently, I once more begged for understanding, for someone else to help him, because I could not do it any more. Everything happened as predicted, well, except the part about the bodyguard's reaction.

I bumped our return El Al tickets up to first class. Home again, more exhausted than elated, I think we both prayed for a second wind — or that the crack, still just a fissure in our marriage, would not grow any larger. "The Changing Book" contains no reference to any of this. "Israel: There's a Crack in Everything" would need twenty years before I could write it.

33: What Did You Expect?

FLIPPING GINGERLY THOUGH "The Changing Book," I see anew how the heartbreak started even before that trip to Israel. By November 1992, after a beautiful morning of Irving dictating a letter to local poet Michael Harris and an afternoon full of affection and ease, the day lurched off the rails. His hearing was by then very poor and required the television to be at maximum volume even though we sat five feet from it. I was making supper, Irving was downstairs watching Dan Rather expound on neo-Nazis kicking a Turk. He kept calling up to me with running commentary the story.

Trying not to drop the roast chicken or burn myself, his comments began to unnerve me. Once settled downstairs with our supper, I calmly asked him not to shout like that, as I could hear every word and it made me nervous. He took it as an attack, and defended himself by lapsing into a shockingly childish cry of "lalalalalala" with his eyes closed, holding both palms over his ears, elbows in the air, fingertips pointing downwards. He then implored me to stop repeating things to him, and bolted upstairs.

It shook me to my core. The pills surely must be to blame. I thought, picking at my supper. Irving knew he was starting that slide into the dark good night. Death, as he told me numerous times, was not an issue for him, but the very thought of losing his memory crippled him with fear, and the pills were making it worse.

After a few minutes, he returned downstairs. We ate in silence. Later, as I did the dishes, he came up to offer an explanation. He had mistakenly thought the neo-Nazis were kicking a Jewish man, and it upset him terribly. "I'm not interested in explanations." I said, cutting him off abruptly. "Oh," he said quietly, and went up to our bedroom. If I could take that moment back, I would. No man deserves being reduced to such a state. I waited a bit before joining him and calmly explaining that, regardless of what's on the news, it does not justify his using that tone and shouting at me, especially after he had been so affectionate a few minutes earlier. We slipped into one of our conspiratorial talks and set things aright again.

The news footage had triggered in Irving the sensation that he was under attack. He saw a Turk being brutalized, but subconsciously interpreted it as himself. Later that night, after his walk and his pipe, he sat me down at the dining room table and shared how one event — perhaps more than any other — had altered his life permanently. At some point during his time with Aviva, he was in need of dental work. A friend recommended a Greek dentist, who, whether incompetent or an anti-Semite or both, extracted far more teeth than necessary, including perfectly good ones that could have been used to anchor bridgework later on. When Irving recovered from the procedure and realized what the dentist had done, he described the effect on his personality and sense of self as devastating. This, compounded with what he described at Aviva's total lack of empathy, had devastated him. As he told me this, he began to break down, his whole body shaking with pent-up anguish. I had never seen him like that and wanted to cry for what he had suffered, but it served no purpose. The journal again records my vow to make his days and nights as happy and carefree as possible.

This remembered injury at the hands of a dentist, like the misinterpreted news footage, falls into perspective only now. Sensing that Time had him in his sights, the recollection of being emasculated by that dentist, so to speak, was akin to what he was feeling then. Time was declawing and defanging him, and he was just as helpless now as in that dentist's chair.

"Face time! I must have face time!" he chimed the next day, keeping me at the breakfast table again instead of upstairs dispatching the work at hand.

Who knows what propels us down any given path. In my case, I can say the weight loss led to the jarring, almost traumatic discovery of my own body at the age of thirty-two. Despite the residual anger, cellulite, stretch-marks, and permanent blue veins like a road map to nowhere on my legs, my body had begun to thrive. I started taking care of it by joining the local YMCA. There, I met a young athlete. The most jejune thing I want to say here is that from the very moment I first moved in with Irving, my intention was to be faithful to him until death did us part. Morality and my personal integrity had nothing to do with it; my loathing for banality had *everything* to do with wanting to stay true to Irving. People expected me to take a lover, and I loathed their presumptuous, filthy little minds. Mother Nature, however, had other plans. It began with me telling Irving I overheard the boy — for that's all he was at age nineteen — talk with his friends about going out. Would it be alright, I asked, if I went out with them one night. Irving readily agreed. There was no place he could take me where I could wear my pale yellow mini-dress. Irving gave me to believe he was actually relieved that I had found someone to take me dancing.

That November, we flew to Chicago on what was, I believe, his last international reading. It went very well, Irving could still enthrall an audience. That night in the hotel, however, I had to steer Irving away from the closet and into the bathroom to his left when he woke in the middle of the night. "These doors all look the same," I said, trying to ease his nerves and repair his dignity. Back home, on November 29, 1993, "The Changing Book" notes:

> In the past few months, several things have happened. Irving was diagnosed with Parkinson's, the kind which also affect the brain's frontal lobes. I succumbed to the strains and pressures of these last few years, also perhaps reacted to the imagined hardships ahead, took a lover, got pregnant and today had an abortion. In a way, I don't feel as if I betrayed Irving, partly because the Irving I knew so well and for so long has gone away. He remains my best, truest friend, but age prevents him from fully expressing and exhibiting all the affection and attention any wife needs. There are mixed feelings all around. I said to myself

I am not really betraying him — I am being loyal to myself. He not only understands, but in a way feels relieved
of the guilt he felt at having taken such a young wife. I am
a very changed person, very much changed. It is late now,
and I can't begin to do justice to my turmoil, my newfound
serenity which is quite likely a profound numbness that is
helping me through these painful days and nights.

Life after that point consisted of trying to keep Layton Enterprizes
going, maintaining my weight with regular workouts (which ultimately
led to me taking up freestyle wrestling), and spending time with my
young companion. That "relationship," if desperation is any basis for
friendship, had more red flags than the Kremlin on May Day. I had so
little faith in myself at that point that I would look at his chiselled body
and wonder if I would ever be that close to physical perfection again. It
dragged on while I looked for ways to break it off. For the record, "The
Changing Book" entries about him are full of romantic flourishes. Even
while writing them, however, I knew that I was doing so to dress up a
brutally unwise affair. Did he permit me to feel happy or whatever? On
occasion yes, but there were no grounds for couple-hood.

By early December of 1993, I was exhausted, angry, bewildered,
and sad. Musia could see the tension and soon became privy to what
was going on. She arranged for a caretaker. Alla, a Russian-Jewish lady,
was wonderful with Irving, looking after him as if he was family. It
eased my mind, and afforded me some respite.

Life was changing too rapidly to take stock of it all. On December
8, 1993, I note how some days Irving was so hyper — whether from
stress or Parkinson's or those damn pills — that I began allowing myself
to contemplate the heretofore unimaginable: moving out and returning
to the ordinary world. I could not sustain the thought for more than
a few microseconds, resolving to manage somehow. A few days later,
I returned very late from my friend's place. Irving was in bed, but a
cough told me he was still awake. He knew where I had been. On most
days, he managed to be generous, philosophical, and relieved. Other
times, he hurled angry, hateful words at me, leaving me mortified and

mute with despair. Our many talks had helped clarify many things, but, obviously, the status quo was becoming untenable by the week.

On December 19, I happened on a newspaper article on the early warning signs for Alzheimer's. Irving's doctor had not used the A word yet. The article described personality changes and mood swings. For the past two weeks or so, I wondered what had gotten into Irving, even telling Musia there were days I did not recognize him. Whether caused by Parkinson's or the pills, surely the stress and pain I caused him made everything worse. I sank deeper into abject wretchedness.

If it was Alzheimer's, I needed to stop arguing with him and cease all self-justifying chronologies whenever he asked me how I was. Perhaps my guilt could be cut in half, my taking a lover almost forgivable.

Then, on Christmas day, "The Changing Book" records yet another turning point:

> That's it. Over. Over. He said he wanted affection and a little love from me. How can anyone respond to a stranger with anything but outraged coldness? The names and scenes have grown so ugly. Worst of all is the roller coaster mood swings. I am fairly consistent — numb, with intermittent attempts at getting him to see my side of the story. But Irving, whether it's the stress, the pills he's on, or what I suspect — Alzheimer's, he varies with an increasing amplitude. Week by week, even day by day it seems the "good" moods have more hysteria than happiness in them. And the bad moods — I don't even try describing them — the ugly words, innuendoes, and the vehemency with which he spits these out, each coated with bitter venom. Have I said this before? Perhaps if emotions had been allowed to develop naturally, this situation wouldn't be so tragic. Indeed, the mistake was for me to have let my personal life bind to his. But even as I write this, I know it could not have been otherwise.

On New Year's Eve, I describe a horrific incident that took place that week. Irving had met a lady. He announced he was going off to see his "companion." There was no torrid affair — she was married and welcomed him as a family friend. It was merely his way of maintaining his dignity and manhood. It may also have been his way to help cleave me from him, knowing I needed to reclaim my independence and that my staying on would destroy us both. That night, desperation now a dull routine, I set off to my friend's place, albeit with a terrible sense of foreboding. Thinking Irving surely must be back, I phoned him. I called and called but he did not answer. "What if he's fallen and is at the bottom of the stairs right now?" I asked my friend, who urged me to go and see. Despite feeling sick to my stomach, I stayed put, dreading a terrible scene, which would double my wretchedness and send me scurrying back to my friend's place like a crazed insect through the darkened streets.

I kept calling. Irving finally picked up after midnight. He'd had an accident, he said, and did not want to tell me over the phone. I assumed it had to do with incontinence. He did not ask me to come home, so I stayed put. Back at the house early the next morning, I bent to untie my hiking boots and saw blood spots on the floor. I bounded upstairs to find Irving in bed. He had missed the last step and careened headfirst into the cast iron radiator. There was dried blood staining his hair on the left side of his head. The cut, some three inches long, was still sickeningly livid. His elbow swelled to the size of a small lime, and an oval bruise about six inches long and three-and-a-half inches wide was clearly visible on the left side of his back. The bleeding had stopped and he refused medical attention.

Despite everything, he was calm, lucid, in fact — the Irving I remembered. We blew off Layton Enterprizes and talked all day, achieving a real breakthrough. After weeks and weeks of hell, of feeling like a pair of lunatics jerking on the steering wheel of a speeding car, we'd finally straightened out. Both of us seemed to accept the fact that our continuing to be "Mr. and Mrs." was no longer possible because we were no longer the same people. The journal entry ends with, "The age difference had finally caught up and posed too great an obstacle, too many pressures. A real metamorphosis took place in front of our eyes and I think we *both* felt something of the burden lifting."

I began 1994 by reminding myself to resist whatever diabolical force that renders intelligent, creative, spirited women useless as wrecked shells. One survival tactic was to pretend I had no needs beyond ordinary ones, and try to fulfill myself whenever and howsoever I could. Even Irving's son David, who visited around this time, suggested in so many words that it was okay for me to look elsewhere for physical companionship. It was impossible to guess whether he spoke from genuine compassion, or if he was laying a trap. It felt as if people were taking bets as to when the paragon of virtue could be induced to fall and stain her name like those who came before her. Up until then, only Irving, Musia, Alla, and later, Aviva, knew my crown had already rolled into a muddy ditch.

That week, Bill dropped by. I disappeared into my study, unwilling to deal with his prying questions. The next thing I knew, Irving was asking his nephew Bill what he would do if he caught his wife cheating on him. I felt sick. Irving and I had sorted it out, but now Bill would assume the worst and perhaps tell everyone of his suspicions. After Bill left, I came downstairs and questioned Irving about the wisdom behind asking that leading question. "Bill raised the subject," he said. Possibly, but it was Irving's voice I heard. Irving was terribly tense.

Things got worse toward lunch. He was agitated, perhaps as a result of how much coffee he had consumed: a pot for himself before I arrived that morning; half of the pot I made for myself; and yet another pot to serve Bill. He had knoshed all morning. Afraid for his overeating, I suggested, "Why don't you have a big piece of pie and milk for lunch, and we'll have an early supper? He blew up, incensed.

"That's not enough for lunch," he raged. I gave in, exasperated at how his will always triumphed when he overate or did something he should not be doing.

My next faux pas was to remark he was pumped up on too much caffeine, which really set him off. His voice became strident, laced with meanness such as I had never heard. "Where are you learning to be so nit-picky, from your *friend?*" he snarled. This after having offered a few months earlier to let my friend move into the basement. Absurd as it was, he had even suggested with wrenching earnestness that my friend and I might raise our child there.

His monstrous jeering was unbearable and almost frightening. I could not cope when he became this hysterical, hurtful, coarse stranger.

Blind with raging despair, I slammed the bag of bread I was about to put in the freezer onto the floor and screamed, "That's *IT!*" Later I recorded the argument in "The Changing Book":

> **THAT'S *IT!*** As I stormed past him out of the kitchen, I spun around and raised my clenched fists to chest height and dropped down into a fighting stance, hissing that I could kill him when he was like that. This provoked him to clench *his* fists and punch me in the head and face, as well as knee me a couple of times in the legs. His hair, spiky and uncombed, flared stiffly around his head. His glasses were slightly askew and his eyes were round with rage, though they looked small in that large head, which was now the head of a madman. I was quite stunned to be punched in the face. Yet, as he rained his blows down on my head, I was almost relieved. Maybe he'd get the anger out of his system at last. In any case, he was lashing out at the world for having brought him to this, and though there was rage and madness in his eyes, there was also fear and it was heartbreaking. He of course apologized almost immediately, though I was in no mood to be the kind, sweet, all-forgiving wife. I was plenty pissed off, and spent the next half hour holding a bag of frozen peas against my bruised cheek.

The year ground on. With my friend out of the country temporarily, Irving and I were virtually two halves of an arthritic knee joint. The slightest contact caused excruciating pain. My face grew gaunt with frustration. Irving was in and out of the fridge constantly — newborns could go longer between feedings. His nervous anxiety, impatience, and general agitation communicated themselves through the very walls and floors of the house. I too began to eat nervously, ruining my appetite and diet until food became repugnant. We were both victims. On good days, the gentle Irving emerged, asking me how I felt, whether I looked forward to the future. "You might just as well have asked that of Dresden or Hiroshima after the war: yes, I suppose one day a flower will grow and life will return, but right now, I am as blackened and bombed out as those two cities were," I answered. He still loved my rhetorical flair, but my words just added to the ineffable sadness.

"You should write this all down! Are you making notes?" he asked other times, still wanting me to write.

"I don't have to, Irving," I quipped one day. "I will be able to read my scars like Braille."

My birthday, like the previous year, passed without a phone call from home. Musia took me out for lunch. She suspected, but did not know the full complexity of our devolution. Sympathetic but concerned only for Irving, she arranged for me to talk to a professional listener at the Herzl Clinic. She also arranged for a social worker, Rose, who encouraged me to repeat my favourite word, "water," when feeling overwhelmed. If I could go anywhere, Rose asked, where would I go? New York City. "Good!" she exclaimed. "You do that. Make arrangements and go. It will do you good."

I bought a guide book, but that is as close to New York as I got. What if someone asked what I did for a living? I did plenty, but nothing that anyone could relate to. They would all think me bizarre. Feeling too shattered to venture further than the 24 bus could take me, I slid into a mute, robotic existence. Eventually, Musia put the unspeakable into words. It was time for me to decide: stay and improve the situation, or move out.

At the height of the crisis, Aviva arrived from Los Angeles. She sat ever so sweetly on the love seat with me, the basement resonating with my sobs. I can still hear that dulcet voice, cooing, "You poor thing! O you *poor* thing, Anna!", trilling away in her Australian accent, "You've got to leave him! You've *got to!* Aw, Sweetheart, you've got to leave!"

Later, down to my last roll of pennies and a few coins, utterly broken, but now on my own, I was stunned by the coldness of the new keepers of the gate. It was as if my visits were begrudged, allowed only because Irving remained as fond of my company as before. They also commanded me to stop telling Irving about my grim reality, even if he asked. Aviva, back in town to check on Irving, sneered, "Well, what did you *expect?* You *left* him!"

Late one night in January 1995, during that brief but intensely un-happy time when I had taken to spending the day with Irving, waiting until he fell asleep before heading to my friend's place for the night, my friend and I set out for an ATM machine. He needed to borrow a twenty. It was 2:00 a.m. The wind cut through our tracksuits, freezing our bed-warm skin within minutes. Somerled was ink black save for gauzy sheets of snow billowing toward us. Each lamppost shook in its own pool of feeble light cast onto the asphalt.

Suddenly, just ahead of us, a small dark figure weaved slowly up the empty sidewalk. My stomach convulsed with such violence that it seemed as if my insides had swallowed themselves. Anguish ripped through me in that horrible instant of recognition. I would rather have looked on anything but this. Irving. Walking alone, in the freezing night, his Greek fisherman's cap pulled down hard to one side, his hair whipped back by an icy wind. One bare hand, luminous against his navy blue pea jacket, pulled it closed against the bitter wind. A forlorn Napoleon, his other hand hidden inside an empty pocket. The care-givers now deprived him of cash, save for a few coins.

I watched, barely able to breathe as he loomed, a small leviathan, out of the darkness. A dark blue presence, aimless against the swal-lowing black and whirling snow, he sidled up along shop windows, holding tight against the cold and wind.

It is one of the last images I have of Irving as still relatively autono-mous, able to come and go as he pleased, that brutal night in January 1995. I cannot now recall whether I approached him, or let him con-tinue his eerie stroll uninterrupted. What I do know is that we were now at the lowest, most wretched point in our lives.

Three months later, after nearly fourteen years, our marriage ended.

34: Goodbye

THERE IS NO DATE on this letter, but it was likely February 1995:

Irving –

Don't you understand? It's precisely <u>because</u> I am so aware of the need here for compassion and gentleness that I see how far away I am from being able to provide these things. It is nearly impossible for me to separate you from "The Situation". "The Situation" / you have reduced me to a perverse caricature of everything I both was and further aspired to become. You or The Situation destroyed me and I am torn by grief as well as by a black, bottomless rage. Something, i.e., someone extremely rare and precious has been killed. Time has done you a dirty — but how do you [think] I feel as a 35 year old who has also been done a dirty? I am truly sorry, very very sorry for everything.

A.

PS: And how do you think I feel, me — who had so much potential and real talent — when I see a ___. Here she comes into my unkempt home (because I am too fucked up at this point to do the damn housework) with her beautiful

clothes, perfect hair, makeup and carefully chosen jewel-
ry and sees me — the perpetual fat ill-groomed teenager
— with her rich husband whose bulging wallet renders
the Mexican cab driver as obsequious as if were serving
a car load of Royals just in from London — and her perfect daughter already grown and on her way to a diplo-
matic career while my child, my beautiful baby has long
since been turned to pond scum and worm food for some
lucky worms in the sewers leading from the clinic to the
St-Lawrence. And she comes in with her perfectly tabulat-
ed, typed, professionally plasticated document-like manuscript while all I can manage — and only on good days
— is to clip the odd coupon from the flyers and staple it
to a hastily, distractedly scribbled grocery list whose items
I rarely am able to collect myself long enough to actually
purchase. Instead of the gourmet meals I used to feel like
making, there are bags of chips and gallons of ice cream I
now devour madly, mindlessly before vomiting the stuff
up into a toilet whose stench alone provides the gag reflex,
mouth open wide as the stained germy bowl over which
I crouch and retch and heave the junk out of my gut. My
gurgling, fucked-up unhappy gut. Compassion? Is there a
God and if so why didn't He create a single human with
compassion for **me?** It is **I** who has given my life to you —
not the other way around. But that no longer matters and
it probably never did.

Truth is, I mattered more to Irving than I had ever mattered to
anyone else.

35: Escape

BETWEEN MUSIA, the social worker, and even a marriage counsellor, I still needed someone to tell me it would be okay to leave. After three visits to a psychiatrist, I received the permission I sought, and began looking for an apartment. On March 1, 1995, Venie, who on Irving's advice had remarried, took him out to a movie. By the time she brought Irving home — as we all knew — I would be gone, moved into an apartment some two kilometres away.

The only reason I got the apartment, a beautiful one-bedroom at 6151 Côte-Saint-Luc Road, was because the owner was a huge fan of Irving's. The affair between me and my young friend had slowed, then crawled to a halt. And though unemployed, the thirty thousand dollars in mutual funds that Irving had given me made me feel rich. So, on that March night, I walked out of my marital home with the clothes on my back, a toothbrush and whatever toiletries fit into a plastic bag, and began life as a single woman.

Readying for the move, I listed my personal effects: clothing, books, photos, papers, journals, pens, stationery, make-up, videotapes, cassettes, a set of Irish linen bedsheets that had been in my mother's trousseau, blue Kenwood wool blanket, a quilt my mother had made, and my camera. Once in my new place, I added a computer and a telephone. I was relieved to have my own place, to see only my things in the medicine cabinet, but with every little flap of my Free Bird wings, the wounds ripped open again. I kept imagining Irving coming back to and being in that empty house. Trying in vain to lessen the pity, guilt, and wretchedness I felt at leaving Irving, I went to the SPCA and got him a cat. Irving named him Walter. At least he had Walter. Guilt and sorrow tore at me for the next ten years. Rumours of how I stole fifty thousand dollars in clothes or money, and had the presence of mind to take some of Irving's millions and bury it in the backyard on Monkland did nothing to sweeten the start of my new life.

I was thirty-five years old, without a stick of furniture beyond a new bed. This was quite different from the twenty-three year old with a world-renowned husband and a home, with neither a mortgage nor a care in the world. Suddenly anonymous, I started over from less than zero. After a trip to Ikea and splashing out on a Biltmore sofa so huge it had to be hoisted from the roof and eased in through my living room window, I sat in my own ivory-coloured bathrobe — rather than in one of Irving's — feet up, coffee in hand. For the first time in nearly fourteen years, I could finally just *be,* tranquillity punctuated only by birdsong. By around ten-thirty each morning, however, I missed Irving's company so much that I dressed and walked back to the house to spend the day with him, occasionally retrieving bits of clothing, my favourite coffee cup and cookbook, or other small oddments. Our union had ruptured, but not the bond between us.

This went on for the first year. Irving had been my entire world. He was grateful for my company, and the entourage, as I had begun to call them, did not yet object. My presence now brightened his spirits, as long as I did not burden him with unhappy subjects. It was bizarre to see letters on the table, unanswered. By unspoken agreement, they were no longer my concern. If Musia or Bill asked things such as how to file dental claims, I told them. Layton Enterprizes had dried up. Several months later, when my finances began to do the same, I confided in Irving from sheer force of habit, having done so my entire adult life. The entourage accused me of looking for a handout, one of several smears. As in practically every divorce, the female gets short shrift, regardless of circumstances. After about a year of my going back for my Irving fix, they hinted it was best I stay away. It was a lose-lose situation. Continue to visit: they will say I am looking for money. Stay away: they will say I am a heartless bitch. I withdrew from public view, falling virtually mute. Since words could not do justice to my turmoil, I took up oil painting instead. Colours worked where words failed.

My leaving Irving meant that five people were hired as salaried caregivers. I was burning through my savings and still too shell-shocked to look for work. Irving could offer only his love and moral support. Thrilled that I had taken to painting, he bought two paintings for something like one hundred dollars apiece. He had *Lady in the Dior Hat* hanging in the living room where he could see it from his chair in the dining room; and *Mavillette Beach* in the bedroom. His pride in my painting recalled those heady days when he read something of mine and said, "Blessed is the teacher whose student surpasses him." Of a small self-portrait, Irving declared I looked as stunned from the victory as from having fought the battle.

Naively, stupidly, I hoped the entourage would perhaps buy my paintings too. Leon and Musia Schwartz, avid art collectors and reputed to be millionaires, were a faint possibility. Had I not toasted them on my thirtieth birthday, thanking them for being my surrogate Jewish parents? Surely, they might purchase a painting to tide me over, salvaging my pride. This hope flared and died like a candle in a gale. I would figure something out. Bill flinched when I got up my nerve to ask for a small loan. "Sorry, but I'm helping my son buy a pizza franchise, and my wife deserves all the comfort I can provide, so no, I can't lend you any money."

I had taken up wrestling by accident through people at the local YMCA. On the mats, I was respected by the Russian, Georgian, Iranian, and Armenian wrestlers and went full-throttle for each "*horosho*" ("excellent") from the Russian coach. I was also mercifully anonymous, relishing the brute "below the neck" physicality of Turk rides, gut-wrenches, and laced-ankles. I threw myself into it with maniacal abandon, training six days a week with the Montreal Wrestling Club for three-and-a-half years. With little else to put on my resumé, I listed being a member of the Montreal Wrestling Club. It caught an employer's eye, saving me from destitution. The extreme physicality and welcome anonymity brutalized my body while giving my psyche a chance to heal. After living from the neck up for so long, I was now living from the neck down. Only a wrestler would understand the satisfaction of overhearing Coach Victor Zilberman say to the assistant coach, "If only the guys could be more like Anna!", wondering where I got my energy and enthusiasm. His wrestlers included world-class champions in their prime. Chokri was ninety kilograms to my seventy-five. We met on the mats at the Montreal Wrestling Club.

What should have been a brief restorative encounter involving strong arms and a broad chest upon which to pillow my sorrows ended with marriage in a Montreal mosque on November 11, 1996. *Remembrance Day?* The imam, Chokri said, had an opening and they set the date. It was one of several misgivings I let slide for lack of strength. *Misgivings?* Here too I saw a sea of red flags, but a bedraggled need for affection so clouded my judgment that I nose-dived into the catastrophe, still too numb to care.

Despite the fact that Irving understood why I had to leave him when I did, I remained guilt-stricken. Even with his compassionate understanding when he said, "Anna, it's not fair. I've had you all to myself all these years. You have to live your own life." Nevertheless, if I felt anything at all, it was guilt's toxins burning holes through what remained of my soul. An entire decade would pass until I could go a day or so without thinking of Irving.

We had no money for rings let alone a honeymoon, and no guests except Chokri's two close friends as witnesses. Unbeknownst to me, his friends were feuding. Had they remained on the outs, the wedding would not have taken place and perhaps one of us might have spoken our doubts aloud. In the half hour before entering the mosque, we waited in a borrowed car for his friends. Not one word was spoken, not one gesture made. Only after our divorce did he confess how doubt and foreboding had overwhelmed him. He was twelve years my junior, Muslim, unskilled beyond being a champion wrestler, and unemployable due to visa restrictions.

I have no reason to speak ill of Chokri. Rumour had it he married me for the immigration visa, another smear spread by the entourage. Discrediting me was their way of making themselves look like starlets on the Irving Layton red carpet. I had no option but to rage privately.

Marrying such an inappropriate second husband was my punishment and self-incarceration for having left Irving. In ten years: no dancing; not a drop of wine or whisky; no soul-meshing conversation; no hand-holding in public; no French kissing in private; no going to movies; no cavorting in the waves when we finally did get to a beach; no socializing beyond a visitor, or two at Ramadan. Now in a smaller, cheaper apartment at 6010 Cote-Saint-Luc Road, I made do. Every weekend for ten years, I sat home while he went to the mosque and then to play chess at a café. "*Repose-toi*," he'd say (rest), as he left our tiny apartment after his ablutions: me splayed out on the couch, drained, defeated. I was working full-time; training six days a week as a freestyle wrestler (becoming 1998 national champion); teaching myself how to oil paint; and, starting in 2003, going to Concordia University at night, which began with Dr. Michael Kenneally's superb course on James Joyce's *Ulysses* — all while trying to get over the "Irving thing" and its harrowing aftermath.

The years of despair led to an appalling weight gain. Worse still, in an over-zealous attempt to shape up, I'd blown a disc in my back. Nerves leading to my right ankle died, leaving me with a slight limp and a permanently compromised stance. The weekend my back gave out — me speeding to the emergency in an ambulance — is the same one whereupon I told Chokri that, after a decade of self-deprivation, my forties completely wasted, he had to find somewhere else to stay. By August of 2006 poverty, stagnation, and our sad incompatibility had taken their toll, as had ten years of Muslim decorum. He fed, dressed, and cared for me for six weeks as I lay on bed or floor. Wrestling had proven me to have an extremely high pain threshold, but this was beyond pain. On occasion, my screams were so chilling that Chokri feared the police would be called or that my lease would be cancelled. My surgeon said had the disc blown out just a little more, I would have been left without control over bowels or bladder, and paralyzed from the fourth lumbar vertebra down. Chokri's ministrations, extended knowing our marriage was over, is a mercy I recall now with sorrow and silence.

Despite the entourage's preference that I stay away, I continued to visit Irving from time to time over that barren decade with Chokri. After leaving Irving, a couple of tribute nights were thrown for him.

One was at the Centaur Theatre where everyone was told to bring a flower. He seemed exhausted. I was not invited to that event, but went as if I were an anonymous fan.

Irving still knew me, of course. During my visits, increasingly, he asked about my life but then repeated the same questions. On the table next to him, Tadeusz Borowski's *This Way for the Gas, Ladies and Gentlemen*; I realized it was always there because he forgot that he'd read it. He showed me passages, devastated afresh as if reading of the horror for the first time. When it was time to leave, he always insisted on walking me to the door, even with Alla helping to steady him. "It was lovely to see you, Love! Come back soon and join me for a cup of coffee!" I promised to do so, urging him to go inside before he caught cold. After each visit, I would cry for two or three days. Finally, it seemed best to thin these visits down to almost nothing. It was too hard both of us.

The last public appearance of Irving's that I know of was a tribute evening to mark Jewish Book Month in late 1999. He was seated in the front row along with Max and Musia and Leon. Even his daughter Samantha was there. I found out about the event in the *Gazette*, and had long-abandoned thoughts of being offered a ticket or something wildly absurd like a reserved seat. Afterward, I stood in the bright lobby while a photographer documented Irving's final public appearance. Musia and Leon flanked him as the flashes lit up Irving's tired, drained face. They shot me icy looks, daring me to approach. I turned and left, dignity if nothing else intact.

One day in the summer of 2000 I was called and told that the house had been sold. Long since shut out of Irving's private affairs, I only found out after the fact that the entourage facilitated the rewriting of his will in 1996, when he was completely dependent on them. The notarized will drawn up in November 1994, when his accountant, the notary, and myself had no doubt of his long-standing conviction to bequeath me the house and its contents, was now a worthless piece of paper. Irving was in Maimonides, oh, and there was a box of knick-knacks for me and I should come pick it up. Brutal as that. By that time, the entourage had iced me out so completely that I was denied the chance to see Irving one last time in what had been our marital home.

I walked to the house a few days later, having picked up the few knick-knacks, and found garbage bags stuffed to bursting lined up alongside the length of the house. It made me nauseous. Fortunately, I had catalogued the items covering his final productive years for Concordia's last accession. Whatever remained now filled those garbage bags, the entourage having no care for what they were throwing out or giving away. This is how his life was winding down, in garbage bags? I would not visit him in Maimonides. I continued on as best I could with office jobs, painting, and trying to put Irving out of mind in order to move forward, yet thinking of him daily.

The entourage forgot to tell me how ill he was. I learned of his death on January 4, 2006, from the CBC's Peter Mansbridge, his sombre voice announcing, "Irving Layton, dead at ninety-three ... " Montreal turned to cardboard for me that night.

36: Final Scene

WITH THE SAME KIND of chance and appetite that enticed me to braid my life with Irving's, I was able to undo that braid and make my way toward a new life. Eventually, love and landscapes brought me to Utah. I have a good man at my side and am, at last, minutes away from completing this book. As I write, the skies are heavy with rare dove-grey clouds. There is rain in the air. Perhaps it is only my imagination, but I swear I can see Irving and his cohort God on some celestial porch taking their time, waiting, ready to burst into thunderous applause.

How odd to look back and remember with such a vivid, piercing ache of the last time I saw Irving, kissing him goodbye that cold afternoon in March 2001. The Concordia librarians and dignitaries warmly saluted Irving for handing them the last batch of his papers. The reception ended. I collected my coat and hurried outside to find Irving already bundled into the back of the limo. I approached the huge car, its doors still open. *The next time he will be in such a big car, it will be his hearse,* I thought, my heart pounding, my eyes already stinging with tears. I knew then that I would never see him again. My mountain was turning into grains of sand, and I could not bear the weight of such desolation.

I ducked into the limo to kiss him goodbye for the last time. He kissed me back. I can still feel his warm lips and cheek next to mine. And then, with my face still inches from his, he looked directly at me, held me once again with his blue, blue eyes and, gently taking my face in his hands said, "Anna, I will love you until the day I die."

Those were his last words to me.

Epilogue: Idiot Wind: Catharsis

BY THE SUMMER OF 2008, I had left the office world and academia behind, a 3.96 GPA dissolving into the ether. My unemployment benefits expired. Yet, after nearly collapsing from the strain of the past twenty years, I still trusted my latent abilities to carry me through. I now thrived on the explosive joy that came with each step toward the latest version of my best true self. Now, with a modest inheritance from Irving, why not just blow the biscuit and enjoy life. I could suss out a rideshare on Craigslist, write about the experience and break into freelance journalism.

The rideshares out of Montreal were unspeakably dull. New York City, however, rippled with possibility. If I could get to New York, I could get rides to anywhere, including one all the way to the West Coast. Better yet, Ray Tarantino, the thirty-one-year-old Italian-born singer, wasn't even asking for gas money! The travel companion he sought needed only to pay for her hotel and food expenses. For once, a "too-good-to-be-true" scenario proved sublimely true.

Ray was doing an acoustic tour, playing gigs from New York to Portland, Oregon. His call had "destiny" written all over it like gold flecks on a Godiva chocolate. I had just turned forty-nine, had no job, no kids, no pets, no plants. The inheritance was practically screaming *use me*. Ray said little beyond "Meet me at Nietzsche's Bar in Buffalo on Friday and we'll go to Portland." That's all it took. I was good as gone.

I missed the first bus out. "No problem. Take the next one," Ray said. It was the eighth day of the eighth month of the millennium's eighth year. The Greyhound bus rolled into Buffalo at 4:30 a.m., me too excited to sleep through one mile of that first night on the road. I stood under an indigo sky near the Lafayette Hotel, waiting out the hours. And there he was, a tall scoop of earth, rolling toward me, linen shirt open to his solar plexus. Crystal pendants and small amulets on leather strings nestled in chest hair the colour of burnt saffron and umber. His wrists were banded with leather and bracelets of stone beads and shells. We helloed, hugged, took stock with quick laser-beam looks, and fell out into the bright sunshine.

Fact is, we were complete strangers about to drive across America. Standing by the car, him smoking a Marlboro, we chatted somewhat nervously before setting off. "I've never been to Niagara Falls. Let's go see it," he said with a recklessness that mirrored my own. We were equally spontaneous, and truly free-spirited. Despite his charisma and all my unrequited libido, there was erected between us a Great Wall of Chastity, undeclared, but tangible. Our flesh would never come to touch. We sped out of Buffalo, Ray playing me cuts from his *Recusant* CD.

By the time we got to Cleveland, I had become a roadie, me carrying his guitar into The Barking Spider Pub. Martin, the owner, radiated generosity. His classic American countenance made me feel glory-bound, welcoming me to the best of what America means to me then as now. Gig over, we packed up in a torrential rain and headed west. After my "borrowing" a Toledo hotel room that was under renovation, saving myself $109, then his gig at Sylvie's Lounge in Chicago, we hit interstate 80-S. Ray played Bob Dylan's *Blood on the Tracks* album almost continually. As we blazed out of Chicago, the lyrics to "Idiot Wind" began to reach through to me as more than just a song. At first, I resisted the sense of connection as merely incidental brewings of a road-weary, slightly wired mind.

Yet each time "Idiot Wind" played, something cut through me like an Edgar Allen Poe pendulum slicing through the numbness I'd wrapped myself in. Cupping chin and trembling mouth in my hand, I stared out the side window, hiding my face from Ray. By this time, he knew enough of my story to let his intuition take over. "Anna? You okay?" he asked softly. "Yes, I'm fine. It's just this song. The lyrics ... "

I'd had stories planted in the press, and wished "they'd cut it out quick." I hadn't "known peace and quiet for so long" that I'd forgotten what it was like. Chokri had "tamed the lion in my cage but it just wasn't enough to change my heart." Irving: "I followed you beneath the stars, hounded by your memory and all your ragin' glory ... It was gravity which pulled us down and destiny which broke us apart ... "

"Want me to change the CD?"

"No." So he hit replay again. And again, over and over again and again, "Idiot Wind" playing at full volume as the miles rolled out behind us.

"Let it out! Let it all out! SING IT OUT!" Ray shouted as the night-dark wind whipped through the open windows. Learning the lyrics as we drove, I sang with an off-key violence, tears flowing unchecked well into the next day. We'd been on a piece of Highway 61, another Dylan connection. Everything happens on Highway 61. I was about to undergo a life-altering catharsis.

Nearing Davenport, Iowa, on the third day I sobbed from the depths of my very soul. Nearly every line of this song spoke to a hurt as vast as the surrounding fields. My eyes were red, swollen. My voice grew ragged as I sang and smoked and let wracking sobs tear through me and out my torn open mouth. Ray drove on. His soul, ancient as my own, seemed there to bring me through to the other side.

And suddenly, without warning, it was over. The last of the chagrin, pain, rage, and every other long-buried hurt left me. "Double-crossed for the very last time ... and now I'm finally FREE." After "losing all the battles," I had "finally won the war." It was an extraordinary moment, literally feeling the last of the guilt, that profound sorrow concede defeat and disappear. Ray drove without speaking as I sat motionless, letting the newfound stillness flood through me. Wholeness and calm purled over the clean-washed stones in my riverbed self. Catharsis. The crippling soul-ache was no more. Whatever else might happen, I would never stagger under that kind of burden again. Just then, at that *precise* moment, I looked up and there was the sign for Annawan, Illinois. "Annawan." Anna won. "Ray!" I exclaimed, "Did you see that? *Annawan!* We just passed "Annawan! I WON!"

A strange excitement grabbed at us, we were grinning, laughing. "I won, I'm FREE!" I laughed, Ray declaring, "Anna, after losing all the battles, you finally *won!*" We were super-charged and giddy with the realization that something extraordinary had just transpired. I sat back, completely drained and electrified at the same time.

Several miles of cornfields rolled by, me savouring my freedom and feeling magnificently alive. Up ahead against the heavy sky, a large blue ironwork structure loomed up. "What on *earth* do they need a big bridge like that for?" I scoffed, shaking my head at the engineering folly. "Nothing around here but tiny little creeks.... Oh! Ohmi*god*, Ray!" I gasped. The mighty Mississippi lay dead ahead, glinting silver under the afternoon clouds.

I was awestruck at the sight of this iconic, immensely powerful river. We were about to cross the Mississippi. "Oh my god … oh my *gawd*. It's the Mississippi!" is all I could manage. It was immediately ahead, then below, then behind me. Ray offered another cigarette declaring, "Anna, if ever there was a natural dividing line between one's past and one's future, you've just crossed it." My hands were shaking as I, speechless, fumbled with cigarette and camera.

The next morning, we set out for Des Moines. Again without saying a word, Ray veered off the interstate and drove down to the western bank of the Mississippi. We stepped out and walked along a little sand and pebble beach, aware of one another, each alone in our thoughts. There was warm sunshine, the sound of birds, and the river's deep hush. I walked into the water a little ways in my sandalled feet, letting the Mississippi wash away whatever else needed to be swept from me. The river's sheer force was almost overwhelming. I looked eastward, toward the past, for the very last time. Then slowly, deliberately, I turned and looked to the west. That was where my future lay. I reached down for a small roundish pebble, rough to the touch, vibrant reddish brown, tucked it in my pocket, and never looked back.

Acknowledgements

Linda Labadie (née Fitzmaurice) helped me find my voice after years of silence. Her Celtic soul and restorative humour captained me onwards. With each conversation and surreptitious email sent on company time, I felt my voice returning, my heart taking shape again. Much of this book's existence, and my own, is thanks to Linda's boundless capacity for love, empathy, and all things invisible.

Jordan Simms-MacIntyre, the first "stranger" who bought one of my paintings. Our ensuing friendship has been better than sunshine.

Dr. Michael Kenneally, Principal and Chair of Concordia University's Canadian Irish Studies Department, and spectacularly gifted teacher: his course on James Joyce's *Ulysses*, taught with such passionate ease, helped set all my wheels in motion.

Michael Warford's dangerously sharp editorial eye winnowed good from chaff in those first chapters, gaining my trust and admiration with every slash of his pen. As grew the pool of red ink, so too our bond.

Ray Tarantino — singer, musician, recusant — who brought me past Annawan, Illinois; over that dividing line between past and future. Crossing the Mississippi, hitting replay on Dylan's "Idiot Wind," helped snap my last remaining chains. With anyone else, my friend, it would have been just a road trip.

The very late, very great Blaze Foley's music accompanies me still as I too go down to the metaphysical Greyhound station. Thank you Blaze.

Westwood Creative Artists' Chris Casuccio, literary agent extraordinaire, fought for and championed this book the moment it came into his hands. I can neither praise nor thank him enough for his determination and tireless support.

To Diane Young at Dundurn press, thank you for taking a chance on this unknown first-time author. Vision, heart, and imagination will, or should, always trump the balance sheet. I am profoundly grateful to whoever matched me with editor Michael Melgaard, exactly the kind of brilliant challenge-taker this project needed.

To my husband Grant who took that impossible chance, thank you. You have given me a home, a country they call America, and love enough to fill canyons.

Finally, my thanks to Concordia University Libraries, whose dedicated staff provided me with the means to sort through the ephemera of a past life. Concordia's Layton Collection revivified my memories, howsoever bittersweet.

Appendix 1: Yarmouth, NS: Small Town Summer

"SUMMER CLASSIC," one of the poems I brought with me when I first went to Niagara-on-the-Lake, shows Irving's handiwork. Figure 1 is my third draft; Figure 2 shows Irving's edits; Figure 3 is what I sent to *Poetry Canada Review*. They published it, albeit after lopping off the first stanza. The title seems to have changed to "Yarmouth, NS: Small Town Summer."

white wooden houses repose
silent (under) thick damp shade
c. 1941 ~~voile~~ curtains
sigh
(behind) gape (of) slat-bordered screens.

long-legged boys hang
(around) the corner gas station
learning (about) cars and oil
pump pressures
Girls slink and slump past
jaws working double-time
(on) bubble-gum and talk
of the latest, oblivious

(As) the ferry oozes
big late-model cars
Their 5th avenue tourists
all cool (and) powdered in ~~pale polyester sheaths~~
in pale polyester sheaths,
From behind tinted windows They creep
carefully, up the main drag
~~debating Back, lost in maps~~
~~completely out of town~~
lost in filtered Back and maps,
oblivious to the music of a classic
~~of a classic small~~
small town summer.

Third draft of "Summer Classic" (1983), written in Yarmouth, NS, while on lunch break, and one of the poems I included in my portfolio when I went to meet Irving. He circled superfluous words.

Irving's second run at it. The ferry "ejaculates," then "discharges," and finally "oozes" big, late-model cars.

YARMOUTH N.S.

Long-legged boys
whistling from the gas station
at girls slumping past
their jaws working doubletime
on bubble gum

A rusting ferry brings
late-model tourists
cool and powdered
in sensible shoes

Someone raises his baton
and all afternoon I hear
the music of a classic
small town summer.

I preferred the voile curtains to sigh rather than having "gapes of slat-bordered screens." In any case, it was my second published poem.

Appendix 2: Cameronian Bloopers

UPON GOING THROUGH Elspeth Cameron's book page by page, Irving and I compiled lists of her mistakes, errors, and dubious characterizations. She presented herself as a scholar. Unable to pursue her in the courts, Irving decided to dismantle her scholarship. Blooper Lists were sent to numerous critics, reviewers, pundits, editors, and academics. Incredibly, Cameron enjoyed their continuing support for the duration of the battle, which reinforced Irving's accusations of rampant anti-Layton bias. A selection of items from these lists is reproduced here.

1. E.C.: "As soon as Issie learned to read, his interest turned to the erotic. Whenever he had even five cents, he'd buy or trade second-hand boys' magazines like *Fame and Fortune* or *Pluck*."

   FACT: Cameron will find more sex in Paul's Epistle to the Corinthians. (The second title should be *Pluck and Luck*.)

2. E.C.: "Issie was in his twelfth year. He had eluded a Bar Mitzvah."

   FACT: Jewish boys are Bar Mitzvahed at the age of thirteen.

3. E.C.: "He peddled his skills in English and earned enough to give him time to write … "

   FACT: Why "peddled"? Can't a book-loving Jewish youth use his teaching skills — or is that word reserved only for a WASP pedant?

4. E.C.: "When Mr. Astbury, the school principal, demanded that he apologize to Steeves, Lazarovitch angrily strode to the school library and ostentatiously sat reading a book."

    FACT: I refused to apologize and was forthwith expelled from Baron Byng. What is so "ostentatious" about reading a book in a library?

5. E.C.: "He had enjoyed a brief fling with Nina Kaiserman."

    FACT: Another example of Cameron's vicarious enjoyment of the lechery she obsessively imputes to me throughout her book. The "fling" is straight out of Cameron's own fantasy sex life.

6. E.C.: "It was a former classmate from Baron Byng High School, Alec Avarine (with whom Lazarovitch had set up a mutual cheating system) ... "

    FACT: Alec Avarine was my brother Hyman's classmate in public school, not mine. It was he who told me about the low fees at Macdonald College. It was with Sol Berman that I had this mutual cheating system at Baron Byng High School.

7. E.C.: "He and Robert Flood defeated the Oxford-Cambridge team by negating the statement 'It were better to have written Gray's Elegy that to have conquered Quebec.'"

    FACT: We took the affirmative and won the debate.

8. E.C.: "How he must have cursed when he failed his third year."

    FACT: How can I curse something that never happened? I withdrew at the start of my third year and re-registered the following year and completed it successfully.

9. E.C.: "On October 8, 1924, as twelve-year old Lazarovitch was entering Baron Byng High School ..."

    FACT: I entered Baron Byng in 1925, age thirteen-and-a-half.

10. E.C.: "He gave me a book by some Marxist thinker, probably Sydney Hook."

FACT: The book I gave Eugene Forsey was Mehring's biography of Karl Marx. Hook would be very astonished to find himself called a Marxist thinker.

11. E.C.: "Frank Scott had agreed to supervise his thesis on Laski in Political Science."

FACT: Rubbish. My thesis supervisor was Professor Raphael Tuck. Scott was the outside reader.

12. E.C.: "It was 1955, the year after Dylan Thomas drank himself to death; ... "

FACT: Dylan Thomas, according to the *Encyclopaedia Britannica*, died in 1953.

13. E.C.: "He [Layton] encouraged Jonathan Williams to request an introduction from William Carlos Williams."

FACT: Rubbish. Williams' introduction was a complete surprise to me.

14. E.C.: "He [Layton] challenged Party founder Daniel DeLeon, and annihilated the meeting."

FACT: Daniel DeLeon was indeed the founder of the Socialist Labor Party, but having died in 1914, he wasn't around to be challenged.

15. E.C.: "His car has been stolen....There will be a delay while he gives the police the details."

FACT: Cameron gives the date for this "theft" as September 6, 1983. I'd gotten rid of my car in February 1983 and have not owned one since.

16. E.C.: "His mother, her new husband and his two brothers-in-law, especially the belligerent and obnoxious Strul Goldberg, were infused with the capitalist spirit, determined to acquire power and wealth through economic advancement."

FACT: Another example of Cameron's rich antisemitic fantasy life. Poor sick woman. She can't help running off at the mouth when she talks about Jews. " ... infused with the capitalist spirit ... "? My mother was over 75, her "new husband" was in his eighties, infirm, long-retired, and supported by his devoted children.

17. E.C.: "May Day Orators (which reduces his former idols David Lewis and A. M. Klein to sheer buffoonery)..."

FACT: This poem is too subtle for Cameron's intelligence. I'd advise her to get someone else to interpret it for her and never to rely on her own unaided efforts.

18. E.C.: "Dudek sent Layton along to meet Sutherland."

FACT: Since I was the first of the two to meet John Sutherland, it was I who sent Dudek to meet him.

19. E.C.: "He might be Jewish, yet some of his poems took an agnostic and even anarchic stance."

FACT: It may come as startling news to a provincial WASP from Barrie, Ont. that Jews have their fair share of agnostics and anarchists.

20. E.C.: "Layton took a small apartment on Keele Street near York and put in the 1969 winter term as writer-in-residence."

FACT: Having spent many years around university campuses, Cameron ought to know the difference between "writer-in-residence" and "full professor with tenure," which is what my status was at York University.

A selection from the "Yet More Cameron Bloopers" list, these gems:

1. E.C.: "Gone were the enforced kiddish (morning) prayers, the pressure to attend synagogue and the feared visits to mikvah and cheder." (p. 37)

FACT: Kiddish is NOT morning prayers; it is the ritual blessing made over a cup of wine. Mikvah is the purification bath for orthodox Jewish women and ultra-devout Jewish men. Small boys were never to be seen in a mikvah. The image of me being dragged there by my father is too ludicrous for words.

2. E.C.: "He'd sell his children for a paradox," Issie would exclaim, apparently ignorant of [Oscar] Wilde's sexual proclivities. (p. 63)

   FACT: Apparently, the great scholar, highly praised by the WASP literary establishment (Robert Fulford, William French, Phyllis Grosskurth, Pat Keeney-Smith, etc.) is unaware that Oscar Wilde was married with two sons.

3. E.C.: "Lazarovitch attacked the British Cabinet for being sympathetic to Naziism and praised Soviet Russia and France for upholding world peace, a movement to which he was actively committed through the National Committee for World Peace, where Lazarovitch was one of seven elected members." (p. 85)

   FACT: I praised Soviet Russia and France NOT for upholding world peace, but for signing the Franco-Soviet pact to resist Nazi aggression. Whatever the National Committee for World Peace may have been, I was NOT a member of it.

4. E.C.: "Betty was in hospital suffering from Bell's Palsy, a viral infection of the nerves ..." (p. 236)

   FACT: My wife was in the hospital suffering NOT from Bell's Palsy but from endocarditis. It was many years later that she came down with Bell's Palsy, and was never hospitalized for it.

Notes

PREFACE

1. Irving Layton, "The Fertile Muck," *A Wild Peculiar Joy* (Toronto: McClelland & Stewart, 2004), 34.

LEAVE-TAKING

1. Irving Layton, "Keine Lazarovitch: 1870–1959," *A Wild Peculiar Joy* (Toronto: McClelland & Stewart, 2004), 79.
2. Irving Layton, "Elegy for Marilyn Monroe," *A Wild Peculiar Joy* (Toronto: McClelland & Stewart, 2004), 273.
3. Irving Layton, "Keine Lazarovitch: 1870-1959," *A Wild Peculiar Joy* (Toronto: McClelland & Stewart, 2004), 79.
4 "For Mao Tse-Tung: A Meditation on Flies and Kings." Excerpted from *A Wild Peculiar Joy: The Selected Poems* by Irving Layton. Copyright © 1982, 2004 Irving Layton. Copyright © 2007 Estate of Irving Layton. Reprinted by permission of McClelland & Stewart, a division of Random House of Canada, a Penguin Random House Company.
5. Irving Layton, "I Take my Anna Everywhere," *A Wild Peculiar Joy* (Toronto: McClelland & Stewart, 2004), 266.

CHAPTER 3

1. Irving Layton, "The Fertile Muck," *A Wild Peculiar Joy* (Toronto: McClelland & Stewart, 2004), 46.
2. Irving Layton, "Aesthetic Cruelty," *Final Reckoning: Poems 1982–1986* (Oakville: Mosaic Press, 1987). Though written a couple of years later, the poem epitomizes Layton's theory that man has anaesthetized his appetites and desires, that is, numbs himself to the moral dictates that proscribe

barbarity. The poem originated after his reading about Austrian officers in the Second World War. They heightened their pleasure in killing Jewish children by first soothing them with toys, candy, false promises, etc. Only once the children had calmed down would they be shot point-blank. Layton's awareness of this human trait informs many earlier poems.

3. Letter from Irving Layton to Annette Pottier, dated September 29, 1981, Concordia University's Irving Layton Collection, Vanier Campus, Montreal, Canada.

CHAPTER 5

1. Irving Layton, "Tragedy," *The Gucci Bag* (Oakville: Mosaic Press, 1984), poem 89.

CHAPTER 6

1. *CIV/n: A Literary Magazine of the 50's*, ed. Aileen Collins (Montreal: Véhicule Press, 1982).

CHAPTER 8

1. Irving Layton, "New Shining Worlds (for S. Ross)," *The Gucci Bag* (Oakville: Mosaic Press (www.mosaic-press.com), 1984), poem 25.

CHAPTER 9

1. Irving Layton, "On Seeing the Statuettes of Ezekiel and Jeremiah in the Church of Notre-Dame," *A Wild Peculiar Joy* (Toronto: McClelland & Stewart, 2004), 43.

2. *Onion Rings* came about in the late 1980s with a tremendous sense of urgency due to Irving's growing fatigue and fear he would soon be unable to express his vision as in the past. The selections *Tutto Sommato: Poesie 1945–1989* and *Fornalutx: Selected Poems 1928–1990*, appeased his anxiety that some of his favourite, but lesser known, poems might fall through the cracks.

3. Henry Moscovitch (1941–2004) was a Montreal poet whose name is synonymous with genius and heartbreak. Prodigiously talented, and one of Irving's Herzliah students, his startling gift for poetry was known to friends like Leonard Cohen and Howard Aster. In 1956 Irving fought fellow Contact Press editors Louis Dudek and Raymond Souster, and published the fifteen-year-old's first book, *Serpent Ink*. Henry visited us many times in Montreal. Though greatly damaged by schizophrenia, poverty, and neglect, Irving treated him like a visiting prince, making sure to have a pack of cigarettes and a bit of pocket money for him. Mosaic Press published his last book, *New Poems*, in 1995.

4. If more proof were needed that Irving was a poetic barracuda, shying away from nothing in his quest for poems, my PMS episode yielded "Lady Macbeth," poem 90 in *The Gucci Bag*.

CHAPTER 10

1. A Montreal filmmaker who later made a bizarre, egregiously self-indulgent film called *Spotting Layton* claims he saw Irving in the Notre-Dame-de-Grâce YMCA's sauna wearing a red bikini-style bathing suit. The only swimwear Irving owned throughout that time was a pair of baggy turquoise Bermuda-style shorts by Ocean Pacific, which I bought for him.

CHAPTER 12

1. David Solway, b. 1941, poet, essayist, educational theorist. He lived for many years in Montreal's NDG neighbourhood.

CHAPTER 14

1. "Kakania" and a suite of poems including "I Take My Anna Everywhere" were published with a lengthy interview by Cliff Whiten in *Poetry Canada Review*, c. 1983, pp. 8–9. The poems are said to be from the forthcoming book, *While Waiting for the Messiah*, later changed to *Final Reckoning*.
2. Dr. Wynne Francis (1918–2000) began lecturing at Sir George Williams College (later named Concordia University) in 1942, becoming a full professor of English there in 1967. Considered a pioneer in Canadian literary studies, she is now honoured with Concordia's Wynne Francis Award for Graduate Study in Canadian Poetry. Irving often recalled how she risked losing her job by inviting him to speak to her class in the late 1940s or early 1950s. Their friendship endured over the years. She lived near us in the suburb of Montreal West where we visited numerous times.

CHAPTER 15

1. In early 1985, I submitted it to *Canadian Literature*. Irving sent "Leopardi in Montreal" and "Fellini." I recall Irving handing me the March 21, 1985, letter from editor W.H. New, accepting my poem for publication in *CL* No. 106, Autumn 1985. I slid, noodle-like, off my chair while bursting into tears. Irving's laughter and pride as he picked me up off the floor and embraced me remains one of my most delicious memories, as are the times he said to me, "Blessed is the teacher whose student surpasses him."

CHAPTER 16

1. Irving's first wife, Faye Lynch, came from Yarmouth, Nova Scotia. Even before he mentioned this, I looked at a photo of her in front of a building

that I recognized instantly as Yarmouth's courthouse. His left-wing ideals led him to marry her, as he felt it terribly unfair that someone with a glandular condition (which led to her being overweight and infertile, as well as necessitating her shaving her face daily) could not have her pick of well-favoured men. As detailed in *Waiting for the Messiah*, he didn't have the heart to break up with her when they were dating and sought advice from his doctor, who suggested Irving tell Faye he was stricken with tuberculosis. When Irving tried to break up with Faye, she sobbed so hard that he began sobbing from the ignominy of his ruse; and so they wed. The marriage lasted little more than a year, and was later annulled. For all the pity and sorrow, he later discovered she married a furniture salesman and lived a happy life. I never met her, but her relative Hubert Lynch had a weekly humour column in the Yarmouth *Vanguard* for years. The latter part of her life was spent in Yarmouth where she volunteered at the local library, perhaps being the one to order several of Irving's books for their shelves.

CHAPTER 18

1. Letter from Venie to Irving, c. early 1984, which he shared with me and is now in Concordia University's Irving Layton Collection, Vanier Campus, Montreal, Canada.

CHAPTER 19:

1. Irving Layton, "Boschka Layton 1921–1984," *The Gucci Bag* (Oakville: Mosaic Press, 1984), 138.
2. Irving Layton, "Lady Aurora," *The Gucci Bag* (Oakville: Mosaic Press, 1984), 143.

CHAPTER 20

1. John Robert Columbo, *Canadian Literary Landmarks* (Toronto: Dundurn Press, 1984).

CHAPTER 21:

1. Concordia's Layton Collection contains RCMP files on Irving from 1953 to 1972.
2. Lindforss was disappointed that Leonard Cohen showed no interest in the natural world around him, no curiosity, and may have politely declined to write a preface.

CHAPTER 22

1. Only in winter is it grey, but never ugly. I still miss Belleville every summer.
2. In 1984 it was still owned and run by the Kravitz brothers, who had been

schoolmates of Irving's at Baron Byng High School. He took me to lunch there one day, thrilling the brothers by remembering how one of them sank the winning basket against the buzzer in a long-forgotten grudge-match game.

CHAPTER 23

1. I once mentioned this to Bill who instantly recalled seeing a similar phenomenon. Still in their late teens or early twenties, Bill and Irving had just bought the *Keneder Adler* (Montreal's daily Yiddish newspaper founded by Hirsch Wolofsky in 1907). They got to Fletcher's Field, sat on the grass, sharing the paper and discussing the news with their usual zeal. It was a summer day. Bill vowed that he looked up and noticed a bluish cloud, not much more than a colour, floating just above Irving's head. In describing it to me, he actually used the word "halo." It left him startled, a little frightened, but not really surprised. His uncle, it seems, already had the makings of someone not quite like anyone else.

2. Irving Layton, "Fellini," *A Wild Peculiar Joy* (Toronto: McClelland & Stewart, 2004), 287.

CHAPTER 24

1. Irving Layton, *Waiting for the Messiah* (Toronto: McClelland & Stewart, 1985), 31, describing his father's tragedy, like that of many men of his generation, in that they left the Old World (where their scholarship and piety were valued) arriving in the New World only to shiver in "the drench, and raised beseeching orbs to the unanswering skies."

CHAPTER 25

1. "Black Tourist in Tinos," Excerpted from *A Wild Peculiar Joy: The Selected Poems* by Irving Layton. Copyright © 1982, 2004 Irving Layton. Copyright © 2007 Estate of Irving Layton. Reprinted by permission of McClelland & Stewart, a division of Random House of Canada, a Penguin Random House Company.

CHAPTER 26

1. David sucker-punched his father with a cover story in *Saturday Night* magazine. It was unexpected, and so cruel in places that Irving went stone deaf for an entire week from the shock of it. On his next visit to the Herzl Clinic, people came up to offer condolences for his having such a *mamzer* (bastard) for a son. The article later grew into his memoir, *Motion Sickness* (Macfarlane Walter, & Ross, 1999).

CHAPTER 27

1. Judith, a former York University student of Layton's, confided that she had a professional issue with Cameron involving a story that Cameron published and that had garnered her a prize. Judith was not pleased. What angered her even more was Cameron's denigration of her former teacher. Judith interviewed Cameron for the *Windsor Star*. The article, "Two Stories That Don't Rhyme," was published on October 12, 1985. Loyalty to Irving prompted Judith to also give us the recorded interview and transcript of same. Her article contains excerpts from this interview, conducted in September 1985.

2. Judith cross-checked Cameron's assertion that Morley Callaghan did not want her to write about him because he was "working on his memoirs and he wanted to do it himself." Judith interviewed Morley Callaghan in September 1985 and provided the transcript. This quote is from the transcript. It appears almost word for word in the article as well.

3. Direct transcript (provided by Judith Fitzgerald) of her interview with Elspeth Cameron, in September 1985. Italicized portions appeared in the article.

4. Ibid. Italicized portion appeared in the article.

5. Letter from Irving Layton to Elspeth Cameron, March 8, 1985. Now in Concordia University's Layton Collection, Montreal. It was also published in *Wild Gooseberries: The Selected Letters of Irving Layton*, edited by Francis Mansbridge (Macmillan, 1989), 360.

6. Ibid.

7. Along with daily support I lent to Irving, I compiled a nine-page manifesto identifying and illuminating Cameron's slurs and errors, e.g., saying Irving's mother couldn't wait to "get her hands on" her deceased husband's few savings (p. 37), I sent it, along with a "Blooper List" and a Christmas card from Simon Fraser University professor John Mills (flatly denying purported quotes that he "hated Irving and thought him absurd"), to forty-eight people across the country, including the President of the University of Toronto, Peter Gzowski, and William French. It helped prompt supportive articles from Keith Garebian and Joseph Gold, which in turn helped secure our eventual victory.

8. Letter from Irving Layton to Anne Vanderhoof, the editor of *Quill & Quire*, July 17, 1985.

9. William French quote from his year-end column in the *Globe and Mail*,

December 28, 1985. Stunningly, after being apprised of all salient facts, he had the temerity to write that Irving's campaign to defend himself was a "one-sided literary feud" and that Layton "launched an attack by mail on Cameron that has no precedent in this country for venom and scurrilous implications." French also disingenuously characterizes Irving's disclosing of her shoddy, degrading work as a "calculated attempt to damage her reputation." Incredibly, despite all the evidence we sent to him, he shamefully concludes that most of Irving's criticism was based on "alleged [!] factual errors," and that his anger was merely due to Cameron's failure to "rate him as a poet up there with Homer." Our minds boggled at this kind of asinine tunnel vision.

10. CBC *Arts Report* broadcast, December 9, 1985.

11. Along with a stack of "Cameronian Bloopers," which I distributed just before Cameron emerged, I brought a cassette tape of interviewees expressing their disgust at how their words had been twisted by Cameron.

12. Irving Layton, *Wild Gooseberries: The Selected Letters of Irving Layton*, ed. Francis Mansbridge (Toronto: Macmillan, 1989).

13. Ken Adachi (1929–1989), editor of the *Toronto Star* book section from 1976 onwards. Though fired in 1981 following a plagiarism accusation, he was later rehired as a book columnist and reviewer. A second accusation of plagiarism in 1989 may have been a contributing factor in the suicide pact he entered into with his wife Mary. She recovered.

CHAPTER 31

1. Irving Layton, "Keine Lazarovitch: 1870–1959," *A Wild Peculiar Joy* (Toronto: McClelland & Stewart, 2004), 79.

Index

Also Available from Dundurn

Margaret Laurence
The Making of a Writer
By Donez Xiques

Margaret Laurence: The Making of a Writer is an engaging narrative that contains new and important findings about Laurence's life and career. This biography reveals the challenges, successes, and failures of the long apprenticeship that preceded the publication of the *The Stone Angel*, Laurence's first commercially successful novel.

Donez Xiques demonstrates the importance of Margaret Laurence's early work as a journalist in her development as a writer and covers her return to Canada from Africa in the late 1950s. She details the significance of Laurence's "Vancouver years" as well as the challenges of her year in London prior to settling at Elm Cottage in Buckinghamshire, when Laurence stood on the verge of success.

The Margaret Laurence known to most people is a public figure of the 1960s and 1970s; matriarchal, matronly, and accomplished. The story of her early years in the harsh setting of the Canadian Prairies during the 1930s — years of drought and the Great Depression — and of her African years has never before been chronicled with the thoroughness and vividness that Xiques provides for the reader.

John Buchan
Model Governor General
By J. William Galbraith

An accomplished Scottish journalist, soldier, head of intelligence, and Member of Parliament, John Buchan (1875–1940) is best known for penning thrillers such as *The Thirty-Nine Steps*. However, as Canada's fifteenth governor general (1935–40), Buchan, First Baron Tweedsmuir, played a significant leadership role as a statesman and diplomat.

Buchan was the first governor general appointed after the 1931 Statute of Westminster, which gave Canada constitutional equality with Britain. He worked tirelessly for Canadian unity and promoted the sovereignty, and loyalty to the sovereign, of Canada. In 1937 he founded the Governor General's Awards, still Canada's premier prizes for literary achievement.

Lord Tweedsmuir helped draw Canada, Britain, and the United States closer together to strengthen the democracies threatened by Nazism and Fascism. He was an inspiration to several of his successors and still inspires us today.

Available Soon from Dundurn

'Membering
By Austin Clarke

Austin Clarke is one of Canada's most distinguished and celebrated novelists and short-story writers. His works often centre around the immigrant experience in Canada, of which he writes with humour and compassion, happiness and sorrow. In *'Membering*, Clarke shares his own experiences growing up in Barbados and moving to Toronto to attend university in 1955 before becoming a journalist. With vivid realism he describes Harlem of the '60s, meeting and interviewing Malcolm X, and writers Chinua Achebe and LeRoi Jones. Clarke went on to become a pioneering instructor of Afro-American Literature at Yale University and inspired a new generation of African-American writers.

With a writing career that spans more than fifty years, Clarke has been called Canada's first multicultural writer; and has been awarded the Giller Prize (*The Polished Hoe*), the Commonwealth Writer's Prize, the Toronto Book Award, and the Martin Luther King Junior Award for Excellence in Writing.